Bankrupt Education:
The Decline of Liberal Education in Canada

Canada has see   teaching
methods in the   in education reflect the   h the
times and uncl   Newell
make a provoc   ion. The
authors believ   ducators
to promote lite   character,
but who find t   rent system.

Taking as its   aming
and 'transition   principles
involved in the   nd the
economic and   incongru-
ity between th   in a liberal democracy   e current
debate, the aut   ssical tradition of libera

In the tradit   Bloom's
Closing of the   cy, *Bank-*
rupt Education   s excellence in educat   reading
for parents, tea   oncerned
about the crisis

(Toronto Studi

PETER C. EMI   fessors in
the Department of Political Science, Carleton University. They have published extensively in the fields of education, ethics, and contemporary
thought.

PETER C. EMBERLEY and WALLER R. NEWELL

Bankrupt Education: The Decline of Liberal Education in Canada

UNIVERSITY OF TORONTO PRESS
Toronto Buffalo London

© University of Toronto Press Incorporated 1994
Toronto Buffalo London
Printed in Canada

ISBN 0-8020-0435-0 (cloth)
ISBN 0-8020-7224-0 (paper)

Printed on acid-free paper

Toronto Studies in Education

Canadian Cataloguing in Publication Data

Emberley, Peter C. (Peter Christopher), 1956–
Bankrupt education : the decline of liberal
education in Canada

(Toronto studies in education)
ISBN 0-8020-0435-0 (bound) ISBN 0-8020-7224-0 (pbk.)

1. Education, Humanistic. 2. Education – Canada –
Aims and objectives. 3. Educational change –
Canada. I. Newell, Waller Randy. II. Title.
III. Series.

LC1024.C3E5 1994   370.11'2   C94-930380-1

University of Toronto Press acknowledges the financial assistance to its
publishing program of the Canada Council and the Ontario Arts Council.

To the students of Canada

Contents

Acknowledgments

We wish to express our gratitude to a number of people who read all or a part of this book and helped us with their comments. We reserve the greatest thanks for our wives, Cheryl Emberley and Jacqueline Newell, not only for their insights, but for their patience and encouragement. Our friend and colleague Tom Darby knows what part he has played in crystallizing our views on these matters. For the enthusiasm and encouragement offered to us by Ron Schoeffel, editor-in-chief of the University of Toronto Press, we are especially grateful. We found the comments and suggestions of our reviewer useful and sound.

We would also like to thank the Dean of Social Sciences, the Dean of Graduate Studies, and the President of Carleton University for their support of this project. Finally, we are grateful to our student Michael Reid for his energy and diligence as a research assistant. None of these individuals bears direct responsibility for the views expressed in this volume.

Ottawa
October 1993

BANKRUPT EDUCATION

And we are here as on a darkling plain
Swept with confused alarms of struggle and flight
Where ignorant armies clash by night.

Matthew Arnold

1

Introduction

Our Canadian educational system is in a shambles. We are progressively dismantling one of the finest public school systems in the world. As never before, there is a zeal for revolution – 'destreaming,' 'learning outcomes,' 'child-centred schooling,' 'continuous learning.' Nearly every day another crisis is exposed. Unlike earlier periods of re-evaluation and accommodation to changing circumstances, today's overhaul goes root and branch. The responsibility for all social ills is being laid at the door of education. Radical educational reform is to be the panacea for curing an ever-expanding collection of grievances and complaints. At the behest of far-ranging sectarian interests and radical reformers, the principles of the curriculum and teaching practices which have brought us world acclaim are being repudiated and overturned. Under the banner of 'excellence,' 'value for money,' 'equity,' and 'competitiveness' we are allowing the curriculum and traditional teaching practices to be trumped by politics.

Education stands or falls by the principle that virtue can be taught. Different ages have understood the content of 'virtue' differently, but there is broad agreement that certain talents and aptitudes can be taught and that the teaching craft ought to be directed to nourishing and forming a human being who will take his or her place among the responsibilities and possibilities, the freedoms and risks, of the world. Today we are observing a vehement assault on that principle. In brief, the current agenda of reform is an attack on the substance and dignity of liberal education.

At the core of liberal education was the duty of the teacher to impart and cultivate those talents and excellences which would prepare a student to bear the obligations of citizenship and to begin the exploration of the intellectual and spiritual life. Liberal education spoke to human equality and freedom.

The early architects of the Canadian educational system understood that.

They put in place a curriculum and an educational program which illuminated the distinctness of Canadian political culture with the insights of antiquity, the humanist renaissance, and early modernity. They adopted the principles of the Scottish commonsense tradition, of Burkean communitarianism, of Presbyterian and Methodist moral restraint, and of Hegelian transcendence. Yet, in their attention to disciplined freedom and individuality, the early Canadian educators were also open to the modern reforms of Pestalozzi and Froebel. They sought to balance the legacy of the ancient world with the achievements of the modern age. But they explicitly disavowed the educational philosophy of the United States in its pragmatism, utilitarianism, and scientism. A liberal education, they believed, was a balance of tradition with freedom, and of openness with the forms of civilized life. In fostering this type of education, they saw themselves as sustaining the Victorian ethos of Canada's founding fathers.

The educational revolution occurring around us, by contrast, aims at nothing less than a denial of the principles and practices undergirding the traditions of liberal education. The litany of the revolutionaries is uniform even though its sources are many: much of what transpires in the schools, they say, is irrelevant, parochial, and ethnocentric. The revolutionaries demand radical reform. They desire education to be used as a technique in the service of social reconstruction. They insist that education should furnish only those skills and behaviours whose universality and flexibility permit them to be jettisoned whenever circumstances demand. For the revolutionaries, education at its best is a process of sensitizing students to the injustices of the past and the range of possible complaints about the present. All past moralities and spiritual understandings, political categories and intellectual forms, must be transvalued.

The principle guiding the radical reforms could be aptly conveyed by the term 'disentanglement.' The student is to be disentangled from any substantive or concrete conditions defining human possibility. Under the new reforms, this process of disentanglement is proceeding apace. In place of the unity of the free mind, the object of education is becoming a vague assemblage of skills and sensitivity to fashionable issues. The student is being encouraged to fuse with his or her environment. Its requirements and pressures and the student's attunement to its demands are to constitute the whole of reality for the student. Instead of providing the foundations of intellectual and spiritual life, the new educational reforms are creating adaptable problem-solvers and socially integrated team-players fearful of giving offence. The schools, instead of being communities dedicated to the equality of opportunity and the freedom of the mind, have increasingly become ghettos or theme parks of 'identities' – race, colour, ancestry, religion, disability, gender, sexual orientation, age – and promoters of 'sensitivity' to the totality of ecological existence. Their orientation is wholly towards a future, dynamic fluidity, an orientation built on the wholesale abandonment of performance and achievement-based education. Traditional 'results-based' education presumed a stable curricular foundation. The new 'outcomes-based' education calls for endless mobility and infinite adaptability. One school superintendent in Calgary captures the mood very succinctly: 'we can't look at the future by going back to basics.'[1]

No wonder angry parents feel that the school system has abandoned its responsibilities. Their anger is particularly poignant since for decades parents were told that, unlike professionals, they lacked the understanding required to educate their own children. Now parents are discovering that the schools have not been educating them either. What the future promises, parents fear, is a situation in which their children have neither been prepared for life's practical necessities nor supplied with the moral substance associated with a meaningful existence.

And it is even less wonder that teachers are angry. The understanding of education they have acquired from years of classroom experience is being declared less important than the first principles driving the radical reforms. Their authority in the classroom is being taken away from them. The knowledge with which they were furnished in their training is being dismissed as anachronistic. The ministries of education, which were intended to *represent* their perspectives and insights in forming public policy, do not support the teachers, but rather contribute to the general abuse aimed at them.

Our aim is to resist these reforms by restoring the classical ideals of liberal education. Our study takes the perspective that the practices and philosophy enunciated at the origins of the Canadian public school system constitute a balanced, judicious account of human longing and possibility, of citizenship and responsibility. Our research has left us impressed by the fair and challenging system of liberal education put in place by the architects of Canadian schooling, based on their sober assessment of the human character. These architects understood the founders of Canadian Confederation and thus the distinctiveness of Canadian political culture. They produced a standard curriculum and teaching practices which united the particulars of our historical existence with the universal yearning for transcendence, or, stated otherwise, they united civic-mindedness with the deepest aspirations of the free mind. We urgently need to reflect on their efforts at seeking to combine the virtues of a classical liberal education with the freedom of modernity.

In our view, the revolutionaries have a deluded belief in the power of the will to engineer society and human souls, as if a wholly new age and a wholly new humanity can be brought into being. This will to reconstruct education is frequently conveyed by the mentality expressed in the statement 'The system's broke so let's get on with fixing it.'[2] In our view, the animus driving the reforms is an extravagant expectation of how much education and technical prowess can do to remake human life. We see danger in the reformers' intolerance for the conditions under which human existence has been given to us. The will to negation which underlies their every denunciation and deconstruction reflects an inability to live with the everyday. What we mean by the 'everyday' is a web of human relations which inevitably entail judgments of higher and lower, inside and outside, noble and base, anger and loyalty, friend and enemy, self and other. The revolutionary will relentlessly proceeds, believing that the tensions and contradictions which necessitate such judgments can be superseded. Underlying this hope is the Rousseauan view that human relations should resonate with an authenticity richer than our observable and customary interactions as members of society – as husbands and wives, as mechanics and politicians, as soldiers and poets, as teachers and pupils, as skilled craftsmen and apprentices. These roles and functions are 'inauthentic,' it is said, and the source of invidious distinctions which produce hurt and offence. Since the revolutionary sees reality as purely linguistic, he looks to a new language to evoke the new humanity where such hurt and offence are replaced by human encounters which are always pleasant or neutral.

The revolutionary dreams of a world where no one has to pronounce judgments, where no one must be ostracized, where no one fails to live up to expectations, where everyone extends warm effusiveness to all others, and where human beings are quietly submerged among the rhythms of natural growth and decay. Cardinal aspects of reality are obviously conveniently forgotten. The world invoked by the revolutionary is a dream because it eclipses the reality where the burdens of existence have to be nobly and justly shouldered – disease, labour, early death, injustice at the hands of the stronger, pragmatic compromise with others, tragic judgments, painful choices. In our view, the dream-world of the reformers gives rise to an education which does not exercise its responsibility in forming those characteristic virtues – charity, forgiveness, honour, righteous anger, compassion, dignity – through which we express our humanity.

What is alarming to us is that this same utopian animus has been evident in our politics, most strikingly during our recent round of constitution making. The enthusiasm to fix the political realm with certainty into a constitution which covers all contingencies matches the revolutionary process unfolding within the educational system which seeks a curriculum appealing to all constituencies and affronting none. It has contributed to political instability and intellectual confusion, not to say extravagant hopes and skewed judgment.

This book is an appeal to liberal education in its full meaning. Our aim is to help retrieve what is of enduring worth in our political founding as Canadians and in our public school system and explain why this core is worth defending. We believe there is a need to expose to reasoned debate the tactics of 'progressives' who claim to take the high road and to occupy the higher moral ground, pretending to align themselves with the forces of freedom and rationality by denouncing all criticism of their innovations as reactionary. We wish to show that traditional liberal education properly understood is not only democratic in the best sense, but also most likely to contribute to a society which is not deeply divided by race, class, and gender.

The showy and faddish gestures of educational radicals towards global competitiveness and redressing inequity are, we argue, no substitute for the freedom of the mind and balanced political judgment aimed at in a liberal education. This is an education which is without ostentation, an education which through the gradual and sequential formation of habits and talents produces a critical and impartial mind. Liberal education, as Leo Strauss once remarked, seeks the light and shuns the limelight.

At the same time, this study is a call for the return of responsibility for education into the hands of those who know best what is good for their children, namely parents and teachers. Parents and teachers know best how the longings and passions of children take shape, what talents and aptitudes prepare them for their lives as citizens and human beings, and what tensions lie ahead for a child as it grows to participate more fully in reality. The reformers see parents and teachers largely as impediments to the success of their agenda. We want to show that there is dignity in the anger of teachers and parents. It has such dignity because it speaks in the cause of justice.

As this book was nearing completion, it was reported that 40 per cent of Ontario high school students are 'dysfunctional.' Because of the problems they encounter in earlier years – the stress of the recession and the increasing number of split families – by the time they reach high school, it is argued, large numbers of students suffer from feelings of alienation, loneliness, and drift. The response to this news was characteristic of educational debates in Canada as they are framed by the educational establishment. Schools, it was said, must make greater efforts to impart 'social skills' to help students deal with their problems. If necessary, imparting 'social skills' must take priority over imparting a basic education. As one high school English teacher report-edly put it: 'What's more important, that we graduate a kid who can read or a kid who can be a good citizen?'[3]

But we ask: how did we reach a point where a high school English teacher can suggest that somebody could be a good citizen without knowing how to read? It is precisely this kind of attitude, we believe, that endangers education in Canada without promising to make any serious contribution to solving the personal and social problems students are facing. We argue in this book that there can be no essential conflict between good education and good citizen-ship. One cannot exist without the other. Neither good citizenship nor per-sonal fulfilment is possible without a good education. Students who are unable to clarify their problems and to articulate their instinctual responses to the world in the light of reason, history, and the known record of human experience and speculation will become neither informed, thoughtful citizens nor innovative and productive workers. For these reasons, liberal education as we explore it in this book is not a luxury or a matter of nostalgia. It is the indispensable condition for a young person's growth to responsible maturity and a chance to excel in life.

Moreover, we believe the latest trends in curricular reform – the culmi-nation of some twenty years of child-centred, process-oriented learning – may well exacerbate young people's feelings of alienation and inner frag-mentation, contributing to 'dysfunction' rather than alleviating it. This pos-sibility needs urgently to be explored. Might it not be the case that a contributing factor to the drift and emptiness felt by many students is our current education system's excessive emphasis on empowerment, group-think, advocacy, and agendas of the left and right that seek increasingly to convert school curricula to their own partisan purposes? Important as these facets of life are, when pursued too zealously, they can operate at the expense of the wholeness, balance, moderation, and sense of obligation toward family, friends, and fellow citizens that should be at the heart of a young person's education.

As our readers will see, we believe there are some genuinely positive fea-tures to the new pedagogy. But we also believe that, taken as a whole, its defects far outweigh its achievements. As a conceptual and practical whole, child-centred, process-oriented learning has had long enough to prove itself. In fact, the period of its mounting predominance pretty much corresponds with the documented decline in learning and literacy among Canadian stu-dents. Is it not ludicrous to argue that the problems largely created by this trend in education can be solved by going further in the direction of this same trend? The verdict would seem to be in. And yet our educational establishment responds to the crisis by radicalizing its pursuit of the innovations most likely to be responsible for the crisis in the first place.

Our book is meant to address the concerns felt by so many students, parents, and teachers about the decline of Canadian education. Unlike many treatments of this subject, however, we are concerned with the universities as well as the schools. This reflects our conviction that the problems faced by schools and universities, however they may differ in specifics, are related aspects of a single crisis. This crisis is the decline of liberal education in Canada under a lethal combination of pressures from the left and right, and – more strangely – from a convergence between their goals. At bottom, the debate over education is inseparable from the vast political, cultural, and economic changes taking place in Canada and the world, changes as yet dimly perceived, disturbing, and perhaps best summed up by the recent fascination with 'the end of history.' We will try to connect the education debate to these larger global processes.

Others have narrated at greater length than ourselves the specific policy controversies over curricula, funding, teacher training, and so on. Although we examine the new curricular reforms in considerable depth and detail, we believe that the problems besetting Canadian education cannot be reduced to conventional policy debates over methodologies of teaching or the constraints of funding. Important as these are in context, when they are allowed to define the debate in their own terms, these policy options foster the impression that the concerned parties disagree only over fairly narrow technical issues which, if clarified by further empirical study, will at length be resolved. We would be happy to think so, but we seriously doubt it. Liberal democracies generally tend to convert debates over ends into debates over means, and this is almost always a healthy practice. But sometimes debates over ends are unavoidable. Behind the mountain of studies, statistics, and task forces, we have in Canada today a fundamental debate over the intellectual and moral purposes of education, and the sooner we face it, the likelier we are to achieve some real results. Indeed, as we argue, it is the essence of liberal education to prepare us to undertake such a debate without rancour or the shrill posturing and professional advocacy that increasingly characterize public discourse in Canada.

We are arguing that no thorough and lasting beneficial reform of Canadian education will occur until we recover what it means for a person to be liberally educated. The crisis in education is a crisis in the souls of young people. It is most immediately manifested in the poor preparation they receive in high school for the transition to university, but it goes far beyond such measurable indicators. Liberal education, we will argue, is an education in wholeness and balance. It enables us to cultivate our moral and intellectual capacities to their fullest, thereby achieving the satisfaction of a just, stimulating, and productive life. Liberal education is, above all, a civic or political education, an education for citizenship. Such an education has nothing to do with the kind of *politicized* education that we increasingly impart today to young people through 'socialization' and 'social skills' that frequently serve some partisan agenda of the left or right. A liberal education must be non-partisan. Its aim is not advocacy, but instead to provide a haven where young people can acquire the depth of thought and observation that will equip them to choose knowledgeably among the political alternatives that will compete for their attention as citizens.

While we maintain that there can be no essential conflict between good citizenship and a good education, we also argue that liberal education is the key to practical success in life while at the same time opening us to spiritual satisfactions that transcend practical success. Liberal education includes – but is not reducible to – what we now call the 'basics' of mathematics, science, and literacy. The 'basics' are the means to a good education, but not an end in themselves. They are necessary but not sufficient conditions for the pursuit of full human satisfaction. If you are liberally educated, you will also be a more productive and creative worker and, more importantly, a decent human being who respects the rights and achievements of others.

Although it might seem to some as if our vision of liberal education is impossibly outdated and antiquarian, this is most emphatically not the case. Indeed, we believe it is fundamentally in harmony with the views of education emerging from Canada's growing counter-culture of parents, students, and teachers who are dissatisfied with the educational establishment. The essentials of liberal education as it is discussed in this book were, until just yesterday, leading features of what is best in Canadian education. From Aristotle to D'Arcy McGee and Egerton Ryerson, down until the late 1960s, liberal education has had a more or less continuous pedigree (which is not to say there was not an intense debate about its precise meaning and content). Indeed, the kind of history of ideas that we present in this book was once taught in many Canadian high schools, although it has all but disappeared in recent years. Many people in their late thirties or early forties fondly remember the excerpts from the Greek and Roman classics they learned in school, or the ancient history they were taught, and are appalled to find that these studies have virtually disappeared from the schools their children attend today. The traditional ideal of a liberal education still sustains much of what remains strong and worthy in Canadian educational life, although we are rapidly losing it. Traditional liberal education is not the whole solution to our current problems, but it is the necessary starting-point. Without it, the ship is rudderless. In the light of two thousand years of accumulated wisdom and experience about learning, the last twenty years constitute a highly eccentric interval.

Many classical allegories for a liberal education – for example, the voyages of Odysseus or Telemachus – represent a journey of the soul from one's particular time, place, and attachments to the universal and back again to one's own. The same cycle of transcendence and return is sketched by Plato in his Image of the Cave. In our experience as teachers, we find that young people are still naturally inclined to fall in love with this journey to the stars and back. Education, as one of its Latin roots conveys, is the art of leading forth. The core purpose of a liberal education, we shall argue, is to lead a young person on just such an odyssey of the mind and heart, which is really to lead them to themselves as they can hope to be at their very best. This journey to the great ideas liberates us from the unthinking conventions and orthodoxies of the day, but only so that we can return to our own way of life better able to appreciate both its defects and its virtues. Liberal education is unconventional, but constructively so. It avoids both revolutionary nihilism and philistine conformity, which is why it is under increasing assault in a culture whose particular brand of philistine conformity is to believe itself to be the one truly liberated, unconventional society that has ever existed.

In our book, we have tried to imitate this classical form of a journey from the love of one's own toward the Good and back again equipped with a new insight into how to be a decent and reflective citizen. Chapters 2 and 3 are an examination of the debates over curriculum, finance, and social and economic policy in the schools and universities. Chapters 4 and 5 set forth a selective archaeology of the meaning of liberal education to serve as a critical foil for the educational abuses and inadequacies we analyse in chapters 2 and 3. Finally, in chapter 6, we return from the universal standards of liberal education back to our own Canadian experience. We try to show that, until just recently, Canadian educational theory and practice had evolved their own rich application of the universal standards of liberal learning to suit our country's specific circumstances, a unique hybrid of Anglo-European influences including Hegelianism and Scottish commonsense philosophy that is open to yet further enrichment and evolution from other traditions and cultures. In journeying to the stars, we conclude, we find we have been at home all along.

We believe our readers will share our view that, before one can defend traditional standards of excellence, one has to recall and reflect on what they are, and how they are integrated in a comprehensive account of human character and learning. Whereas many critiques of current educational practices invoke traditional ideals and lament their passing, they often do little more than nod in that direction. We go further by providing a sketch of the history of liberal education that tries to show what it is, suggests to some extent how to go about teaching it, and invites the reader to reflect on its ambivalent status in the modern world. Our account of liberal education is meant to show how, despite enormous differences between ancient and modern accounts of the human personality, nature, and history, the essential aims remain the same, at least among its greatest defenders and exponents. In the spirit of liberal studies, we are more concerned with posing questions than attempting definitive answers. Liberal education could indeed be defined as the art of learning how to ask questions. But questions are not the same as whims or unprompted impulses. Questioning is an art that imposes its own discipline so that the mind can be free.

Although all of the ideas we discuss in this book are relevant to the meaning of education, not all of them are benign ideas. A reverence for tradition must always be balanced by scepticism and thoughtful criticism. Although there is a more or less continuous pedigree for the main ideas of a liberal education from Aristotle down to the present, it is not a smoothly untroubled history where everything is wonderful until the Hall-Dennis Report. Our readers will see that we mean nothing so platitudinous. Today's child-centred and process-oriented concepts of educational reform derive from a decayed remnant of German Idealism. Today's educational experts are unlikely to know or care much about Hume, Hegel, or D'Arcy McGee. But they are steeped in the deconstructionist vulgate they receive second or third hand from devotees of Derrida and Foucault in the universities (who sometimes receive it second or third hand themselves). In order to understand how this has come about, we must return to the Hegelian and post-Hegelian roots of that thinking. Although the connection between the traditional ideal of a liberal education and contemporary Canadian education has not yet been severed, it has been weakened to the breaking-point. Hence, we need to think through the crisis in the meaning of liberal education in the Western tradition as well as the restorative possibilities of that tradition. This is the dual aim we have tried to pursue in this book. Reflecting on how and why liberal education has been subjected to intense challenges from within the very intellectual tradition that gave it birth is an essential component of the meaning of liberal education itself, if it is not to decline into mere antiquarianism and museum-going.

Liberal education is seriously endangered by the current reforms, and the danger is growing. But there remain many serious teachers, parents, and students, and they are waking up to the danger. These are the people we are writing for, and they exist everywhere in Canada, in all communities and both genders. We write from a sense of crisis, but not from a sense of despair. Our aim is to help save what can be saved, and – above all – to provide some encouragement and solace for students.

2

The Crisis in Canadian Education

The Public Decline in Confidence

When we look past the official pronouncements and bulletins of the provincial education ministries, what we see going on across Canada today is a battle between the voices of common sense and experience, on the one hand, and those of vague abstractions driven by an agenda for social experimentation, on the other. Students and teachers, unfortunately, are to be the guinea-pigs. Let us begin with a representative sampling of the debate. In doing so, we will also introduce some of the themes that will recur throughout this book – the meaning of education, and its connection with citizenship, and with liberal democracy in the Canadian context. Then we will turn to a detailed examination of the new curriculum, the controversies surrounding it, and their connection to the universities. For although most discussions treat the controversies over secondary and post-secondary education as if they were separate issues, they are in fact intimately connected with one another, representing related aspects of a single educational crisis.

In Ontario as in other provinces, parents and teachers are often stunned to find that vast and radical new initiatives are being foisted on them from above. By the time they reach the public, they have already been thoroughly planned down to the smallest details of implementation. Parents and teachers thus suspect that when ministry officials present these plans for 'feed-back' or 'full public consultation,' they are participating in a ritual whose outcome has already been determined. Even the Ontario government, however, was unprepared for the wave of indignation and criticism that greeted its proposals for destreaming and the rest of the new curriculum. Parents and classroom educators sensed that the government was ramming the reforms through with such unseemly haste because it feared that the more people found out about them, the more opposed they would be.

As we will see later in this discussion, destreaming is but the tip of a radical pedagogical iceberg, and must be considered in connection with a number of other issues. But because it has become such a powerful symbol of discontent with the school system, it is worth dwelling on for a moment by way of introduction to the larger consideration of curriculum reform. When first unveiled, the government was straightforward about the fact that destreaming was based on its ideological conviction that streaming constituted 'institutionalized racism.' As public criticism mounted, the reforms were also defended with conservative-sounding slogans about competitiveness and the need to educate people for the global economy of the twenty-first century. In the next section of this chapter, we will examine the detailed inadequacies of the Ontario proposals, so typical of the thinking of educational mandarins and bureaucrats across the country. But, preparatory to that examination, let us begin with a more general reflection. Even taken at face value, are these reforms really likely to make our workforce more competitive? Before the Hall-Dennis Report, the mainspring of all the current child-centred, process-oriented approaches to learning, Ontario's last major educational reform began in 1960. There as elsewhere in Canada, an effort was made to enhance pure and applied research in universities and technical and vocational training in the schools.[1] Much of the developed world moved in the same direction, and the United States was particularly concerned about the Soviet Union's launching of Sputnik in 1957 and the decline of the liberal democracies' technological and economic prowess that it appeared to symbolize. Although the Soviet edge proved to be illusory, education benefited greatly. In Ontario, the reforms aimed at enhancing technical and vocational training in the schools were made in addition to, not at the expense of, the traditionally strong core curriculum in the sciences and humanities stretching back to Egerton Ryerson. The period of those reforms roughly corresponded with the longest period of sustained economic growth in North America, a period of prosperity and opportunity we now look back to as a golden age.[2]

We ask our readers to join us in asking some questions. Isn't it likely those high standards of scientific, technical, and traditional learning were at least a contributing factor to that economic prosperity? And as we face new global economic challenges, aren't we more likely to prosper as a country by increasing the meritocratic dimension of education as we did after Sputnik, rather than decreasing it? Is teaching our children to work in teams and submerge their own individual strivings for excellence really likely to produce a dynamic future economy? Or are we in fact training people to be docile group-workers in low-paying service-sector jobs? This might suit the short-term, and short-sighted, self-interest of businesses pressing the school system to be more relevant and responsive to their needs.[3] But should our schools be cooperating in furnishing drones for our service economy, or should they not rather be working to recapture a leading role in developing new technological and scientific capabilities? Our mainstream educational gurus sometimes claim that we need to teach our future workers to imitate the team-oriented, consensual work style of the Japanese and German economies. But the Japanese and German public education systems make little use of child-centred, process-oriented learning methods. On the contrary, they are far more meritocratic and competitive than our own. Shouldn't that tell us something?[4]

Indeed, to the extent that child-centred learning is justified on the grounds that it will contribute to a better trained and more competitive workforce, its claims seem especially hollow. For, while it depicts itself as an innovative new approach responding to the changed global economy of the eighties and nineties, it is in fact the continuation of a project that began in the late sixties with the Hall-Dennis Report. And ever since the guiding concepts of Hall-Dennis began to hold sway over the high school curriculum, student performance has steadily declined, especially in the areas of mathematics and science that are arguably the basis of a technically competent workforce in a competitive economy.

The dreary results are summarized by Dennis Raphael, director of the Coalition for Education Reform:

The poor performances of Ontario students in mathematics and science were first identified in 1984, and have been replicated time and time again ... I have watched these events unfold with a sense of despair and resignation. The reasons for Ontario's poor performance were outlined in George Radwanski's ministry-commissioned report in 1988: Ontario's educational philosophy is focused on activity or process ...[5]

But the response to this evidence has been to go further down the same road:

Despite all that was going on elsewhere in Canada, and despite the increasingly poor achievement results of Ontario students, the recent Ontario document *Everybody's Schools: The Common Curriculum* suggests the Education Ministry is moving even further toward watering down the educational curriculum. Particularly disturbing is the plan to implement de-coursing (in which subjects such as maths, sciences and technological studies are put together) and de-streaming (which, in Ontario's version, appears to involve not a systematic raising of standards and instruction, as outlined by Mr. Radwanski, but a confused emphasis on `cooperative and holistic learning,' left undefined).

It is little wonder that this wilful ignoring of reality – a reality demonstrated by the government's own studies – has led parents and educators like Mr Raphael to begin forming their own educational counter-culture. For they see in their homes and classrooms what the evidence also shows, but what the provincial ministries bury in a blizzard of psycho-babble and empty conceptualization. Dennis Raphael observes:

As the research literature shows, an effective school system is one where a core curriculum of traditional subject matter (math, science, geography, history) exists with clear, high expectations for all students; where methods are in place to evaluate the implementation of this curriculum through student assessment; and where teachers are given the instructional tools to help students reach these desirable levels of achievement if the goals are not being met.

'When,' Mr Raphael understandably laments, 'will we ever learn?'

But economic competitiveness is not the sole – or even the main – motive behind destreaming and the rest of the new curriculum. One of the most disturbing features of the new curriculum is how it manages to serve the worst instincts of both the left and the right on educational issues. For the same new structures that claim to imitate Japanese-style teamwork will also implement the ideology of victimization that views any assertion of individual merit as being necessarily at the expense of the government's approved victim groups. Unfortunately, while the deconstruction and fragmentation of the curriculum is unlikely to help create a more competitive workforce, it will be all too effective, one fears, in achieving this inner ideological imperative. The rhetoric of fiscal responsibility can be used to disguise the use of public funds to promote politically correct trends while repressing others. Hence, the government of Ontario, recently embarked on budget trimming to convince the electorate that it is a centrist party worthy of the majority's trust, used fiscal austerity as a justification for ending public funding for University of Toronto Schools. When pressed, however, Ontario Education Minister David Cooke reportedly admitted 'to being uncomfortable with the idea that the public should finance a high school that caters to the intellectual elite.'[6] And this brings us to the heart of what is behind destreaming. For University of Toronto Schools is a purely meritocratic institution.[7] Whereas Canada's old-line prep schools still have a heavily Anglo-Saxon and Protestant flavour and are often ferociously expensive, UTS was designed to allow young people from all backgrounds the chance for a prep school education in the heart of a great university in a sophisticated urban setting. Any student who meets the school's entrance requirements is admitted whether he or she can afford the fees or not. Asian students form the largest single ethnic group at the school, and as many girls are admitted each year as boys.

But a meritocratic admissions standard is not enough for our educational mandarins. For behind the current debate about curriculum reform and teaching methods lies a huge moral divide between the vast majority of Canadians – of both genders and all ethnic origins – and the people increasingly in control of educational policy. This moral divide is rarely discussed in a full and frank way, not least because the education planners have a vested interest in confining the debate to a technical discussion of pedagogical methodology as a way of keeping the larger agenda under wraps. But it is impossible not to spot it, and parents' groups are becoming increasingly vocal in their opposition to the ideological manipulation of education.

Most Canadians believe that government should maximize the equality of opportunity so that individuals can compete on a level playing-field to demonstrate an earned inequality of result. They believe that merit should be rewarded regardless of race, origin, gender, or background. That is what liberal democracy is all about. As citizens we are equal. We are equal before the law and equally free to participate in political life, and we have equal civil rights. But economically and culturally, we are free to excel as individuals. Moreover, in Canada, we have always properly been concerned to prevent the rights of the individual from becoming too sharply corrosive, paying special attention to every individual's basic material and bodily needs and fostering the autonomous identities and special arrangements of linguistic and ethnic communities wherever possible. Our Canadian version of liberal democracy not only allows, it actively requires, that remaining obstacles to true equality of opportunity be removed wherever they remain, for women, visible minorities, or anyone else.

True equality of opportunity can be achieved by increasing equal access to our education system, not by dismantling it. But our education planners increasingly reject the very idea of merit. It is not merely the inequality of opportunity they reject – we all agree this can and should be remedied. They reject the earned inequality of result as a sign of (to quote the 1992 party platform of the Ontario NDP) 'institutionalized racism' and 'classism.' The drive to end streaming is, at bottom, part of the drive to convert Canada from a country based on the equality of opportunity for the meritocratic inequality of result into a racialist and sexist state where the government distributes

entitlements, jobs, and status so as to exactly replicate at all times the distribution of the two genders and visible minorities in the population at large.[8]
The effect on education will be to demoralize students and teachers alike, flat-
tening levels of achievement and making a high school diploma of increasingly less value in what remains of the competitive world outside the
classroom. Meanwhile, the children of the well-off (including, not infre-
quently, those of our politicians and mandarins) will continue going to private schools and on to expensive American universities, where streaming is
practised with a vengeance. The new curriculum is in this sense profoundly
undemocratic and patronizing, treating public school students as if they are
fit only for a general mediocre training for the service economy, not worthy
of the traditional education in the sciences and humanities that their betters
will go on acquiring in private schools. It was once the right of every student
to have the opportunity to acquire such an education.[9]

The proponents of the new curriculum will, of course, deny that it leads to
mediocrity and protest that they are the ones who are truly concerned for the
individual development of each student. But why, then, do they view merit as
a zero-sum game?[10] The new curriculum proposes that, in place of streaming, students work cooperatively so that the more gifted students can help
out students having difficulties. To some extent, this is a laudable aim. But we
still have to wonder whether it is right for young children or teenagers to be
burdened with the responsibility of doing what teachers themselves should
be doing. Even children who perform very well academically are vulnerable
to the whole range of stresses and emotional problems produced by adolescence and the often bewildering pace of change in modern life. Should they,
in addition, be conscripted as assistant teachers? Taken too far, the concept is
an unwarranted intrusion into the realm of private freedom. It implies that
gifted children are somehow operating at the expense of the less gifted, which
implies in turn that merit is a collective rather than an individual quality, so
that one person who demonstrates more than the average amount of it owes a
kind of toll or surcharge of social responsibility to the others. This critique of
individual merit in turn stems from the neo-Marxist theory that all apparently innate differences in ability are in fact socially 'constructed' in order to
bolster an unjust and oppressive class system. Because the injustice is 'systemic,' the remedy must be to deconstruct the inequities through the agency
of the state.

These are the theories, originating in the universities but now spreading
throughout the world of university-educated social engineers, that are being
practised on our students. One is entitled to believe in them if one wishes.
But is one entitled to implement them to the exclusion of every other

approach? We believe that every identifiable injustice and defect in the schools today could be remedied without departing from the liberal-democratic ethos – that is, by better funding, by more individualized attention for students with learning difficulties, and by improving access to our schools for the disadvantaged and the disabled. But the new curriculum is not about justice so much as ideology. This is why the Ontario government, for instance, is bent on getting rid of the enrichment stream. Since it only involves an estimated 2.3 per cent of the student population, it obviously is not a financial or instructional drain on the school system.[11] Moreover, there is no contradiction between retaining an upper stream for the most gifted students while raising standards and improving instruction for all the others – partly so as to bring more of them into the enrichment stream. But doing that only makes sense if one believes in the opportunity of every individual to seek his or her own highest level of achievement. It makes no sense if, like the Ontario government, one believes that the very idea of an enrichment stream is an affront, because the very idea of individual merit is a justification for oppression ('parasitical elitism,' as one of our own colleagues once charmingly termed the concept of merit pay). Hence, the enrichment stream will be abolished.

The foregoing overview gives a sense of the broad parameters of the debate going on across Canada over education, and the grave concerns and strong feelings it has aroused. Now let us turn to a more thorough consideration of the proposed curricular reforms and the reasoning – stated and sometimes unstated – behind them.

The Curriculum under Siege

Nowhere has the furore to overturn past educational theory and practice taken as strong a bent as in the area of curriculum reform. Whereas change in teaching techniques, in external organizational forms, and in grading practices may scratch against the surface of schooling, curriculum reform goes root and branch to the core of education. It is here that the battle over the substance and the formal structure of education is being fought out. 'There is a fundamental decline in confidence in the public education system,' argues David Cooke, Ontario's minister of education, echoing ministers across Canada. In his view, it is clear that

our society is currently undergoing far-reaching changes in the structure of families, in the composition of the population, and in the nature of the economy. Other trends, such as the information explosion, the impact of new technologies, changes in the workplace, the increasing fragility of the environment, and concerns about changes in the values and institutions that have formerly been a source of stability in our society, all dictate a review of traditional models and approaches in education. Responding successfully to these changes ... requires new ways of thinking about and organizing curriculum.[12]

The curriculum has become the object of such scrutiny and reformist enthusiasm because activists seek to place upon it the full burden of the social, personal, and moral crises they have determined are the source of all human malaise.

For the last thirty years, we have observed many similar efforts, as ministries of education, teachers' federations, and school boards made powerful efforts to demonstrate the relevance of their curriculum, their value for money, their capacity to supply the engine for social reform. In the 1960s the favoured means was 'values-education.' During the 1970s the catchword was 'skills.' Throughout the 1980s the solution was 'back-to-basics.' In all these cases, school reform focused on adding to or supplementing existing programs and courses. But today we are undertaking a wholesale *restructuring* of the school curriculum.

It is important, if we are to have clarity in these matters, to start at the beginning. The curriculum is to schooling as the constitution is to politics. It sets out the fundamental principles of order and thus supplies the authority by which teaching practices and assessments of achievement are legitimated. If the curriculum is to have this authority, like a constitution, it must be seen to be above sectarian interests and the ongoing techniques of social organization. Its measures, moreover, must transcend the means by which the ends of education are implemented. Otherwise, teaching practice, transmitted knowledge, testing techniques, and the recognition of merit are simply reducible to power, where might makes right. And the curriculum will then be thought of as an arbitrary arrangement, subject to ceaseless changes and politicization. Success at the task of elevating the curriculum to an authoritative status does not come easily. It assumes the capacity to understand what a human being is, in his or her actuality as well as in potential. It must, of necessity, adopt a specific perception of reality. These are ponderous responsibilities. Thus, undertaking reform is a serious and painstaking effort. It is laborious because what is at stake is not only how many skills and learned behaviours and how much knowledge a student will have by the end of his or her schooling, but the nature of his or her participation in reality itself. Schooling is not the only formative influence on the nature of that participation, but it can be the most important. The curriculum sets in place the principles and forms of lifetime experience. Curricular reform, evidently, must address the broadest and deepest of questions. How should it be undertaken? Upon whose authority do answers to these questions rest? There are many claimants among those currently expressing their dismay with the curriculum.

Before we attend to this discontent, one matter of terminology needs to be resolved. The battle over the curriculum has produced a polarity between 'traditionalists' and 'progressives.' The first, it is said, wish to preserve the static, hierarchical, content-burdened curriculum, while the latter focus on dynamic interchanges, democracy, and process- and student-centred learning. We hesitate to embrace this distinction in our discussion. While there may be extreme advocates of one alternative or the other, and while public polemic is made more colourful by these caricatures, our view is that educational debate is flattened when these alternatives are posed. The polarity needs to be dismissed if there is to be responsible discussion of the purposes and means of education. The sound 'traditionalist,' after all, while demanding performance related to content, and linking such performance to knowledge of a legacy of cultural and scientific achievements, is also concerned with freedom, equality, and relevance. The thoughtful 'progressive,' while championing creativity, self-esteem, and relevant skills, does not thereby abandon an understanding of standards of achievement based on potentiality and development. Simply stated, balanced 'traditionalists' and 'progressives' do not disagree fundamentally about the nature of education, even when they dwell on different events in the process of education, or employ distinct techniques. A preponderant number of 'traditionalists' and 'progressives' will agree that a sound curriculum balances order with movement, structure with process, authority with creativity, knowledge with judgment. Few teachers or parents among the 'traditionalist' or 'progressive' camps deny that there are many human longings, a plurality of perspectives on reality, and the ineluctable fact that each of us is a unique being. They will each admit, at the same time, that there are essential principles of order, that *human* life is always embedded in political and cultural worlds, that there is a human need for meaning, and that there is a legacy of works speaking to human excellence and achievement. They will agree that curricula should lay out the conditions which must obtain if we want to educate human beings who can exercise their freedom to think independently, who can be enriched and contribute to a collective good by participating in enterprises with others, and who have some preparation for answering the complex questions of meaning which arise in response to the mysteries of our origins and our mortality.

But increasingly, public debate *is* polarizing teachers and parents into camps, and drawing battle lines between them, thus driving 'traditionalists' and 'progressives' into tight corners of polemic. And this is occurring, we believe, because of the nature of the current clamour demanding a wholesale restructuring of schools and the curriculum. There is a serious battle occurring over the nature of the curriculum, but we will argue that it stems, at bottom, from a position more radical than that held by most so-called traditionalists and progressives, confounding debate about the essential purposes and ends of education.

The current clamour for curricular reform comes from many sources. The persistent theme among those lobbying for curricular reform is that the existing structures and objectives do not adequately correspond to the reality of Canadian society. The curriculum embodies outmoded cultural practices, while the world is becoming more cosmopolitan, ethnically and culturally diverse, and fluid. While the curriculum, it is said, reflects the monochrome of an Anglo-Saxon understanding of knowledge and culture, and Protestant middle-class morality, Canada is a secularized, pluralistic society that must respond to the information-age upon which humankind is collectively embarking.

In this view curriculum revamping, if it is to prepare students for a new world, must encourage an extensive withdrawal from specific tasks, knowledge-bases, and outdated behaviour. 'Much of our curriculum needs less content,' advises the Carleton Board of Education, 'More emphases on skills, attitudes, and process are necessary.'[13] 'People who demand a back-to-basics education,' explains Andy Hargreaves, of the Ontario Institute for Studies in Education (OISE) and one of the chief architects of the new reforms in Ontario, 'will prepare students for a back-to-basics traditional manufacturing society that's no longer there. Seventy percent or more of jobs are now in the service industries and demand a very different set of skills.'[14] 'We can no longer rely on teaching dead certainties of uncontested fact,' Hargreaves continued, 'in an age of rapid discovery that changes those facts.'[15]

The clamour for curricular reform can be said to arise from five evident sources. One of these is business. One businessman, Angus Bruneau (president and chief executive officer of Fortis Incorporated and chairman of Newfoundland Power), stated baldly: 'The province's education system, on its own, cannot and does not meet the biggest challenge in today's increasingly information technology–based society – producing learning rather than learned people.' Bruneau expanded his critique of current schooling practice by denouncing the 'central command and control system,' a system which is out of step with 'a society organizing itself amidst the movement of information and technology.'[16]

In a similar tone, members of Newfoundland's advisory council on the economy expressed incredulity at the aims and objectives listed in Newfoundland's curriculum ('to develop the individual – religiously, morally, mentally, intellectually, culturally and for the enjoyment of leisure – in order to participate as a member of society'). 'We all recognize the linkages between education and economic development,' said Christine Howlett, executive director of the council, 'but in the aims and objectives of the Newfoundland school system, there's very limited reference, if at all, to economic development, productivity, and the working individual.' Japan, by contrast, the business group advised, states its objectives more appropriately: 'to build a satisfactory and spontaneous life for adapting to social reality and for the creative solution of difficulties.'[17]

Some business groups have advocated an even more drastic means to assure 'value for money' by proposing the elimination of the school as it exists today and the formation of 'virtual schools.' These would take their bearing from radical experiments in the business world known as 'virtual corporations.' Such corporations are temporary companies that are nothing more than the aggregate of boutique firms working together to respond to a temporary market demand. Like 'lego bricks' these firms will be unlocked from one another and re-aggregated in another configuration when market demand shifts. 'Virtual schooling' would be similar, a temporary arrangement which could shift the ideological flavouring or the technical performances it taught depending on the prevailing political mood. Schooling would be tailor-made to the needs of the individual, and one student's draw on the resources of the school could be played against another's: the funding from the six months saved on the gifted student could be reallocated to the extra time needed for the challenged student. Teachers, on short-term contracts, would be enlisted for their specialty and called in to satisfy any given requirement as it emerges.[18]

The pressure for curricular reform has also come from ethnic advocacy groups. For them the curriculum is fundamentally flawed because in structure and content it is 'Eurocentric' and thus biased and discriminatory. They are opposed to studies of history which are essentially Western in content and theoretical focus. They find offensive the depiction of their peoples as having been colonized by Western imperial powers. They are hurt by their portrait in many textbooks as non-scientific, despotic, or 'traditional.' They find it degrading that they are depicted as the 'Other' of Western culture. They find little for themselves in the presentation of the achievements of British North American culture. They find the predominance in existing curricula of reasoning skills, or facts, or models of communication, foreign to their native perspective. They see little in the curriculum that causes respect for, and acceptance of, their cultural practices. Indeed, for these advocacy groups an implicit racism characterizes the curriculum. They say that the specific contents of school subjects perpetuate stereotypes, cultural generalizations, and discriminatory distinctions. Such racism is institutionalized by a curriculum which pursues its aims by individual achievement, or by competitiveness, or by grading, or by streaming. This argument dovetails with the position held by other advocates who see all 'labelling' as offensive and thus argue that the distinctions and judgments set in standard curricula are inherently socially divisive.[19]

The third pressure applied to the curriculum comes from within the educational discipline itself, though less from classroom teachers than from educational theorists and administrators. The reforms they want must exhibit the most advanced findings of educational theory. Today's vogue is for 'outcomes-based education.' The aim is not to have students master subject content or even acquire skills, but to display complex role performances by the time they leave the schooling system. These performances can be activated, the latest findings purport to demonstrate, only if teachers and curriculum designers introduce considerable fluidity into their notion of time. Simply stated, not all learning can be compressed into evident time-frames, and the succession of performed tasks over time does not translate into high-level performance, according to the studies done. An outcomes-based education, then, Bill Spady notes, is neither time-based nor curriculum-based.[20]

Orienting the curriculum according to what the student's performance should be at the end – determined by examining future trends and the conditions required when students enter the 'real world' – means that the mastery of traditional subjects and content of the curriculum can come to be seen as a 'transitional outcome,' and may even be dispensable, while 'effective adult functioning' is seen as an 'exit outcome.' Spady argues that outcomes-based education links traditional curriculum content to 'significant spheres of successful living' rather than to separate disciplines and subjects. 'Certain musical knowledge, certain aspects of philosophy, great works of literature and art,' he comments by way of illustration, 'they'll be taught, of course, but they won't be segregated into separate subject compartments and they'll be linked more to the quality of life experience.' Mathematics, for example, is an 'enabling outcome,' useful not in itself, but as a way of functioning effectively in many life roles. So, there is no point in teaching it separately but only in such 'ways that it is linked to real-life problems, issues, and challenges, so that it becomes the tool it was intended to be.'[21] 'We must rethink and reconfigure present disciplines into interdisciplinary packages which focus on learning at the higher levels of application, analysis and synthesis for skills workers actually use in their adult lives.'[22] Teachers 'must understand that their present courses and assessments are simply means to an end, not ends in themselves.'[23] And thus, 'should kids take a separate course called history every year that starts at some ancient time and moves forward to the present? No. Should they thoroughly examine current problems, issues, and phenomena in depth and ask why, why, why, about their origins and relationships? Yes.'[24] Spady concludes: 'when Mr. and Mrs. America get up in the morning and go out into the world, they don't do social studies, they do life. Parents are very responsive to these ideas.' Only an outcomes-based education can truly 'prepare for life.'

The fourth pressure for reform comes from radical intellectuals at universities and colleges across Canada and in diverse government ministries or offices (multiculturalism, immigration, the National Action Committee on the Status of Women), who view themselves as activists on behalf of social change. Not too many years ago, this same generation was attracted to the Frankfurt school and its synthesis of Marx and Freud, finding there guidance for reforming society. Then, social revolution was to release the 'polymorphous perversity' repressed by capitalist domination. In the language of Herbert Marcuse and Norman O. Brown were found the tools to produce a therapeutics for a new 'authentic' self and the insight that the freedoms and rights of liberal societies were in fact forms of 'repressive de-sublimation.' The 1960s reforms in education and social policy, including the Hall-Dennis Report, are filled with the result of that influence. The current appeal is to French 'deconstructionism' or 'post-modernism' (despite the rather hasty abandonment of this craze in the 1980s by French intellectuals themselves), for what North American intellectuals believe it advances is a creative release of 'marginalized voices' and the critical apparatus to destroy 'social hegemony' on behalf of a 'new pluralism.' 'Race, gender, and ethnicity' have become the operative terms of social redemption. In the 'social movements' spawned by a new activism affirming these 'identities' lies the salvation which Marxism and Freudianism have been unable to provide. Many of these intellectuals have played a large part in 'raising the consciousness' of advocacy groups; that is, making them aware of the political capital in announcing their distinctiveness.

We do not deny that there is some value in the claims made by these advocates. A balanced curriculum cannot encourage dogma, privilege, and archaism. Mechanism and antiquarianism are the death of the vital presence which is education. If the achievements of the past are to be recognized, the past must become a living part of the present. We agree with those advocates who believe it is appropriate to prepare students for the range of experiences to which they will be exposed when they begin to work and have families, as it is sensible to expect that students will have the skills to work effectively and in collaboration with others. We do not deny that those who pay the fiddler can expect to have their interests play a part in what is taught. We also think that, in so far as a sound perception of reality arises in the exchange of reasoned opinions among a genuine plurality of human beings, it would be narrow to exclude the depth and critical possibilities arising from alternative cultures. We also agree that it is necessary to renew teaching practices with more effective techniques. And finally, we agree that there is a place in education for contributing to thoughtful social change. As human beings we have moral duties, such as charity, and their enactment includes social reform. We agree with George Grant when, referring to those who immure themselves from the world, protected by their scholastic jargon, cynically watching over the detritus of our technological destiny, he writes: 'Let none of us who live in the well-cushioned west speak with an aesthetic tiredness about our "worldliness".'[25]

But we think, too, that there are limits to how much the curriculum can represent the multiplicity of sectarian interests. Our concern is that the idea of liberal education is being fundamentally eroded when curricula become hybrids of social grievance, workplace behaviours, sociological experimentation, and intellectual fashion. Liberal education has traditionally held out two promises. First, it undertook to equip all students with basic knowledge and understanding so that their opportunity for achievement was equal. Second, it saw its objective as freeing students from the opinions and fashions of the day by exposing them to the deepest and broadest human possibilities, so that in detachment each individual could judge what was important. This is how liberal education liberates. Neither promise can be fulfilled if there is no agreement that education's task is to shape and sublimate a student's longings in the service of a thoughtful civic decency. The lobbying of advocacy groups to have curricula reflect their desires has, in our view, two results. On the one hand, it denies the freedom and equality which liberal education held out, implying that all standards and principles are mere values or ideologies masking a ceaseless struggle for power at the expense of the marginalized. We see this as the path of cynical despair. On the other hand, it believes that the curriculum is a tool-box whose instruments can be shuffled around, removed, and reinserted as long as it serves the pragmatic task of engineering the reform of society towards its perfection. We see this as the route of dangerous presumption and utopianism.

The advocates who today monopolize debate in the public domain speak in one voice when they demand that the curriculum mirror the stresses and solutions-at-hand of contemporary society. For them the curriculum serves only to make students more responsive to social immediacy. Indeed, it is this capitulation to 'relevance' which explains the theme of anti-foundationalism which we find in all these advocates' positions. What we mean by 'anti-foundationalism' is the repudiation of stability, permanence, and order, even when symbols like 'equity,' 'liberation,' and 'plurality' are evoked whose prescriptive power, one would think, rests on a substantive idea of human character and of a stable order of reality. What is celebrated by nearly all the reformers is fluidity, mobility, and perpetual overcoming. Their visions are of a world devoid of models and archetypes, essential experiences and substantive meanings, and where human longing is never directed and formed, but permitted infinite metamorphosis and play. Their anti-foundationalism is a position counter to the very idea of a curriculum. There cannot be a statement of essential principles and aims, serving as the authoritative measure for assessing the extent and purpose of pedagogically forming a young mind, if the curriculum is nothing but a mirror of social alteration. Infinite adaptability in the curriculum translates into dissipated schooling. In our view the consequence of this anti-foundationalism is that education simply becomes a patchwork of discontinuous themes, producing a student who lacks all unity and balance.

Not surprisingly, there has also been a backlash against what passes for progressive reform. A fifth expression of discontent and demand for curriculum renovation is coming from activists who seek a return to 'Judaeo-Christian values,' to strict discipline, to rote-drills and formal testing, and to 'old-style' civics. Some have demanded the ban of books (a demand not unique to this group), the restoration of school prayer, and an ethics-test for teachers.

But nostalgia and regret are ultimately cynical and self-defeating. The rigidity of antiquarianism is no answer to those needs to which education responds. We have acquired over the centuries a more nuanced and dynamic understanding of the means by which education's purposes are fostered. We need to absorb the important discoveries of the last decades in comparative religion, philosophy, classical literature, and history in our teaching methods and objectives. But we have also forgotten that at the origins of liberal education lie comprehensive teachings which speak to the widest amplitude of human possibility, but which regrettably, through neglect, we have allowed to petrify into dogma. In subsequent chapters we will try to retrieve the experiential core of some of these teachings and consider whether liberal education is not still a living alternative for us.

Our public debate increasingly exhibits a loss of balance. It is polarized by

appeals which amount either to fascination with total fluidity or to a reasser-
tion of dogma. The advocates of curricular reform are either putting forward
chiliastic proposals for total transformation, or renouncing the responsibility
for education and capitulating to social processes. Such imbalance has distorted our capacity to see what is healthy in liberal education and what is
moribund. We must see if we can walk between the presumption of perfection and the slough of despair.

3

The Assault on Education

New Directions: Destreaming, Transition Years, Learning Outcomes

In January 1992, the Ontario minister of education announced, on behalf of the New Democratic Party government, a major 'restructuring initiative' for Ontario schooling. Then education minister Tony Silipo introduced the reform in a letter to teachers on 20 November: 'Exciting changes will take place in your school and others like it across Ontario. We will embark on a three-year process aimed at increasing the opportunities and educational challenges for students in the Transition Years (Grades 7, 8, and 9).' This exciting new era in education will 'guarantee all children an education that prepares them for their lives in an ever-changing world, but also ... guarantee them an equality of outcome.' It will 'take education from the 19th century to the 1990's,' from an industrial society to a postindustrial society. And it will lead to 'the elimination of poverty, illiteracy, and violence.' The reforms involved a major restructuring of the curriculum, of teaching practices, and of evaluation procedures. The principles underlying the reform towards a 'meaningful curriculum' were 'student-centred and integrated, developmentally appropriate, ones that allow for continuous learning, relevant and meaningful, accessible to all students, premised on the belief that all students can learn and be successful.'[1] The new direction would lower the number of school drop-outs and be a reply to accusations that the prevailing schooling system was unfair in 'labelling.' Not only was the government displaying leadership in advocating progressive measures designed to take Ontario's schools into the future, Ministry of Education officials suggested, but the shifts in society and technologies themselves had made possible new ways of organizing the curriculum. The NDP government was thus riding the crest of a historical transformation, at once medium and advocate.

The four pillars of the initiative are 'excellence,' 'equity,' 'partnerships,' and 'accountability.' To achieve these, the plan entailed destreaming and dela-belling Grades 9 and 10, the elimination of traditional subjects in favour of 'holistic education,' the establishment of 'benchmarks,' the elimination of specified hours of study, a new curriculum and a new system of evaluation, 'anecdotal' rather than graded report cards, the elimination of separate classes for exceptionalities (extreme hearing, visual, and behavioural and learning disabilities), and plans for a closer alliance between schools and the work-place. The way to make the structural changes needed, advised the minister of education, evoking the appropriate mood for the revolutionary call to a *novum saeculum*, was through 'new ways of organizing time and space.' Much of the inspiration for the initiative came from a report of a task force of the Carnegie Council on Adolescent Development in Washington, DC, enti-tled *Turning Points: Preparing American Youth for the 21st Century*, and the work of Jeannie Oakes.

Many teachers were outraged by the initiative. Parents were utterly per-plexed and in resistance formed the Organization for Quality Education. Immediate pressure was applied on the ministry by the Ontario Secondary School Teachers' Federation, with the support of the Ontario Teachers' Feder-ation and the Ontario Public School Boards Association, both at the New Democratic Party convention that summer, and through such resource books as *Grass Roots Up*. The OSSTF demanded Silipo's resignation. The opposi-tion was noted. The original initiative was modified and the incumbent min-ister was shuffled. The restructuring would now occur over a three-year phase-in period, local schools could control evaluation procedures and retain subject areas, exceptionalities and remediation programs could continue, and a royal commission would be struck to test the public waters. These conces-sions aside, later that year and in early 1993, the *Policies and Program Requirements for Transition Years: Grades 7, 8, and 9* were made public.

The restructuring initiatives had been percolating in the research and development stage for many years previously. The Ontario Liberals proposed the educational reforms in 1989 based on a 1987 report which had expressed dismay at the number of school drop-outs and the unfairness of streaming into 'dead-end' classes. That report, the Radwanski Report, compiled statistics to show that a disproportionate number of students from low-income fami-lies and immigrant or non-white families were represented in basic and general-level classes.

But despite the claim that the curricular reform was based 'on sound edu-cational theory and research' and that its goal was 'better learning opportuni-ties for all students through improved instruction and curriculum,' the ideological backdrop to the policy was obvious. It is well conveyed by the telling resolution of the 1992 Ontario New Democratic Party Convention directed against streaming students: 'this system has grown into an institutionalized form of racism and classism where black and poor students in southern Ontario and native and poor students in northern Ontario are directed into the general and basic streams because, even though unspoken, the ideological underpinnings of this is that these students are intellectually inferior and thus deserving of their lot.' Tony Silipo echoed this assessment when he stated that he would pursue 'aggressively' the proposal that teacher-training positions be reserved for members of Ontario's visible minority communities. Affirmative action in teacher training is, he commented, only part of the government's drive to ensure that 'all education in Ontario will become anti-racist education.' Wholesale curriculum revision was also necessary: 'Curriculum materials are usually written from a Eurocentric perspective with other groups assigned stereotypical and inferior roles.'[2] In July 1993, the NDP government, acting on Bill 21, made it mandatory for school boards to have an antiracism and ethnocultural equity policy approved by the education ministry. The strategy was to apply to all features of schooling: curricula, report cards, guidance counselling, hiring practices, staff development, student languages, and anti-harassment programs. David Cooke made it clear that his government was particularly keen to see changes in the teaching of history. Instead of forever reading about Europe's contribution, he stated, it was time to learn of the many contributions African nations have made.

Response to the 'restructuring initiative' was swift and vehement. The Ontario Secondary School Teachers' Federation accused the government of 'using our students and our schools in an experiment to implement social change through one institution, the educational system.' Many teachers felt that the proposals were placing undue burdens on them. How would they hold together a blended class of 'exceptionalities,' average learners, and 'gifted' students without teaching to the lowest common denominator and creating boredom among the better students? More specifically, how would they produce the 'enabling environment' required for exceptional students 'to reach their fullest potential' while challenging everyone else? They were being asked in effect to be private tutors to twenty-five students and to produce an individual program of studies for every one of them. Where would they find the time to collaborate with other teachers under the new plan of curriculum integration? How would they master the distinct subjects, outside of their own training and expertise, which now were being fused into 'supersubjects'? How would they keep abreast of studies correlating the minutiae of classroom conduct with future adult roles, being demanded under the 'learning-outcomes' approach? How would they have time for the extensive form of evaluation they were being expected to perform – continuous observation and check-lists; interviews; self, peer, and teacher evaluations; portfolios; informal and formal tests? The teachers' anxieties were not without substance. The directives to school boards stipulated that teachers would have to assume a broad accountability for student achievement. Objective test results would not be sufficient; teachers were expected to be responsive to, gauge, and bear responsibility for a wide range of behaviours and attitudes. The responsibility of producing 'comprehensive achievement profiles' was a minefield of limitless and extravagant demands for teacher accountability.

Parents were angered about the lack of consultation. To many, what they heard was confusing and jargon-laden, but it seemed to confirm their worst fears and to justify the actions observed last winter in Toronto suburbs of parents standing in overnight line-ups hoping to register their children in the few high schools known to cover the basics adequately. It substantiated many parents' frustrations about the quality of the schooling their children received. Many parents were left to reconsider private-school enrolment, especially those already concerned about the lack of discipline in public schools and the lack of a moral focus.[3] Others, looking to the success of parents in British Columbia, Alberta, and Quebec in having province-wide testing restored, lamented its absence in Ontario since the 1960s despite an Angus Reid–Southam News poll in February 1993 showing a 77 per cent support for standardized testing.[4] Administrators responded that universal testing was discriminatory in a multilingual society and that such exams as the Scholastic Aptitude Test were culturally racist.[5] Parents seemed less concerned about 'institutionalized racism and classism' than mediocrity. They did not deny that there were social problems, but they rejected the assumption that education should be the engine of reform. 'Laudable social objectives,' commented David Hogg, vice-president of the Organization for Quality Education, 'are driving our educational system instead of being derived from it.'[6] Most parents were not particularly heartened by Andy Hargreaves, of the Ontario Institute for Studies in Education, when he retorted with jaunty vulgarity to the concern that there were no new textbooks ready for the implementation period: 'Of course we don't have textbooks, we don't bloody well want them for multi-ability classes.'[7] Finally, parents felt they were never consulted. Of forty-eight advisory councils reporting to the minister of education, none represented the exclusive interests of parents or taxpayers. In June 1993 David Cooke, bowing under pressure, finally formed a *single* 'parents' council.'[8]

Gifted students judged the new curriculum to be a pointless exercise. 'Since there is no credit, and there is almost no way for a student to fail,' asked Brenda Noble, of Dalkeith, Ontario, 'where is the incentive for students to do homework, tests, or try to do their best?' Richard Martin, at Saint Lawrence High School in Cornwall, wrote: 'The government seems to have confused equality in treatment with equality in benefits ... De-streaming will break down the equality of students in education, replacing the recognition of different aptitudes and interests with the enforcement of a standard template.' Tim Pearce, at Bell High School in Ottawa, commented: 'The highly ambitious plan is trying to create an ideal teaching system – but ours is not an ideal world ... You should not try to live in some false reality where all students are equal.' Other students questioned the elimination of gifted-student courses and the proposal to withdraw gifted students from regular classes for a short period each day: 'Withdrawal from class,' commented Alison Burnell-Jones, 'creates more elitism than offering courses for gifted students.'[9]

Who was going to pay? asked parents, teachers, and school boards. The province pledged $2.75 million for the 1992–3 year to prepare teachers for the new curriculum, and $1.5 million has been set aside to improve teaching to eliminate racism and bigotry from the classroom. Any additional costs, David Cooke made clear, will have to be borne by school boards. 'They are going to have to redirect existing funds,' he ordered.

The ministry knew that the reforms would be controversial. They anticipated the observation of Caroline Orchard, Ottawa Carleton Board of Education teacher, who commented: 'I have been teaching for 20 years and I don't remember any change to the educational system having so little support in the educational community.'[10] Support from teachers' federations, local school boards, municipalities, teachers, and parents would have to be garnered. Teachers and school boards seemed to present the most immediate impediment. Tony Silipo stated that he would like to work 'co-operatively' with them, 'rather than hold a club to their heads,' but that he had legal authority 'which I won't hesitate to use' against those who oppose.[11] Not that they couldn't be 'persuaded' to see the importance of the reforms. In a report commissioned by the Ministry of Education, the principal investigators identified the conditions that had to be met for the reforms to be advanced: teachers would have to see reform goals as their personal goals, teachers would have to see a gap between current practices and the reform, and teachers would have to see the reform as achievable and needing to be done, and anticipate the steps needed for implementation.[12] 'Transformational' leadership would be required – a clarion call harking back to the 1960s idea of teachers as 'change agents.' Ongoing in-service education of teachers would be necessary. Such in-service sessions would aim at reminding dissenting teachers of the primacy of collegiality and collaboration, the vitality of experimentation and risk-taking, the value of incorporating new knowledge-bases and new learning, and the importance of their leadership role. A pseudo-scientific distinction of leadership styles was invoked: there had to be a 'ground shift' from Type A leadership (top-down) to Type Z leadership (consensual). The crass 'gee-whiz' reformism is obvious:

This type of leadership offers a vision of what could be and gives a sense of purpose and meaning to those who would share that vision. It builds commitment, enthusiasm, and excitement. It creates a hope in the future and a belief that the world is knowable, understandable, and manageable. The collective action that transforming leadership generates empowers those who participate in the process. There is hope, there is optimism, there is energy. In essence, transforming leadership is a leadership that facilitates the redefinition of a people's mission and vision, a renewal of their commitment, and the restructuring of their systems for goal accomplishment.[13]

Recalcitrant teachers had to be 'brought on board.' They had to 'put aside emotion and be rational,' and thus be brought to accept the higher wisdom of an educational system which was based on 'ways to enhance equity and provide quality programs for all learners including Native students, racial minorities, and exceptional students,' which advanced teaching and learning strategies 'that are relevant to the diversity of learning styles, [and] linguistic, geographic, ethnocultural, socio-economic and learning backgrounds,' which sought for 'innovative ways to enhance equity of outcomes for both male and female students,' which looked for 'different ways of organizing time and space within a school,' and which found 'new ways of creating school/community partnerships for preparation of career, work and life education.'[14] The resource materials teachers were provided with consist of books (a great part of them American) on empowering minorities, holistic learning, antiracist education, and global education.[15] Henceforth, as Bob Zacour, coordinator of the Ottawa Board of Education's transition team, says, the teacher would not be a 'sage on the stage' but a 'guide from the side.'[16]

There are three major areas of reform in the 'restructuring initiative': destreaming, learning outcomes, and core program areas. Accompanying these are also the principles of integration and partnership and the flagship of the reform – the transitions year.

Before we examine these closely, however, it is important to address the motivation behind the initiative. There is fundamental agreement between the NDP government and the author of the sources of many of the ideas underlying the new curriculum, Jeannie Oakes, that the central problems facing schools are low academic achievement and high drop-out rates, problems which are directly linked to the growing incapacity of the school to deal with the economically disadvantaged, with multicultural diversity, and with racism.[17] It is also commonly held that enhancing the 'effectiveness' of the schools will remedy these flaws. 'Effectiveness' has become the buzz-word for closing the distance between schooling and the larger social environment. Oakes approvingly cites Yale psychiatrist James Comer's view that this distance is the most serious problem facing today's schools. Specifically, then, there must be an enrichment of the curriculum with a more real-world focus, and a stress on creating supportive environments and on fostering partnerships that provide social and economic opportunities for the disadvantaged. Directing resources to gifted students, to the support of higher-quality schools, or to a 'traditional curriculum,' though, is unacceptable 'triage.'

The question should be raised as to whether a model designed to deal with inner-city deterioration and the disaffection of the urban poor and minority children in the United States is even appropriate for Canada. But our concern is different. There is no consensus that the progressive alternatives work in achieving their own professed goals and growing evidence that traditional 'direct instruction' is more effective not only in producing better performance but also in reducing inequality and low self-esteem.[18] We contend that ideological enthusiasm and educational fashion, in opposition to the interests of parents and the experiences of teachers, are being permitted to dictate the methods of education. Moreover, we argue that these reforms are robbing liberal education of its foundation, the balanced and wide-ranging assessment of human purposes and ends that have guided education in the past. What is at stake here is not merely debate about technique. The new curriculum is the fulfilment of those radical departures in education that began in the 1960s.

However visible the words 'excellence' and 'quality' are in the new reforms, they do not represent the idea of schooling most Canadians would associate with them. Just as in the 'enriched courses' drive in the 1970s, and in the 'back-to-basics' movement of the 1980s, the educational establishment is attempting, in widely publicizing the return to a 'core curriculum,' to deflect parents' criticism that today's schooling lacks substance. But this curriculum, based on child-centred and process-oriented learning, bears as little relation to a 'core curriculum' as 'back-to-basics' or 'enriched courses' meant the restoration of the aims of liberal education. There is something disingenuous going on when educrats come out with such slogans as 'Teaching lasting concepts rather than changing facts' when the concepts being referred to are those of flexibility and adaptability, and the facts being jettisoned are the concrete particulars of history and culture. 'Relevance, Rigour, and Imagination,' the catchwords trumpeted in the new curriculum, convey the idea that ballast is being restored to education, whereas in fact they signal the willingness of the educational establishment to go against its profoundest mandate and capitulate to social pressure.[19]

Let us now examine the particulars and see if the evidence bears out this contention. The point of departure for the restructuring initiative was 'destreaming': 'Beginning in September 1993, the organization of classes in Grades 7, 8, and 9 shall not be determined according to perceived student ability, and the program in Grade 9 shall not be organized according to levels of difficulty.' Placing students of varying abilities in the same classroom, we recall, was a key plank in the NDP government's platform: streaming of students is class biased, denying students' full educational opportunities as future workers. 'Multi-ability' or 'flexible groupings' was a signal that heterogeneous classrooms better reflected the real workplace in which students would find themselves.

In our view, there are commendable aspects to the idea of destreaming. We cannot condemn it unconditionally despite the ground swell opposing it. If we wish students in their education to become attuned to reality, then we cannot create enclaves of existence which fail to acknowledge that the human world is a plurality and hierarchy of talents and aptitudes. The fact that human beings are a *plurality*, which encompasses a diversity of interests, understandings, motivations, and achievement possibilities, means that, as human beings who must be educated to civic maturity, we must learn to accommodate ourselves to the differences that belong to human association. The world is not simply one perspective or one interest multiplied many times over. A heterogeneous, or 'multi-ability' class corresponds to the most evident facts of our human existence. To consent to otherness is one of the hardest and most exalted of human possibilities. It is the source of many of the distinctive human virtues – tolerance, patience, forbearance, humility, charity, and forgiveness. Such consent demands moderation, but also fortitude in overcoming excessive pride. If, and to the extent that, destreaming produces this cultivation of virtues, we agree with the hope that the demands of justice are being furthered.

But, as it now stands, destreaming is a denial of the equally evident fact that otherness is not uniform heterogeneity, that consent to otherness must include consenting to the longings of the best. The otherness of which destreaming seeks recognition is one that yields only to what we are in common – humans who are vulnerable by virtue of their physical and emotional needs. Destreaming does not acknowledge that we are also different because we have a longing for perfection, a desire to excel. At its height, such a longing is the source of vital discoveries (in the sciences, in medicine, in religion) and of creativity (in art, in music, in literature), of heroism and martyrdom, of leadership and exemplary conduct. This longing is the source of virtues through which our humanity expresses itself, and in this sense it reunites us at a higher level of our human association. In failing to acknowledge this longing, destreaming falls short of the demands of justice. This side of justice was, we recall, recognized by the student Richard Martin, who questioned the government's confusion regarding the distinction between equality in treatment and equality in benefit, and thereby reconfirmed Aristotle's point that 'The worst form of inequality is to try to make unequal things equal.' Why should the best rise only to the mediocre mean? Is the more sensible route not to upgrade the teaching standards for the disadvantaged, if the amelioration of their condition is one's true concern, rather than to lower the opportunities for the more advantaged? And, equally important, is it not necessary to educate and form this longing for perfection, this desire to excel? For it will be there in the classroom regardless of whether the curriculum reformers want it there or not. Moreover, it can so easily degenerate into a bullying craving for recognition, or an inclination to resent the less gifted, or boredom and day-dreaming, because, frustrated, it sees no other avenue for its satisfaction. The highest potential of the idea of destreaming is not being aimed at. There is no program here that encourages the formation of the virtues appropriate for living in a plural world. Moreover, as we shall see, the highest purpose of destreaming is being vitiated by another component of the restructuring initiative which reduces otherness to the mere fact of multiplicity by imposing a single, restrictive model of what a human being is.

The second component of the new reform is the 'learning outcomes' approach. 'Learning outcomes,' to be clear, is quite different from results-based educational objectives, at least those found in a subjects-based curriculum. Its aim is to make education more closely approximate 'real life.'

This reorientation permits, the guidelines state, de-emphasizing contents in the interests of 'a standard of excellence identified by the learning outcomes and the accompanying benchmarks.'[20] The new objectives will be those that the ministry identified as 'essential cross-curricular learnings,' based in considerable part on the Canadian Conference Board's identification of 'Employability Skills.' 'Benchmarks,' the ministry made clear, unlike standardized testing, would not measure students in relation to other students in the province, but would still provide assessment of students in light of 'given standards and examples.'[21] Unlike traditional curriculum objectives, though, they would be more fluid, more holistic, and more interactive. They are standards related to 'values, skills, and knowledge required for success in a rapidly changing world.' A 'learning outcomes' approach means producing a 'learning environment that promotes hands-on and relevant problem-solving' as a replacement for an allegedly static, increasingly irrelevant, demonstration of competence in knowledge or facts. 'In order to encourage our students to stay in school, we need to convince them of the RELEVANCE of education,' says one ministry circular. 'Facts change; information expands; concepts are the constant.'[22]

In itself, the principle of coordinating schooling with the demands and problems of 'everyday life' is unexceptionable. We do not deny that the primary task of the schools is to foster those talents and aptitudes which are relevant to the student's place in the world. Moreover, we are in agreement that the purpose of education is 'success' in a world 'subject to change.' Antiquarianism and archaism, mechanism and dogmatism, ought to have no place in education. A concern with how society is organized to correspond to human needs is essential to good education. We do not dispute that the full range of responsibilities and aptitudes needed in a full adult life ought to be the final end governing the means and contents of schooling. Indeed, as we will see in later chapters, this is the core of what is meant by a liberal education.

Yet, it seems to us that the 'learning outcomes' approach is, in the first instance, an excessive concession to the business advocacy groups. Of course, 'learning outcomes' does not refer exclusively to workplace behaviours; it is meant to address generally what is needed to 'function effectively in everyday life.' But the very idea of 'partnerships,' central to the 'learning outcomes' approach, applies particularly to the school-to-workplace transition. Partnerships with labour, the public service, government, and business sectors are to provide 'real-life incentives' for school success. The question we ask is whether it is appropriate for schools to take on the providing of job skills. As a financial matter, many schools which tried to simulate the variability of the work world are now learning how costly such a project is. Moreover, the goal of maintaining relevance in job skills may be inevitably self-defeating. A statement made by Willard R. Daggett, guru of learning-outcomes education, is telling: 'Skill requirements on the job,' he writes, 'changed at a rate four to five times faster than curriculum and organizational changes in our schools, leaving a gap between what students learn in the classroom and what is expected of them in the workplace.'[23] While this might be an argument for continuous renovation of school curricula, as Daggett would have it, to us the opposite conclusion is more obvious. Is it not more sensible that job skills should be learned on the job, even if this requires a more comprehensive apprenticeship program, rather than having the schools continually retool to try to keep up with the perpetual changes in the workplace? Moreover, to return to finances, why should the taxpaying public subsidize business productivity, which it is doing when school funds are diverted to repeated curricular engineering on behalf of businesses?[24]

Let us examine further what business advocates are saying. They point to two major principles in contemporary manufacturing strategy: zero-based defects and just-in-time delivery. Daggett, for example, wants schools to replicate these principles in their teaching components, ensuring a more productive workforce. But human existence, unlike the motions of a machine or an automated organizational process, is filled with contradictions, impassioned attachments, unfulfillable longings, mysteries, and anxieties. An inability to accommodate this human complexity and imperfection simply ends in ruthless management, like Taylorization (the enhancement of productivity by close control of space and time), which is nothing more than trying to reduce humans to a bundle of predictable reactions. Good managers know this and they make allowances. This is why good judgment – in business management, in employee labour – is more than the mechanical application of universals to particulars. It is the formation of principles amidst complex circumstances. Good curricula, teaching, and education are not formed like mathematical models. They acknowledge that human life consists of diversity, develops, and is filled with those contingencies that erupt from the fact of our individual uniqueness. We plan for the future, we make provisions for the long term. Human minds are not like warehouses, where rapid turnover and reinvestment are the only prudent strategies. What Daggett does not comprehend is that human reason is not simply an instrument for a quick return. In 'stockpiling' knowledge and artefacts of our historical and cultural existence – if we want to continue the economic metaphor – we are making investments from which we seek lifetime dividends in terms of meanings and truths.

The business advocacy groups are particularly impressed by Benjamin Bloom's taxonomy – awareness, comprehension, application, analysis, synthesis, and evaluation.[25] For them, everything can be broken down to its simplest parts and re-aggregated to achieve maximal performance. Using these criteria, work-world advocates like Daggett recommend the priority of reading for information and reading for critical analysis, but point out the unimportance of reading for personal response. They see the value of writing for information and for critical analysis, but not the importance of writing for personal expression and social interaction. They praise the basic operations of logic, probability, and measurement in mathematics, but see minimal significance in algebra and geometry. They radically downplay personal and civic responsibility, in favour of team-working. 'We must place far greater emphasis on fostering a learning environment where students function as active workers,' Daggett concludes, 'and teachers as managers of the instructional process.'[26]

We have noted our agreement with the idea that education should be relevant, that its purpose is 'success' in a world 'subject to change.' What we question is the definition of 'relevance' and 'real world.' Our concern is that a single and restrictive construct of human possibility is being imposed on education. That construct begins with the integration of the global environment, not questioning whether its growing interdependence is either necessary or good, and derives from this global paradigm the goal of the educational process – the learner as adaptable problem-solver. It further assumes that perfect coordination and symmetry ought to link all forms and practices in between these two poles of worker and global economy.

We doubt whether this approach responds to the amplitude of longings and passions which constitutes a human being. The construct upon which it rests may claim a monopoly of what we mean by reality, but it is manifestly denying the reality of political passion, of intellectual achievement, of historical awareness, of cultural sensibility, and of the need for meaning. The only features of reality acknowledged are those associated with a producing and consuming society – with those skills, behaviours, and values required to 'function effectively.' An audit of what great thinkers of the past have recognized as powerful and disruptive passions – the desire for glory, the lust for domination, the longing for total satisfaction, or the human will's proclivity to weakness and despair – displays a rich and comprehensive attentiveness to the nature of human beings. Behind 'learning outcomes' lies a simplistic optimism regarding human behaviour and a reductionist account of human longing.

The learning-outcomes approach might recognize the multiplicity of different consumer tastes, and the most elementary differences of our natural facts of birth, but it denies a more essential human plurality. It sees a world in which everyone confirms everyone else's fundamental perspective on the purpose of existence.[27] It sees simple contentedness with modern technological society, and its means of integrating individuals and defusing their resistance, as praiseworthy. Against this vision we agree with George Grant when he notes that the diversion, and concentration, of human activity towards mastery of the world through technological control, and its accompanying loss of more profound intellectual and spiritual possibilities, 'may have made us oblivious to the true eternity; but it more and more opens us to an immanent sempiternity of the same.'[28] 'Learning outcomes' is in fact rooted in some of the darkest processes of modernity, and in later chapters we will follow it down those dark corridors, as we try to think through the meaning of liberal education since the Enlightenment.

We are not necessarily repudiating the idea of 'learning outcomes.' As before, we are arguing for the deeper potential that we believe lies within the idea. The notion of unity advanced by the integrated holism of 'learning outcomes' is spiritless. Education does have as one of its tasks the promotion of the capacity for success in a world 'subject to change.' But we would broaden 'success' to 'happiness,' by which we mean the intellectual and spiritual substance that comes from openness to the amplitude of human experience, from politics to the life of reason. And thus we would argue that the best response to a world of change is not the *frisson* of perpetual mobility, but attentiveness to the durable structures of order. We think that common sense and decency, the guarantors of political order, are otherwise at stake. In the rest of this book, when we defend the traditional idea of liberal education, it is not primarily because we are defenders of tradition, but because, as educators, we are primarily concerned with the *happiness* of our students.

In our view, it is not the outstanding students who are the main victims of the learning-outcomes approach. These students will go on to colleges and universities and obtain an education which speaks to their desires and longings. The 'learning-outcomes' approach short-changes the average and the disadvantaged students who intend to work and who will not pursue postsecondary education. By depleting the substance of public school education and making its contents reflect nothing more than the school-to-work transition, we are leaving the average student equipped with minimal academic talents, little experience of the life of reason, close to no moral ballast, and nothing meaningful with which to fill his or her leisure time. Liberal education leavened the preparations for vocational life with a fermenting intellectual curiosity and spiritual yearning. 'Learning outcomes' produces a drab paste which simply bonds the most elementary ingredients of life – the need to labour with the satisfaction of consumption.

'Learning outcomes' satisfies the business and ethnic advocacy groups as well as many of the objectives of radical intellectuals. It stipulates that education is meaningful only so long as it is relevant to the progressive trends of social life. But, in our view, it thereby eclipses cardinal aspects of human reality – it does not elicit and form the civic virtues; it does not form the substance of faith or trust or friendship, without which no true justice is possible; it overlooks the longing for transcendence; and it ignores the intellectual and spiritual response to the mystery of existence. Why should we disqualify the assumption that what human beings need to be and do transcends the particulars of their social environment?

The third component of the reforms is the 'core program areas.' Separate subjects like history, business, geography, family studies, and physical education will be integrated to create modules where sets of problems can be negotiated and solved in interdisciplinary creativity. Four such core programs are designated: Language; Arts; Self and Society; and Mathematics, Science, and Technology. Core program areas, the reformers propose, permit more flexible and integrative use of data, skills, values, and meanings. Continuity of programming will mean that learning in one subject is 'reinforced' by learning in another. And, advancing this idea one step further, in time students will no longer be exposed to a specialized teacher in each subject, but will have an instructor capable of fusing a number of disciplines into the day's lessons.

Once again we see some merit in this proposal. Disciplinary boundaries were created in universities to reflect apparent differences, first of all between the natural sciences, the social sciences, and the humanities, and then within each of these, under the assumption that the dimension of reality investigated by its researchers was *the* cause of all human phenomena and the one to which all others could be reduced. Thus, we have disciplines of psychology, sociology, and political science, and organic, biochemical, and physical sciences, each separately vying to be the queen of knowledge. Each has become a paradigm with its own construct of reality and its own problems which it believes need to be solved. These paradigms, as Thomas Kuhn portrays them, can become institutionalized barriers to thoughtful and creative integration. To see existence as an orderly whole, whose various forces intersect and reciprocate, is to be more responsively attuned to reality. But even if the dimensions of existence we seek to understand do not naturally display a changeless or self-evident order, failure to see the relations and resonances from one field of experience to another denies the active historical work of human beings which has gone into forming unified cultural worlds. Lack of interdisciplinary attentiveness leads to the perception that reality is radically fragmented and that all is chaos, or that one method and set of facts suffices to explain a purposeless whole – the charm of technical competence.

'Core programs' and the principle of the 'integrated curriculum' attempt to redress the problem of fragmentation. But they do not overcome the charm of technical competence. The purpose of interdisciplinary education was not to reinforce a single objective or impression many times over by more data from different fields, as the designers of 'core programs' intend. Instead, it supplied a check on the specialized focus furthered in any one discipline. It did so by making researchers aware of alternative methods, findings, and explanations. From the best in interdisciplinary studies emerges a more comprehensive understanding of a reality that reveals itself as multidimensional. To be responsive to other disciplines checks the subjective certainty of technical competence acquired by researching within any one paradigm. In their best form, interdisciplinary studies produce a sense of humility, for they moderate the presumption of competence with the recognition that reality is always somewhat ambiguous, contradictory, and paradoxical. Humility and wonder before the whole are the core of a well-educated person.

But 'core programs' and the 'integrated curriculum' do not, despite the promise of their titles, provide this deep core of learning. They are set up so that all things present themselves as problems to be solved. Instead of conveying the facts of understanding, these programs present everything as an object of wilful experimentation. Instead of acquiring an awareness that distinct subjects reflect permanently distinct structures in reality or culture, the 'learner' is to have the maximum flexibility to integrate reality to his needs. For example, the major reading strategies are identified as prediction, confirmation, and self-correction. This is a model of verification based on scientific ideas of research and data, and of logicality, where truth is predicated on self-certainty. Reality consists of objects to be manipulated and controlled. Hence, the guidelines propose the following strategies for promoting cross-curricular learning: problem solving, product development, independent research. Informing these strategies is the imperative that 'meaning' be 'actively constructed.' To take one illustration from *The Common Curriculum*: 'reading is essentially a problem-solving process. The reader interprets or constructs meaning from a text by applying language, knowledge, and meaning-making strategies, as well as personal experience, to it.' Students are expected 'to understand that texts reflect the point of view, biases, and strengths and limitations of the author, and understand and appreciate the importance of reading independently and critically to further their own learning and to develop strategies for analyzing text.' In other words, before reading a text, we possess a dogmatic certainty that we cannot learn anything from it that will make us better persons.

Consider the accompanying diagram from *The Common Curriculum*. At the centre is the 'self-directed learner.' As his 'learning outcomes' are formed, that learner will increasingly apprehend what is of importance to him

The Transition Years

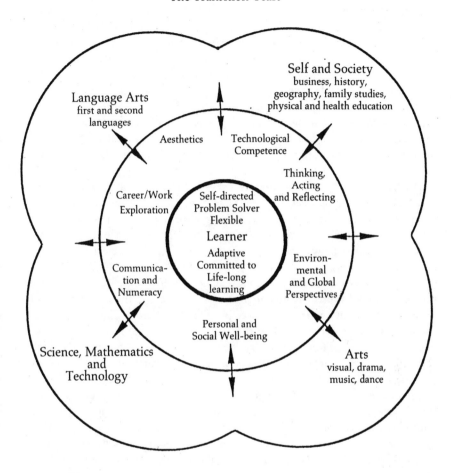

through logical self-certainty and resourcefulness on the one hand, and creativity and adaptability on the other. He is also provided with two sets of linguistic and thinking skills: critical and creative. He will exercise his problem-solving skills and his flexibility in integrating technological competence, aesthetic judgment, communication, personal and social well-being, and environmental and global perspectives in the effort to 'manage change' together with other like-minded learners. One field of inquiry after another will be used to reinforce the 'holism' of the integrated system he calls the world – adjustment and normalization become his moral imperative. The process he undertakes, and the objectives by which he is 'empowered,' mean that nothing that the student uncovers in his process of 'self-discovery' and research supplies him with an opposing perspective. What emerges is his understanding of a global environment, as the product of technical construction and creative projection, whose universal laws are validated in the inner certainty of his mind, and in the reinforcement supplied by other identical beings.

Instead of having been given a reserve of options and possibilities for an informed and independent judgment, the student of *The Common Curriculum* will have been launched on a single trajectory of global reform. He will not be in a position to question the assumption that an interdependent world demands an education like that set forth in *The Common Curriculum*. He will have no standpoint from which to ask if the fact of global integration implies its necessity, or whether its necessity implies that it accords with what is best for human beings. The 'holism' of *The Common Curriculum* is an empty parody of the authentic holism of a liberal education: while the latter makes us whole by enabling us to transcend the demands of the here and now, the new pedagogy promises a spurious wholeness of abject conformity to the here and now.

The Common Curriculum is not a balanced curriculum. It does not give the amplitude of human reality its due. A balanced, and thus educated, soul harmonizes identity with difference. It finds continuities and connections, but it does not render everything the same. It notes discontinuities and distinctions, but it does not allow everything to fragment. It finds interrelationships but it also acknowledges dissonance and contradiction. In the chapters to come, we will recover the central themes of liberal education to see how it helps provide this sense of balance. *The Common Curriculum* does not do this. It does not aim at reciprocity. What we mean by 'reciprocity' is the mutual action of order on the openness to the whole, and of process on measure. One illustration of this kind of reciprocity is harmonizing the claims of the particular with those of the universal, illuminating, for example, the love of one's own with the love of the good. Another illustration is the harmony of principles with judgment. The height of a liberal education is achieved when orderly thought harmonizes with responsiveness to mystery. This understanding of reciprocity is the opposite of what *The Common Curriculum* aims at. When its authors explain 'learning outcomes' as bringing together 'managing change' and 'adaptive creativity' they merely conjoin technicism with an effusive poetic longing. The consequence is that it produces the polarity of character types which Max Weber saw as representing the most dangerous tendencies of our age: 'specialists without vision and voluptuaries without heart.' Both are profiles of activists who are not content to live in their private dream-worlds, but who undertake to make us all partake of them. One demands an excessive mathematical precision. The other romantically dreams of an impossible wholeness. Such persons betray in their utopianism a lack of a balanced education, for they ignore important aspects of reality. The results of such imbalance are the dreams of wholesale reform of an imperfect existence, called millenarianism. Millenarianism cannot tolerate the contradictions and tensions of existence. It seeks a radical upheaval, for it denies that perfection is unrealizable. Millenarianism will make of perfection a world-immanent project. A fictitious construct of reality replaces the everyday complex world where human judgment and virtue were necessary.[29]

The political danger of individuals or groups acting on fictitious constructs of reality has traditionally been blocked by promoting a vigorous public life where opinions are daily held up for public inspection. But in *The Common Curriculum*, the conjunction of universal skills with self-empowerment and ethnocultural identities bypasses the institutions once understood as mediating between the world and the individual – the independent state, or concrete political community. What we have in the 'restructuring initiative' is a simulacrum of liberal education's understanding of the intellectual and spiritual universality of humankind and the concrete particularities of beings participating in political and cultural worlds. *The Common Curriculum* links global consumerism with the inward focus of isolated beings, vulgar cosmopolitanism with tribalist roots. There is very little left here either of the transcendent power of reason or of the fact that we live in nation-states whose purpose is realized in the formation of a 'civil association.' 'Civil society' is not recognized as a civilizational achievement. *The Common Curriculum* designers therefore see no point to forming the virtues required for public existence, that public space in which a plurality of human beings engage one another and in which private perspectives are aired and measured against the common sense and common reality which are both its context and its product. In its stead, *The Common Curriculum* locates the source of truth and value in the self's inner certainty. At best the self may reinforce its certainty by listening to other isolated individuals. The dangerous implication of this is that *The Common Curriculum* holds out no possibility of transcending this solipsism or social conformity. It locks individuals in their own private worlds or, worse, merely mirrors back the tastes of global society.

The Common Curriculum is a puzzling document. It claims to embody noble principles which are also at the core of liberal education. It acknowledges that the basis of our society is respect for other persons; that basic skills are important; that 'values' are more than personal preferences; that there are spiritual aspirations in the capacity for self-fulfilment; that the past is an inspiring record of human achievement; that there is a place for the arts in the full experience of everyday life; that family, community, and nation make meaningful contributions to life. But, more visibly and more relentlessly, it initiates processes which remove the substance and intelligibility grounding these principles. *The Common Curriculum's* racier elements – destreaming, learning outcomes, core programs – seem fair indication to us that its politics are dissolving its educational substance.

Like so much in contemporary society, the new curriculum conjoins high-minded idealism with narrow technicism. Magisterially it announces its compatibility with the fundamental principles of Canadian life, yet at one fell swoop it undermines and excoriates those principles through its millenarian reformism. It does not recognize the incompatibility between self-centredness and spirituality, critical problem-solving and intellectual meaning, managing control and aesthetic attunement, values and structures of order.

We are not surprised that a document which is millenarian in intent – and whose designers are so evidently in revolt against reality – and which undertakes to extinguish liberal education should nonetheless touch on experiences and principles that accord with a truly balanced liberal education. The reform activist, after all, if he is to be successful in overthrowing reality, and imposing his dream-world, must cover the general scope of human experiences and commonly praised principles sufficiently that those he seeks to persuade to his cause do not reject it as utopian, for having omitted cardinal aspects of reality. Eric Voegelin has analysed with unsurpassed clarity the sequence through which this deception proceeds. The account of reality given by the reformer must present the kind of comprehensiveness that, in line with prevailing norms of scientific analysis, will make it appear true. Yet it must be sufficiently obscure so as not to appear as a dream-world. The operation involves describing three phases: first, the times as we experience them are ending; second, the times as we know them are a prelude to a true time of perfection about to begin, and the tentative efforts and struggles to know the true principles of social order are about to be completed; third, the new age to be established fully endows all humans with their perfected state so that no further historical action or intellectual questioning is needed. In the process of this historical and social analysis, commonly held experiences and principles undergo revision and are transfigured into the operational tools of the revolution the activist requires to produce his dream-world. While the words may remain, their function has been annexed to the cause of revolution.[30]

The whole rich burden of being human – asking questions, responding to the mysteries of life and death, struggling against injustice by the stronger, accepting the limits and burdens of existence – is about to become superfluous. *The Common Curriculum* has many typical features of a millenarian movement.

In our view, the school is being used as a laboratory for radical social reform, guided by a messianic impulse that a wholly new world and a new humanity can be produced. The choice of the symbol 'Transitions Year' is illuminating, evoking as it does the sense of a rite of passage or a rite of initiation – as it indeed is, from childhood to adolescence, and from elementary school to high school. And like all rites of initiation, the processes that go on within 'Transitions Year' accentuate the liminal quality of passage, where structures, gradations, and identities all evaporate into fluid play. During that year of self-discovery and new relations with others, the initiates acquire a new life, that is, a new perspective or preparedness for 'living in an ever-changing world.' Many educators have used a similar creation-imagery to evoke the transition from one stage to the next, but nearly all saw the purpose of passage as elevating the student to a higher and more complex dimension of reality – the passage from physical to civic maturity, from play to work, from opinion to the search for knowledge. What distinguishes 'Transitions Year' from these is that the longing which it taps is not guided towards what transcends the immediacy of the student's physical and emotional existence, or what moves the student from flux to stability, from fluidity to order. On the contrary, it is a preparation for wholehearted participation in the permanent revolution of radical social reform. The Grade 9 student is to be a microcosm of the social experiments humanity as a whole is invited to undertake. His classroom has become a crucible wherein the natural diversity of existence, the complex forces acting on humans, and the accumulation of historical accident can be melted down and transmuted into a golden state.[31]

The construct of reality upon which this dream is based is one that takes the tensions and contradictions of human existence and assumes that they are capable of resolution by applying technical means to external social and economic phenomena. Empowerment and management are the operative tools in this dream. Such a focus is anti-political, as well as anti-intellectual. It disputes the reality of plurality. It blithely neglects many human passions and operates with the naive Rousseauan belief that, left to their own spontaneous expression, human longings will naturally form a harmonious whole. The reform brings together an emboldened sense of technical competence with a poetic vision of global wholeness. Eschewing eternal archetypes, stable reference points, and permanent structures, it nonetheless puts forward its own vision of society as the completion of a history of political action and critical questioning.

We all have to live with the acted-out dreams of many people. Usually we can try to avoid their company. The misfortune here is that the reformers advance one perspective on education, while shutting off all others. It would be one thing if the 'restructuring initiative' was an experiment at a select number of schools, and parents had a choice as to how their children will be educated, while teachers could elect to teach elsewhere. But the public school system as a whole is being made over to become homogeneous, consonant with universalizing trends worldwide.[32] And we argue that *The Common Curriculum* risks producing a generation of students severely impoverished by the bankruptcy of their educational experience.

Alberta has backed away from its ill-fated experiment at 'program continuity.' British Columbia is undertaking a major reassessment of its commitment to 'continuous learning.' Both have had to respond to the affront felt by teachers, who had been told that they were not educating to the best of their capacities, and to the demand for performance-based schooling. A confusing dual focus on process and on result has emerged in those provinces. Both provinces' education mandarins have learned the dangers of experimentation where there is an inadequate body of research demonstrating its success. They have also learned their lesson about the baleful consequences of excluding parents and teachers from the ongoing appraisal of the school's ability to educate students. The question that remains is why a generation of students, and all who will be touched by their acts and judgments, should bear the cost of these mistakes.

The Link to the Universities

The crisis in public education is linked to the universities in a number of ways. To start with the most obvious and the most important, universities receive their students from high schools. Hence, how well they perform in university depends to a large degree on how well they have been prepared for university by high school – and this in turn decisively shapes their life prospects for employment and for the satisfaction that comes from being a liberally educated citizen.

Unfortunately, but not surprisingly, child-centred concepts of learning put Canadian students at an ever-increasing disadvantage when they enter university. Since these concepts have failed to equip them with basic skills of reading, writing, and analytical self-distance, universities find more and more that they must provide these skills for students so as to give them a chance of succeeding and finding employment. In other words, the job that should be done by our high schools is being bumped up to the university level, decreasing the cost-effectiveness of their increasingly strained resources.

The problem is grave, and it is already here. In 1992, the Economic Council of Canada estimated that a million Canadians will leave the school system in the coming decade functionally illiterate. David Warrick, a teacher of communications and humanities at Humber College in Toronto, puts his finger on the origins of this crisis:

About a third of students entering Humber College who take our placement test fail because of their inability to recognize mistakes in English composition. This is the generation educated in child-centred, discovery learning. This is the generation which is supposed to have developed self-esteem through process learning. But, in fact, this is the generation that has been deprived of a sound education because of a misguided ideological revolution, which began with the Hall-Dennis report 28 years ago and continues today ...[33]

In the world of common sense as opposed to the world of educational theorists, we know that self-esteem comes from understanding how to make an argument based on reason and experience, rather than just reacting emotionally to whatever whim predominates. But, as Warrick observes: 'Objectivity and documentation are foreign concepts to most high school graduates. In the absence of rules, our students have a need to reinvent them. This use of language without constraint and guidance is gaining acceptance. Illiteracy is actually defended in the classroom.'

Not only does child-centred learning deprive students of basic communications skills, it actually stunts personal development. Far from liberating students to think for themselves, it narrows their horizons and makes them the prisoners of whatever media clichés and fads are currently most popular. Warrick identifies the heart of the crisis. We are harming the souls of Canadian young people by making them believe that the whims and impulses stimulated by the culture of kitsch and consumerism surrounding them are equivalent to thinking independently:

Pop culture is exciting and fascinating – certainly worthy of study in its own right, but 'temporal chauvinism' which excludes great cultural achievements from other places and times is gaining ground. This 'attitude,' manifested in the behaviour of many high school students, is infectious. The surprising thing is that our school system inadvertently encourages it by neglecting 'knowledge-based' course material that challenges our students to transcend their own world and discover ways of thinking beyond their own ... (T)his attitude can lead to a malnourished society fed on 'fast-food' thinking and 'all-you-can-eat' narcissism.

As university teachers, we are routinely humbled and delighted by our first- and second-year students. For the most part, they blossom when presented with the wider vistas of university learning. Many of them are full of spirit and wonder, eager to learn all they can about the world, and it is always a privilege to try to fulfil their expectations. Students are not to blame for the conditions David Warrick describes. They are the primary victims of these educational abuses. Because they are young and energetic, the harm is not irreversible, and most of them make up for the deficiencies they brought with them from high school. But isn't it an appalling waste of energy, time, and resources that they should have to do so? Imagine how much these fine young men and women would contribute to themselves and to Canada, and how much sooner, if they had arrived at university with educational skills comparable to those of a high school graduate of twenty years ago.

In light of these problems, one might expect that provincial governments would be particularly supportive of the universities and sympathetic to the increasing pressures on them to do both their own job and that of the high schools as well. But quite the reverse is the case. All across Canada, universities are being subjected to the same fiscal and ideological pressures that have produced child-centred learning processes in the schools. Far from being encouraged to remedy the defects of those processes, they are under pressure to introduce them into their own courses of study. Alberta, Saskatchewan, Manitoba, Ontario, New Brunswick, and Nova Scotia have all been conducting extensive reviews of post-secondary education. Common to the reviews is the contention that provincial governments must 'develop a fuller range of performance indicators' for universities and involve themselves directly in micro-managing them, including the rationalization of programs on a province-wide basis to end 'unwarranted' duplication and proliferation. 'The provincial reviews indicate that universities may well have permanently lost their place as an unassailable priority on the public agenda,' concludes *University Affairs*, the main professional affairs journal of Canadian universities.[34]

One might suppose from reading this that the Canadian public is as dissatisfied with the universities as it is with the school system. But this is not the case. A recent Angus Reid/Association of Universities and Colleges of Canada survey shows that four out of five Canadians believe universities are doing a 'good or very good' job.[35] This is a rating that could only be dreamed of by the politicians who affect to be serving the will of the people by calling the universities to account. Moreover, two-thirds of the respondents believe that universities are doing a better job than primary and secondary schools. There is, in fact, no ground swell of dissatisfaction with the universities because they are, despite growing political interference, still managing to do what they have always done. The pressures are largely manufactured from above. Educational bureaucrats and their political masters are bent on bringing the universities under direct government control out of a combination of fiscal mismanagement of their own resources and ideological pressure to make universities 'accountable' to government-approved victim groups. One can spot this lethal combination of left and right behind the bloodless bureaucratese of *University Affairs* (May 1993): 'Chief among the factors that determine the new context is the government's need to confront the fiscal crisis of the state while promoting economic restructuring. The emergence of ever more diverse expectations and pressing demands on universities is closely linked to this new context. It has also brought governments to ask themselves whether obtaining "more of the same" from universities will satisfy the needs of society.'

One might wonder whether our provincial politicians are particularly fit to set standards for financial accountability, let alone determine whether physics and Chaucer are being properly taught. Even on narrow grounds of fiscal management, the average university would surely stand up well in a comparison with Ontario Hydro or any provincial budget brought down in the last ten years. Universities have neither been major beneficiaries of the fat spending of the eighties (when provincial government expenditures on universities declined both as a percentage of their total budgets and in real terms), nor major runners of deficits among provincial institutions. But there is a broader strategy behind this government-manufactured crisis, and to see its outline, we should look at the recent Smith Report on the condition of Canadian universities.[36]

In the media coverage of the Smith Report, the contention that teaching was 'undervalued' in our universities was often linked with visual and verbal images of crowded lecture halls. The impression was thereby conveyed that the emphasis on research was somehow the direct cause of these crowds of bored and confused-looking students. This impression was underscored by Dr Smith's general reluctance to dwell on the massive decline in funding that Canadian universities have had to cope with in the last decade. But, after the students themselves, professors are the victims, not the cause, of this decline in the quality of classroom time. When enrolments double or triple while faculties remain the same size, the result will inevitably be mass courses with their attendant feelings of alienation and drift. Professors feel this keenly. When we teach introductory courses that used to have fifty students and now have two hundred, our own ability to reach students cannot help but suffer. For our provincial governments to cause this state of affairs through their funding policies, and then blame academics for it while posing as the student's friend, is a perfect example of trying to have your cake and eat it too. Such obfuscation will not aid the difficult task of finding new sources and structures of funding.

Lest we be misunderstood here, let us add immediately that we do not belong to the chorus of those who constantly whine about cut-backs and imply that simply spending more money on universities is the solution to all their ills. On the contrary, massive new infusions of public money into the universities will do no good at all unless they are preceded by a spiritual reawakening of the university's dedication to liberal education and its responsibility for helping to shape thoughtful and responsible citizens. Indeed, there are reasons for entertaining the idea of a full or partial privatization of the university, or perhaps the introduction of a national voucher system enabling students to choose where to spend their money among universities competing for their patronage.[37] But the Smith Report is a representative sampling of bad ideas from both the left and right ends of the political spectrum, and we will have to confront them before any genuine progress can be made.

The whole issue of teaching and its relationship to research was distorted by the Smith Report, and in ways that will retard rather than assist our efforts to deal with the university's real problems. The report was characterized by a disproportionate emphasis on those who profess to find teaching slighted in comparison with research. But with all due respect to their feelings, we believe that academics who are worthy of their positions find that teaching stimulates their scholarship, and that what they publish makes them more stimulating teachers. We have met very few academics who feel compelled to churn out publications for no other reason than to get tenure. There are far easier and far more lucrative ways to earn a living than writing books and articles if one's heart isn't in it. No one who dislikes teaching should even consider becoming a professor, because that is where one's prime responsibility rightly lies. But it is equally the case that no one who lacks a deep and lasting interest in scholarship should become an academic either. The spread of knowledge through independent thinking and writing is at the core of the university's mission in all civilized countries. Canada's contribution to this universal mission has been second to none. Just think of the names: Charles Norris Cochrane, Harold Innis, John Grube, C.B. Macpherson, Hilda Neatby,

Marshall McLuhan, Northrop Frye, Robertson Davies, Margaret Laurence, J.L. Cameron – one could go on and on tracing the stars in this dazzling galaxy. And yet when one looks at Canadian education today, one increasingly finds a dispiriting retreat from this heritage of universal scholarship, a narrow bureaucratic nationalism and inward-looking philistinism masquerading as fiscal conservatism or political correctness.

In truth, the notion that we must emphasize either teaching or research is a forced dichotomy not borne out by the experience of the majority of academics or students. It is true that there are productive scholars who are unsuccessful as teachers. But it is also true that there are academics who disguise their disinterest in scholarship by claiming to care intensely about teaching – and some of them are unsuccessful in the classroom too. In a pinch, a student can get more out of a productive bore than an unproductive one. But the best academics tend to be good at both teaching and scholarship. At bottom, you cannot be an effective teacher of university students if you are not active to some degree as a scholar. Professors have a responsibility different from that of high school teachers. Our students are young men and women expecting to hear something original and thought-provoking in their courses. We do not merely impart information according to a uniform curriculum devised by experts. We are, or should be, the experts. We write the books and articles that are used in our courses. Doubtless every professor could improve his or her classroom skills, and more attention should be paid to this in the training of graduate students. But no amount of caring-and-sharing therapy or techniques for better packaging of xeroxed materials or colour tabs can replace the fact that a university course must engage young adults in serious thinking about the greatest issues of the mind and heart. There is no a priori method or technique, no regimen of communications skills, that can replace this age-old encounter between teacher and student.

For these reasons, it would be a big mistake to abandon the traditional attempt at a balanced assessment of teaching and research, forcing academics to opt for one or the other. The notion of a two-tier university system that continues to float around the provincial ministries is an even worse idea, if this means a division *between* universities rather than *within* them. No university can be designated simply as research-oriented or teaching-oriented. Departments within a single university have widely varying national and international reputations. The same is true of individuals within a single department. To force a university into one mould or another would be like tending a garden with a sledgehammer.

But it would be even more unfair to the students, who should always be our central concern. For, regardless of whatever rhetoric provincial governments might devise to justify dividing universities into tiers, the end result would be that students attending the 'teaching' universities would be considered second-class citizens, while the students of the 'research' institutions would be considered the elite. And this would be to remove one of the few really effective means for meritocratic upward mobility in our society. The affluent would continue to send their children to Yale or Princeton, or to their alma maters like Toronto, Queen's, or McGill. These latter would, of course, magically show up in the 'research' tier. But the blue-collar or working-class student at Brock or Trent would find herself consigned to what everyone would know was an inferior system, though it would be dressed up with a lot of earnest rhetoric about 'our deep concern for teaching.' We suspect this was in the minds of the provincial officials who carped anonymously for the Smith Report about those wicked professors and their disregard for teaching. Behind the masquerade of 'dynamic innovative thinking' lies a remarkably shabby proposition: save money by creating a mediocre bottom tier with heavy teaching loads, and call it 'valuing teaching'; shovel a portion of the savings into a few remaining institutions of the sort that mandarins' children attend and call it 'creating a Canadian Harvard and MIT.' We believe this approach to be transparently wrong-headed. Instead of hiving off a few showcase institutions and consigning the rest to mediocrity under the cover of a pseudo-populist rhetoric, we should be strengthening the standards of meritocracy within *each* university. Doing so would be more cost-effective, since it would produce more highly educated people for every dollar spent. More importantly, however, increasing meritocratic standards in all universities would make each university more truly fair and democratic by expanding the equality of opportunity for an earned individual excellence of result to the entire student population, regardless of background or origin.

Proponents of educational reform are fond of invoking American comparisons, but in discussions of the Canadian university, this is rarely done in a knowledgeable way. Between us, the authors of this book spent twelve years in American academia before returning to Canada. We have taught at, or been a visiting fellow at, an Ivy League school, a nationally reputable small private college, and a couple of major public research universities. American post-secondary education is wonderful for those students who are wealthy and talented enough to go to Harvard. It is not so wonderful if you are at the bottom of the pecking order – say, in one of the local branches of a state university system. The nobility of our Canadian educational experiment has resided in the fact that we conjoined superb universities with universal public funding. This has resulted in a high average quality in our universities that the United States cannot match.

The maundering in recent years about the need for a 'Canadian Harvard' is largely from people who are dazzled by Gothic spires and snob appeal, but who know little about how universities actually work. They might be surprised to learn, for instance, that a representative number of the books and articles studied in elite American universities were written by Canadian academics. Below the level of administrators and provincial ministries with their increasingly parochial concerns, and increasingly unappreciated by them, Canadian scholars engage in a rich and lively international community of learning. By the same token, places like Princeton or Yale have their share of middling talents. They have no monopoly on scholarly brilliance, as their own best talents are the first to admit. We already have Canadian equivalents of the best that such institutions achieve. But one must wonder if we hold our own universities in increasing contempt precisely because they are financially accessible to the majority. In the money-besotted eighties from whose dreams of limitless wealth we have yet to recover, how could a Chevette compare with a Jaguar?

If we do decide to create elite universities on the American model, one thing is sure: it will not be achieved by giving more pubic funding to some universities at the expense of others. Here is where the carping of certain Canadian corporate executives and other representatives of the business community strikes us as especially misinformed. They claim they want Canadian Harvards, but – in marked contrast with their American counterparts – they appear to want the government to do it for them. It is perhaps just another instance of their tendency to profess their fealty to market forces and competitiveness while conniving to get public funding. Places like Harvard and Yale were not created by state planning, or by financially squeezing less-favoured institutions. The source of their freedom to expand and experiment and to admit only the best students is their enormous privately raised endowments (Harvard's is worth $4.6 billion, Yale's and Princeton's about $2.5 billion each, larger than the annual budgets of some sovereign countries). In general, Canada's corporate elite looks pretty stingy toward its own country's educational and cultural needs in comparison with the astonishing generosity of American business at all levels of education and the arts. Only when our corporations realize, as do their American counterparts, that it is a privilege and an obligation to contribute generously to the education of their own country's young people will they earn the right to complain about the results.

Let us try to sum up the crisis facing Canadian universities. Because of the restless desire of politicians to show their innovativeness in a cash-strapped environment, we are endangering one of the best and fairest university systems in the world by using it to pursue non-educational goals that the government cannot find money for elsewhere. Behind the confusion sown by the Smith Report lurks the same combination of pressures from the left and right that threatens what remains of the excellence of our schools: using the rhetoric and techniques of fiscal conservatism to implement a politically correct social agenda.

Politicians today find that there are no financial resources for expanding existing social welfare programs or devising new entitlements, even badly needed ones such as government-regulated day-care. They see the huge sums spent on universities, and are increasingly tempted to redeploy these funds to try to achieve their social and political agendas by other means. Many of these aims are worthy. But they cannot help but come at the expense of existing programs, already battered by the constant attrition of faculty and increase in class size. This is why there is something disingenuous about government demands that universities manage their finances in a more business-like way, responding to market forces and adjusting their course offerings accordingly. University enrolments have doubled in the last thirty years.[38] The market for courses is definitely there, as much for the 'soft' humanities and social sciences as for the hard sciences and engineering. But we doubt that the provincial ministries have any real intention of allowing universities to become financially independent. The capping of tuition fees removes much incentive for universities to reach out and tailor their strengths to market forces. In an age of shrinking budgetary resources, what government will give up a chance to disburse such huge sums and be seen as the student's benefactor?[39]

The confusion sown by fiscal downsizing and restructuring allows pressure groups to demand that the university be reorganized to implement their partisan goals, and this tends to happen whether the government of the day wholeheartedly shares these goals or not. Consequently, the university is vulnerable as never before to politicization at the expense of learning. For example, the Ontario government has served notice that it intends to restructure all university governing bodies to make them reflective of government-approved advocacy groups. In the usual style of this government, and as with its new curriculum for schools, the concerned parties are not so much being asked for their response as being informed that the restructuring will take place by legislative or administrative fiat.[40]

However well-intentioned, this is a dangerous and unprecedented intrusion by the state into traditionally autonomous institutions of learning. The leadership groups who would thereby likely gain control are, on a number of issues, arguably as little reflective of Canadian society at large – including the sections of it they claim to represent – as were the special interests who dominated the Charlottetown Accord. Canadians generally believe in the equality of opportunity for women and minorities without subscribing to the view that Canadian society is systemically racist and sexist. Indeed, they have the common sense to realize that if Canada were systemically oppressive, it would be impossible either to protest the fact effectively or to expect the redress of injustice. The ideology of systemic victimization is hopelessly self-vitiating, its shrill rhetoric exacerbating the tensions it claims to abhor and distracting our energies from the sober, detailed work of finding procedural remedies for the real injustices.

But the leaderships of government-approved single-issue advocacy groups have tended to absorb this ideology from the universities. Far from giving the community at large a greater say in how universities are governed, therefore, they will – following the pattern in the Charlottetown process and elsewhere – very likely further alienate the university from the parents and students it serves. For, behind this threatened legislative fiat lies the critique of the university curriculum as being 'Eurocentric,' a critique that is both misleading and harmful to liberal education. Its most radical advocates use the rhetoric of diversity to disguise an illiberal impulse to stifle debate. They are all too often bolstered by academics and administrators who themselves believe that the very idea of the university as a haven of non-partisan scholarship is illegitimate – or, if they do not believe it, know of no way of disputing it. These pressures are only made more dangerous by the growing contempt among Canadian elites for our university system (reflected in an infatuation with the American Ivy League school), and by the all-too-frequent absence of vision and leadership among Canadian university administrators and presidents.

All in all, the financial dependence of our universities on the provincial governments has proved to be a Faustian pact. Who now recalls the Ontario government's assurances, when large-scale public funding of universities was first introduced, that it would in no way detract from the corporate privileges and independence of the universities? We have almost forgotten that our universities began as private, autonomous institutions. The sceptre and other regalia still on display at commencement ceremonies bear silent testimony to the connection of our universities with a thousand-year-old enterprise of higher learning, and with the privileges of a special corporate body within the larger civil order. Nobody in a position of authority seems to remember this today, or to conceive of making such an argument. Governments routinely assume that universities make up a single administrative 'system,' their own creatures every bit as much as a bridge or power plant, to be included in whatever restructuring is deemed expedient in the public sector as a whole. Universities urgently need to remember and reassert their traditional corporate identity, and to make it clear that they are not the administrative creatures of the ministries. As we have observed, this has to go hand in hand with a serious consideration of the full or partial privatization of the university to recapture its fiscal autonomy and free it from the grip of administrators who view themselves as extensions of the ministries. In the meantime, we can only lament the passing of one of our country's oldest, most successful, and most genuine human associations. As Tocqueville observed, the modern state tends to gobble up all genuine sources of local communal loyalty and replace them with its own bureaucracies.[41]

Complex and difficult as these issues are, they would be easier to deal with if it were not for the fact that the harshest critics of liberal education are often to be found among the ranks of academics themselves, mainly in the social sciences and humanities. They are still a minority, but a vocal and relentless one. In their view, the university is merely an extension of the more or less repressed power struggles going on throughout society between classes, races, and genders. A professor who believes she is giving one student an A and another a B because the first student has learned more than the other is deluded. What she is really doing is reinforcing, in a subtle way, the selfish hierarchies that dominate society at large.

But there are just and unjust hierarchies. A meritocracy is a just hierarchy. It is based on ability and performance, hence to be distinguished from an unjust hierarchy – a hereditary caste – based on arbitrary factors such as inherited wealth, social status, or religion. As we observed earlier, there is no contradiction between meritocracy and liberal democracy. On the contrary, one entails the other, for the publicly established equality of opportunity implies the socially sanctioned inequality of result. As an ideal to be striven for as against continuing arbitrary restrictions on meritorious upward advancement, meritocracy is also compatible with the occasional intervention of government in society to curtail excessive concentrations of established wealth and power that are unfairly restricting further upward mobility – the liberal-democratic emendation of liberal democracy's own shortcomings that informed the establishment of the social welfare safety net and other social programs. We are equal as citizens and equal before the law, and we possess equal civil rights as members of a regime that allows us to excel in every just way as individuals in society. Thus, as citizens of a liberal democracy, we should defend and extend the opportunity for meritocratic upward advancement as opposed to continuing unjust restrictions on a person's ability due to race, religion, gender, or poverty – a test we as a country have all too often in the past failed to pass and have still not passed today.

Defending and extending the equality of opportunity for meritorious achievement is central to the liberal-democratic ethos. But the notion that *all* hierarchies – the meritocratic as well as the arbitrary – are unjust is a Marxist rather than a liberal-democratic conviction. One is entitled to it, and there are reasons for entertaining it philosophically, since two of its original proponents, Rousseau and Marx, are arguably among the greatest of Western thinkers. But it should not be institutionalized as the guiding premise of higher education. Young people should be given a chance to think these issues through for themselves. They should not be told by university administrators or residence councillors as a part of their orientation as undergraduates that university life is about 'learning to be less competitive,' or that the university is a reflection of the systemic sexist and racist hierarchies governing Canada as a whole, hence one of the greatest bastions of reaction. It is pure indoctrination. One need not embrace any of these tenets in order to believe in greater freedom and opportunity for women, visible minorities, or other unfairly treated or disadvantaged people.

As for professors, for them to stigmatize their own universities as 'elitist,' as if to imply that *all* hierarchies, including the meritocratic, are unjust, is to engage in a fraudulent and hypocritical activity. Every time a professor – or, worse, a university president or administrator – loosely throws around this term, calling for less 'elitism' when what he or she really means is less injustice, the enterprise of liberal education is corrupted. Words have meanings, and we cannot escape from them. If we employ a certain rhetoric thoughtlessly, it will begin to take over our actions and define them. Every university is meritocratic, hence hierarchical, by definition. When a professor gives a student an A, that means that he is making his soundest considered judgment as to the superiority of that student's work over the work of a student who gets a B. One should not make such judgments without carefully considering the distribution of grades and the performance of the whole class. But to go on giving ranked grades while cavalierly calling for the end of elitism implies that one does not know what one is doing or is, quite simply, a hypocrite who enjoys the kick of exercising authority over people while asserting in principle that all authoritative hierarchies are oppressive. If you really believe, with Foucault, that all authorities are masked systems of arbitrary power, and you go on failing some students and praising others, what does that make you? Are you not the embodiment of what you profess to oppose?

These reflections are sufficient to establish that the debates over destreaming and other curricular matters that we have considered so far cannot be properly addressed if we confine ourselves to the methodological controversies, or to the economic and political pressures being exerted on schools and universities today. These are important, to be sure. But they are rooted in a far more important debate about the meaning of liberal education itself *sub specie aeternitatis*. Behind the policy wars is a deeper, less obvious, far more grave and difficult argument. What is the best condition for the soul? How and what should people learn in order to be mature and responsible citizens?[42] We can limn the outlines of this deeper debate by looking briefly at the issue of what has come to be known as political correctness in the universities. Specifically, let us look at the allegation that the current curriculum in the humanities and social sciences tends to be 'Eurocentric' and hence against 'diversity.'

There are two sorts of arguments for diversity in university course offerings and their content. One is genuine; the other is misleading and, at worst, disingenuous. The point of a course in the Western tradition is not to try to convince students that it is superior to other traditions and the only one worth studying. That would be impossible if one taught it knowledgeably and honestly, since many of the philosophers and writers who belong to it are radical critics of the status quo. Plato and Aristotle were trenchant critics of Greek political, religious, and cultural mores, including the idea that Greeks, as a Western race, were superior to Oriental peoples or that women and foreigners deserved to be treated as slaves.

Moreover, the Western tradition is not a monolith – it has no single teaching that one could try to impose on students even if one wanted to. Indeed, to study it is to sample some of the most widely diverging, principled oppositions about the meaning of justice, morality, and the good life. Aristotle criticizes Plato; Machiavelli opposes them both. Hegel says all three are wrong for believing in a stable human nature. Nietzsche excoriates Hegel's belief in the rational progress of history. Unless one has already closed one's mind and cast these great thinkers as bit players in an ideological melodrama of Eurocentric, phallocentric oppression, they cannot be conscripted in the service of propaganda for any dominant class structure, race, or gender. Indeed, reading and studying these thinkers – learning what it means to debate profoundly opposing understandings without rancour – is the surest guarantor of liberty, which is why whenever real tyrannies like Nazism or Bolshevism have come to power, they have done their best to suppress them.

The very term 'Western tradition' is misleading if it is taken as anything more than a loose spatiotemporal categorization. There are spiritual and mythological motifs in Homer and Plato that are paralleled in Vedic or North

American aboriginal theology. Knowledge of classical Greek philosophy was often revived in the Islamic world before it reappeared in Europe, so that the debate in the Christian West over the proper relationship between reason and revelation was indebted to the Moslem East for its translations and for the superb commentaries of Averroes and al-Farabi. Machiavelli was similarly influenced by the Latin Averroists. Right down to the present, non-Western countries like India have had their own distinguished scholarship on Western thinkers, shaped by their own concerns. The Japanese produce superb scholarship on Western literature and philosophy without any sense that they are losing their identity to a project of Western cultural genocide. Even a passing familiarity with this tradition shows how utterly parodistic is its detractors' depiction of it as an ideology of cultural domination. Moreover, we find it astonishingly patronizing of these detractors to assume that a student from a non-Western background will, once exposed to this tradition, lose all sense of his or her own. This is to underrate vastly the intelligence and independent-mindedness of the average undergraduate. Some of our keenest students have been people from non-Western backgrounds and religions who are interested in learning about Western beliefs precisely so as to sharpen their own insight into how and why their beliefs are different.

Learning cannot harm anyone. The demand for deconstructing courses in Western civilization to make each one reflective of every possible viewpoint and opinion is the most narrow-minded philistinism masquerading as liberation. Each of the world's great traditions is a loose and delicate unity, within which thinkers and artists debate and disagree with one another over a set of common starting-points. The disagreement between Aristotle, Machiavelli, and Nietzsche over the meaning – or existence – of human nature forms a coherent whole, not because they all say the same thing, but because there is a textual pedigree to their divergences, just as there is within Hinduism, Judaism, or Islam. We urge our students to balance and complement their study of the Western classics with as many courses as they can find on non-Western traditions, or courses that criticize the very idea of the Western tradition as we have just sketched it. Then they will be equipped to judge knowledgeably for themselves, which is what liberal education is all about.

This is genuine intellectual diversity, and it is the heart of what universities have always tried, with imperfect success, to promote. But in the politically correct version of diversity, instead of a diversity of substantively different courses, every course must be restructured and censored to represent the viewpoint of every tradition and every self-identified or officially designated victim group. Instead of being able to experience different traditions with a sense of the discrete inner articulation of each one, students would hear the same slogans of systemic racism, sexism, and homophobia in every course they took. No real encounter, therefore, would take place with non-Western traditions, for in this version of diversity, every form of authority including an intellectual or moral tradition is an ideological camouflage for oppressive class or gender hierarchies.

Indeed, for the politically correct agenda, there is strictly speaking nothing to teach and no one capable of teaching it. Traditionally, liberal education is an encounter between a teacher and a student, in which the teacher's actual superiority of knowledge in the present is placed at the service of bringing forth the student's potential superiority of knowledge in the future. It is a rare form of altruism because it is also selfishly satisfying – every real teacher longs for a student who will go further.[43] But, according to the politically correct version of diversity, to argue this is to support what some have called 'definitional autocracy' or some similar sin of logocentrism. The traditional teacher-student relationship must be replaced by a kind of transactional therapy in which all (including the instructor) share their feelings about how they are oppressed by patriarchy, ageism, or any kind of natural or cultural constraint. The outcome, in the post-modernist vulgate, is for everyone in the encounter group to realize that all of life is about power – you are dominated by power structures (however benignly disguised as parents, religion, and tradition) and the only solution is to shatter their power and assert your own.

It is a dismal view of life, utterly counter-productive to real learning, and it is, thankfully, confined to a minority of the social sciences and humanities. Most professors, like most community college and public school teachers, do their best to provide a good education for their students. But the politically correct version of diversity is spreading, and it has the courage of its fanaticism. Implementing it would produce the very opposite of genuine diversity, and for the simplest pedagogical reasons. The authors of this book between them read several languages, including French, Latin, classical Greek, and German. We know a couple of dozen books well enough to feel that we can teach them rigorously. If every course were to reflect every tradition equally, as well as every minority and advocacy group, each instructor would have to possess a combination of talents and training which no human being has as yet been able to achieve. How likely is one person to achieve a really deep grasp of both Western metaphysics and Vedanta, or of the *Upanishads* and *Measure for Measure*? The traditional academic division of labour is itself a salutary confession of human limitation, an ongoing reminder to professors and students alike that we do not know as much as we think we do and so, like the needy lover depicted in Plato's *Symposium*, must seek it from others who know more than we do.

The politicized and ideological critique of 'cultural relativism' is often as shallow as the attack on traditional liberal education. We do not align ourselves with those – too frequently including academics who should know better – who make a purblind defence of 'Western civilization,' as if the great thinkers and artists we have mentioned are marble busts in a hall of unremitting, self-satisfied success. Really reading the books or reflecting on the art is the best antidote to such complacency. You cannot read Plato or Nietzsche and remain as you were before, or be a booster for the status quo. But there is a profound as well as a shallow relativism, and we are arguing that only traditional liberal education can sustain the adventure of the former. There is a profound relativism whereby a student, having absorbed a deep and rigorous insight from one tradition, can begin to lay the grounds for really interesting questions to ask of another. Having read and reflected on St Augustine on time and eternity, one would be ready to study the Buddha, Confucius, or Ibn Taymiyya – selectively and painstakingly – on the same question. Having reflected on the ancient Greek myths about the forest goddess Artemis, whom Homer calls 'the lady of wild things,' one would be ready to begin exploring the North American aboriginals' legends of the Wild Woman of the Woods, arriving at a richer insight into both traditions by trying to see how they compare and how they differ. That is how liberal education liberates, by small steps building slowly to a flash of insight, as in Plato's *Seventh Letter*. The politically correct proponents of pseudo-diversity have no interest in these still, quiet encounters with the truth. Courses reformed and censored according to their dictates would have to be reduced to the lowest common denominator of derivative chatter and second-hand information. The university would in effect be reduced to the level of a high school course on 'cultures of the world' with a smorgasbord of colourful parochialisms.

Professor Leah Bradshaw of Brock University describes the ideal of a liberal education as well as anyone we have encountered: 'Simply, this means that my students read excerpts from Plato, Aristotle, Rousseau, Marx and so on, and we talk about the ideas. Some of the ideas run distinctly counter to the prevailing culture of contemporary Canada.'[44] This kind of teaching, she goes on, is relevant in a way deeper and more meaningful than anything to be found in the partisan debates of the day:

Students are always astounded to find that many of the notions we hold as the fundamental grounding of our own society were present in the minds of political philosophers 2000 years ago. They can see how the tension between the theoretical disposition and practical demands is as old as Western civilization. They can see that the conflicts between body and mind, female and male, one race and another, are perennial conflicts. Most important, they can see the range of solutions that have been proposed to the fundamental paradoxes of being human (none of them permanent, or lasting, or philosophically satisfying).

And yet, '(i)ncreasingly I am called upon to defend my teaching ... Demands are being made on the university to be socially and politically relevant. This can mean anything from teaching students a more practical course of instruction to working actively toward eliminating sexist and racist biases in society.' Ironically, these demands have the effect of threatening one of the few environments where prejudice is relatively successfully transcended and real multicultural community achieved:

The university classroom, as I see it, is a model of equality. Every year I face a new crowd of students, unknown to me. They are a diverse lot: some female, some male, from varying religious, economic and racial backgrounds. I am not interested in their backgrounds. I am interested in how we can come together for a few hours a week and talk about political theory. This kind of neutrality is no longer in vogue. Rather, the tendency these days seems to be to treat everyone in his or her particularity, to let everyone tell his or her 'story.' The idea of equality is attacked as a liberal scam, in which the powerful dominate and the weak are submerged.

In attacking the aspiration to impartiality of a traditional liberal education, those who view the university as an extension of society's class and gender battleground are perversely undermining one of the few places where the victims they claim to represent can overcome the disadvantages arbitrarily imposed on them by birth:

There are many students who have substantial suffering to contend with in their lives – abusive families, poverty, the dislocation of immigration, marginalization of all kinds – but the university is a place where they can start anew, questioning and thinking in ways that will give them freedom ... Is the sustaining of an equal, impartial and questioning atmosphere in the university secretly a defense of privileged intellectual, racist, patriarchal institutions? No. What it embodies at its best is a place of repose, from which people can think critically in a detached way. No one with any common sense would pretend that the university is like all of life. Insofar as it provides a forum for reasoned judgement about all things human and divine, the university still reaches for what is best.

We are not arguing that liberal education is the only important feature of a university education. The modern university provides all sorts of scientific, technical, and professional education. But we are arguing that liberal education is indispensable to a university's identity. You cannot subtract it and still have a university. Nor are we arguing that the great books approach to liberal education is unproblematic or the whole answer. The great books canon is not carved in marble – it has changed repeatedly, and will continue to do so. But, having taught at a variety of universities, we can say with some conviction that the average Canadian undergraduate is in no danger of having his or her critical faculties overwhelmed by a passive reverence for old books or any kind of book. The problem that concerned educators face today is that their students are so ill-prepared by their high school education, so bereft of any knowledge of their own or any country's history and culture, that they have little basis on which to make critical judgments. They have nothing to be critical *about*. Leaving these students, out of a fear of seeming too 'elitist,' to flounder in a contentless self-expressionism that is inevitably filled up by the kitsch and consumerism of the surrounding society is the greatest possible disservice to them. By contrast, to see an eighteen-year-old read Plato's *Republic* and respond to its arguments, personalities, and ambiguities as living and important is among the greatest thrills a teacher can have. Today's students need more than anything else to begin with reverence so as to experience the full richness and pain, the rewards and costs, of self-liberation. Pointing these things out to students – which involves pointing out the shallow attitudinizing of our contemporary cult of the self – is the act of a friend who cares enough for you to tell you unpleasant facts.

We believe that moral character remains the basis of a good education, and that moral character is inseparable from our civic character as members of a particular nation-state and political community. The dangers of economic globalism as a form of the 'soft despotism' of which Tocqueville warned have often been observed, and we have already touched upon them. But less attention has been paid to the danger represented by the globalism of social activism to the core of a liberal education. We believe that social activism over issues like environmentalism, while important, cannot be a substitute for traditional liberal education. Indeed, these very issues cannot be properly understood and debated without the knowledge and critical detachment provided by a liberal education.[45] Otherwise, while priding themselves on liberating the human personality, social activists run the risk of narrowing it by making us entirely dependent on the fads and partisan views of the day and the bombardment of the mass media – a kind of 'temporal chauvinism,' as David Warrick terms it, which flatters the young into believing that nothing worth knowing has taken place before their own lifetimes. Only a traditional liberal education can give us the moral ballast, the true independent-mindedness, to confront the problems of the modern world critically and constructively, precisely because it liberates us from the unthinking orthodoxies of our own day.

In order to recapture a sense of why education must be civic education, connected to the kind of regime in which we live and its specific notions of justice and human excellence, we must return to the classical approach to education as represented by the works of Plato, Aristotle, and their heirs. But we must pay equal attention to the connection between education and our specifically modern regime of liberal democracy, with a special focus on the kind of moral character needed for the protection and fostering of human rights. A comparison of Locke and Rousseau, for instance, would show us how Rousseau tried to restore the classical concern with moral psychology on a modern democratic basis, and why, therefore, more recent accounts of rights such as that of Rawls posit too thin and impoverished a notion of democratic citizenship. We must also turn to Schiller's conception of the 'aesthetic education of man' – his protest against Kantian rights-based discourse – in order to reflect on why rights are not the only important components of the good life. Forgiveness, reconciliation, and self-restraint are sometimes as important as what we are entitled to as individuals.

As we have seen, there are pitfalls to the educational approaches of the right and the left, and we need to debate them in a manner which is frank but non-rancorous. The capacity for such a debate is itself a chief demonstration of the meaning and application of a liberal education. On the one hand, market forces, while important, are not the answer to everything. Particularly in the public school system, the idea of vouchers and the rhetoric of 'choice,' while worth pondering, risk abdicating a sense of public responsibility for education, especially toward the disadvantaged. At the same time, the imperative of 'global competitiveness' threatens to turn our schools into training-grounds for what Robert Reich has termed the 'routine production workers' of a low-wage service economy.[46] On the other hand, the left's combination of anti-Americanism and the bureaucratization of dissent is no substitute for a real national identity. Although Canada has often fallen far short of its own ideals of justice, we cannot repudiate every vestige of our heritage as racist, sexist, xenophobic, and genocidal and then wonder, as in the Spicer Report, why we have no binding sense of national unity. These debates over principle may be unpleasant or contentious, but to face them and argue them is the very essence of democratic citizenship. The chief aim of a liberal education should be to equip students with a knowledge of ideas and history, and the ability to debate without rancour so that they can take their place among a responsible and informed citizenry. We fear the current educational climate is contributing to what now dominates public discourse as a whole: shrill advocacy combined with a refusal to debate principles.

Finally, in order to restore the vanishing connection between contemporary education and a true civic education, we must find a way of improving education that draws on the best of our own distinctive traditions and ways of life. As we will argue in chapter 6, Canada was a Victorian founding, not an Enlightenment founding. The primacy of rights was mitigated by a certain primacy of groups. To see this, we can compare Thomas Jefferson's optimism about the joint progress of scientific and moral enlightenment with George Etienne Cartier's altogether more Burkean and Hegelian notion of organicism in both the natural and social worlds, implying that the pattern of a historical community must sometimes take precedence over the universal rights deduced by Newtonian reasoning. Of course, Canada was not entirely organicist. The complement to Cartier's view is George Brown's vision of liberal and capitalist progress through the expansion of the western frontier. The Canadian character springs from this creative encounter and tension between Enlightenment individualism and Victorian corporatism, thus recapitulating in a way unique to North America the fundamental debate within the Western tradition as a whole. By this we mean what Swift called 'the battle of the books.' The debate between our duty to the whole and our rights as individuals is grounded in the underlying debate between science as philosophical contemplation and science as the conquest of nature through economic prowess and political contract for what Bacon termed 'the relief of man's estate.' Canada's political and social evolution has housed the working-out of this debate, the basic spiritual nerve of modernity. Quebec's insistence on preserving itself reinforced residual reservations about American-style liberalism in English-speaking Canada as well, reservations that remain to this day. Conversely, these reservations in English-speaking Canada helped evolve a regime that could house Quebec's aspirations in a way that would never have been tolerated in the United States. The more we know about this unique history of accommodating rights and duties, the more the false alternatives posed by Lucien Bouchard and Clyde Wells are exposed in their one-sidedness, and we can discover within ourselves the possibility of the two alternatives living together in experience. It is because of the enduring character of Canadian small-'c' conservatism as a community of communities that the Mulroney era failed to extend the new conservatism (actually a revived nineteenth-century Radicalism) of Reagan and Thatcher to Canada. Students should be learning about this great national adventure in reconciling principles with practice, not the currently fashionable 'process' approach which urges them to express their feelings about fragments of history or news from the media unconnected with any larger sense of the scope of human affairs and the great ideas of justice, freedom, and morality.

4

Liberal Education and the Modern World

Why Return to the Classics?

In the next two chapters, we are going to examine the meaning of liberal education by discussing some essential themes in Plato, Aristotle, Augustine, Rousseau, Hegel, and Nietzsche, as well as by looking at the place of liberal education in the general movement from classical to modern thought. Our focus throughout is on the human longing for wholeness and its relation to the principles of a just and satisfying political order. This is the heart of what the ancients called *paideia*.

The traditional meaning of a liberal education is beautifully stated by the Renaissance humanist Vergerius:

We call those studies liberal which are worthy of a free man; those studies by which we attain and practise virtue and wisdom; that education which calls forth, trains and develops those highest gifts of body and of mind which ennoble men, and which are rightly judged to rank next in dignity to virtue only. For to a vulgar temper gain and pleasure are the one aim of existence, to a lofty nature, moral worth and fame.[1]

There are two other essential features. A liberal education is also a civic education: 'Respecting the general place of liberal studies, we remember that Aristotle would not have them absorb the entire interests of life; for he kept steadily in view the nature of man as a citizen, an active member of the State.'[2] Above all, it consists of reading great books: '"Never am I less idle," [says Scipio] "less solitary, than when to outward seeming I am doing nothing or am alone"; evidence of a noble temper, worthy to be placed beside that recorded practice of Cato, who, amid the tedious business of the Senate, could withdraw himself from outward distractions and find himself truly alone in the companionship of his books.'³ Reading not only teaches us how to speculate about the good life and put these speculations into practice. Reading is itself one of the keys to a virtuous character. The virtues of patience, discipline, and reflectiveness that it instils are the psychological foundations for the virtues we need as citizens in the wider world:

Indeed the power which good books have of diverting our thoughts from unworthy or distressing themes is another support to my argument for the study of letters. Add to this their helpfulness on those occasions when we find ourselves alone, without companions and without preoccupations – what can we do better than gather our books around us? In them we see unfolded before us vast stores of knowledge, for our delight, it may be, or for our inspiration. In them are contained the records of the great achievements of men; the wonders of Nature; the works of Providence in the past, the key to her secrets of the future. And, most important of all, this knowledge is not liable to decay. With a picture, an inscription, a coin, books share a kind of immortality.⁴

This is where we begin our reflection on the purpose of a liberal education. Its original meaning was, and remains, the attempt to articulate human nature in its fundamental and permanent concerns. Furthermore, it assumes that human nature comes fully to light only when man's relation to the political community is elaborated. According to the classical thinkers, human life is incomplete apart from membership in a civic association, and cannot be adequately grasped on individualistic grounds.

The longing for community is endemic to liberalism, a regime expressly designed to frustrate it. It is thus especially useful for us to understand precisely why the classics extolled the superiority of the virtuous small republic to other kinds of regimes. By taking us outside the horizon of liberal democracy, the communitarian republicanism of Plato and Aristotle shows us possible drawbacks of our own regime. But we also learn from this encounter that the classical prescription (with its restrictions of individual liberty and upward mobility) could not easily be grafted onto our own. Thus, studying the classics also shows us the comparative strengths of liberal democracy. Indeed, when students think about the comparative strengths and weaknesses of classical republicanism and modern liberal democracy, they are led to reflect on the difficulty of finding a single political order that could satisfy every valid human need or desire. The beginning of civic education is to realize that we may have to make hard choices between different kinds of human satisfaction and the specific regimes and laws that best facilitate them. According to the classics, there is not an indefinite plurality of possible political constitutions. Any given regime is likely to correspond most closely to one of a small list: monarchy, aristocracy, or some form of lawful democracy, or, to take the bad cases, tyranny, oligarchy, or mob rule. In light of this tradition, the specific choices of the Canadian or American founding fathers, for instance, stand out in sharper contrast with the other known alternatives. What makes humans most happy? Individual security and well-being, or direct participation in self-government? Which regimes best facilitate these goals, and can any one regime combine them satisfactorily? It may be that not all good things are possible under any one system of politics. This is the core of the classical political teaching, and it is an indispensable foil for prudently assessing the more optimistic or incoherent of contemporary claims to be able to achieve all individual and collective agendas simultaneously. As we will suggest in chapter 6, Canada's constitutional trauma of the last ten years can be directly connected to the decline of this kind of learning.

Of course, even for the classics, it is only a hypothesis that human nature and human excellence remain the same. Since, as Plato argues, philosophy is the ongoing distinction between knowledge and mere opinion or casual observation, we cannot necessarily extrapolate a permanent human condition from the apparent permanence of our own particular time and place. The belief in a trans-historical human nature may itself be a historically conditioned belief. Nor have all the great philosophers ended up agreeing that human nature cannot be fulfilled apart from the duties of citizenship. The classical thinkers gave this view its fullest exposition. But thinkers such as Rousseau argue that human nature is complete in its individuality and can be satisfied outside of civil society. Nevertheless, all serious philosophy about the good life begins with the relationship between the city and man, if only to try to show why it is an illusion.

If liberal education as an ongoing reflection on the fundamental human alternatives is to be possible in principle, then we must be able to distinguish philosophy from ideology. All philosophy has an ideological career to the extent that it has an influence on political and social events. Plato's search for the eternal truth was originally motivated by his disillusionment with the Athenian politics prevalent in his youth, and his search for a new moral and metaphysical basis for good government in an age of disbelief and drift. Machiavelli is both a writer for the ages and an Italian patriot and partisan of Florentine republicanism. But not all ideology qualifies as philosophy. An ideology is the partisan defence of an a priori viewpoint. The difference between Hobbes and Milton Friedman is that, while both conclude that bourgeois security and comfort are the sole and sufficient aims of good government, Hobbes does not take this for granted. He is intimately familiar with the classical tradition he attempts to replace, which claims that government ought first and foremost to educate the citizens to virtue, and he addresses this alternative on its own level.

Of course, these observations are complicated by the fact that some of our greatest modern philosophers – Hegel, Nietzsche, Heidegger – have argued that no philosophy can transcend the limits of its epoch. Since what appears to be human nature in reality changes with history, all philosophy is at bottom determined by a culture, a people, a revelation, or a general will to power for domination and the resulting closure of debate. The status and meaning of liberal education in the contemporary world thus provoke an immensely complicated series of questions. While we continue to ponder the original, classical statements of the relationship between human life, nature, and civic virtue, we are also compelled to think them through in conjunction with the arguments our greatest modern philosophers have made for the impossibility of philosophy in the classical sense. We will try to show, through a selective and necessarily very telescoped sampling of the Western tradition, that even in the face of the profound historicism of a thinker like Nietzsche, the traditional concerns of liberal education endure, although in radically altered forms.

Thus, our provisional definition of liberal education as the study of great books is not as naive or straightforward as it might first appear. Liberal education is, at its core, concerned with the prospect for the reconciliation of human beings with the world, with one another, and with their own inner contradictions. The modern world is shot through with contradictions of the most acute and agonizing kind – between our economic prosperity and the environmental and nuclear dangers of technology, between our craving for contact and our assertion of individual autonomy. The need for *paideia* (to use the classical Greek term) is perhaps even more obvious and deeply felt for us in the late twentieth century than it was in earlier times. But whatever answers we arrive at for the meaning of human wholeness today, we can neither repudiate altogether nor embrace altogether any one component of the traditional meaning of liberal education. Rather, we must look to this tradition for restorative possibilities to aid our encounter with the present.

Since we do not believe it is possible simply to 'return' to the classics – even if it were possible to disentangle the precise meaning of the classical authors from the centuries of interpretation and appropriation of their writings – why do we insist on the classics as the core and starting-point of a liberal education? Simply because the breadth and depth of the historicist repudiation of classical *paideia* have been overlain by the general intellectual triumph of that historicism. Historicism has been trivialized by its own success. To take the converse of our observation that the belief in eternity may be historically conditioned, it is equally possible that it is only the prevalent opinion of our time that all thought is determined by its time. We therefore need to open ourselves to the possibility that there are minds that can rise above their times and speak across the centuries in the ongoing effort to understand the human condition. The purpose of reading the great books is not that the classical thinkers say all there is to say. It is to counteract the historicist dogma that otherwise cuts us off from an incredibly rich source of speculation about human life.

There is no greater stimulus to studying the Platonic Socrates than Nietzsche's polemics against him in *The Twilight of the Idols*.[5] The very complexity, even the savagery, of those polemics shocks us into an appreciation of how justifiably great was the authority of the Socratic legacy that Nietzsche tries to undermine. Nietzsche is the very best inducement to reach behind Nietzsche to the Socratic original. But today's students have lost sight of the many layers of this encounter, a kind of educational Troy where you keep digging in the hope of a richer treasure, because they receive a routinized Nietzscheanism in which the anticlassical teachings that Nietzsche arrived at through a lifetime of pain and torment are blandly asserted as the self-evident insight of any North American teenager. Students are told that the point of Nietzsche and Kierkegaard is simply that 'there's nothing out there in the world, so you have to define yourself.' What is seldom remembered is that, for Nietzsche and Kierkegaard, the rejection of tradition presupposes the highest level of familiarity with that tradition, which is what gives the rejection its originality, daring, and savour. Kierkegaard's meditation on the knight of faith shocked his contemporaries with its implication that humans must define their existence in a void because neither nature nor historical tradition offers us any permanent haven or guidance. But what once shocked has today become often little more than dreary attitudinizing and rote rebelliousness. For students today, reading Kierkegaard should, above all, be a demonstration of how real independence can only be achieved by way of the most painstaking immersion in the tradition that one is moved to repudiate. The same is true of reading great literature in general. Students who arrive at university having never read a novel do not need to be told first and foremost that there is no such thing as a novel – that every novel is really a set of tropes, conceits, and stratagems disguising an ideology of reification more or less directly related to some oppressive hierarchy of class or gender. They need to read Dickens or Edith Wharton and be moved by what their novels tell us of love and depravity before they can deconstruct them.

Plato's Education of the Soul: *Thumos*, *Eros*, and the Dialectic of Speech

The philosophy of liberal education begins with Socrates. In 399 BC Socrates was charged with impiety and the corruption of the young. He was found guilty and summarily executed. The action taken against him followed on many years of his publicly questioning statesmen, craftsmen, and poets as to the nature of their activity. He was known as a 'gadfly' and he often left his interlocutors puzzled and paralysed. His young students found these interrogations entertaining, for many of Athens's figures of authority were incapable of accounting for themselves under Socrates' questioning. Although they charged that Socrates was sophistic, thus capable of making the weaker argument the stronger, it was also true that they emerged from discussions with him appearing misguided, incoherent, and poor guardians of their sons. There was evidently then a history of resentment or rancour against Socrates and his friends. This was aggravated by the suspicion that a number of his associates had participated in the shameless mocking of mystery rites prior to the disastrous expedition against Sicily, and by a feeling of outrage when some of these defected to the Spartans. It also did not help that among the Thirty Tyrants who ruled over Athens after its defeat at the hands of the Spartans were others of Socrates' associates.

After Socrates' death, Plato began writing the Dialogues of Socrates, which he used to provide a defence for the philosophic life and to respond to the charges made by Athens. He explored the meaning of a perfect regime, a sound education, and the requirements of rational speech, to demonstrate that Socrates, so far from corrupting the young, was the sole source of their betterment, and that so far from being impious, he held a profound reverence for the divine good. In thus supplying an apology for Socrates, and showing Socrates to be a model citizen as well as genuinely concerned about the souls of his associates, Plato at the same time formulated the symbolism of the intellectual search for order characterizing the life of reason. He realized that the myth of order which had supplied coherence to the Greek *polis*, linking Homeric religion with the manly and agonistic politics for which the Athenians had been known during the democratic era, had exhausted itself. At the height of one of the dialogues, Plato has Socrates confront the representative of the city sanctioned by that myth and declare Athens to be mad, to have eclipsed reality, or as he says it, 'to have broken partnership with the gods.'[6] The Dialogues of Socrates placed the human search for order in a new light, focusing on the connection between political order and the life of reason. Plato anticipated that a true understanding of the life and death of Socrates would be a prolegomenon to a restoration of sanity, of full human participation in reality. Thus the particulars of Socrates' life became paradigmatic events in the human search for wisdom.

Nothing in Plato's dialogues fails to edify regarding the nature and scope of education. But what emerges specifically from his discussions is his recurring refrain of the one thing most needful in human life – balance. This meant not only a reiteration of the Delphic dicta 'Nothing in excess' and 'Everything in moderation,' but, just as importantly, giving every element of the human participation in reality its due. There would be no cessation of disorder, he realized, if cardinal aspects of reality were ignored: the orderliness of existence, the irreducible human desire for the good, the enduring tension of our composition as body and soul; the presence of the political, or thumotic, passions; the erotic vitality of human speech; the participation of human reason in divine reason; the formation of human knowledge after the model of reasoned experience in the technical arts; the ladder of ascent towards the good constituting the questioning soul; the inevitability of degeneration in the substance of political regimes.

Plato observed around him many examples of a loss of balance. He abhorred the anti-humanism of the pre-Socratic inquiry after the basic stuff of nature; he condemned the intolerance for politics evident in the sophist's delight with clever rhetoric; he wrote against the hyper-perfectionism which grips political activists; he challenged the conceit that technical competence in one sphere confers universal competence; he abjured sentimentalism and rigidity; he tolerated neither reductionism nor wide-eyed awe. In each case where Socrates found his interlocutors with the lie in their souls of one of these disorders, philosophy in both its diagnostic and its therapeutic modes was engaged. A well-balanced soul, Socrates taught, was the hallmark of a flourishing human being.

Four forms of this balance are evident in those dialogues whose subject-matter touches most closely on education. The first is at the centre of ancient *paideia*, the formation of virtuous character. In the *Republic*, Socrates is engaged in the craft of forming balanced souls. As a master of 'adapting speeches to souls,' he uses the hypothesis of producing a 'city in speech' to harmonize the elementary forces of the souls of two of his interlocutors. The elaborate artifice of discussing how a city comes to be, how a city is purged of passion, how its rulers are educated and their well-being satisfied, and what occurs when the principle of a political regime is corrupted conforms to the Platonic principle that logic cannot persuade apart from philosophical drama. For, in the process of enlisting their sense of honour and reason in the service of the principle of order for the 'city in speech,' and thus experiencing directly the effect of the restraints and conditionings they build into the just city, the desires of his young associates are drawn out, sublimated, and transfigured into a composite of a truly balanced soul. They have learned to judge and to reason, to express righteous indignation and loyalty, to intimate the object of their deepest longing for transcendence, because their souls have been made responsive to the comprehensive range of experiences which defines human participation in reality.

Platonic *paideia* focuses particularly on two essential forces of the human soul, *thumos* and *eros*. Each spells the potential for profound human disorder, but each is also a medium of the noblest human experiences. The two cardinal interlocutors of the *Republic* quite evidently feel the allure of pleasure promised them by the sophist's claims to be able to teach them the art of tyrannical rule. Socrates helps them to find a higher satisfaction of their deepest desires.

Our first care is our preservation. So elementary is this animal need that its human form is nearly always enlarged by the desire for recognition by others or by the longing for unalloyed pleasure. The latter interests Socrates, for his two young associates evidently find the tyrannical life in which this promise is held out for them attractive. This is the longing which is the cause of the greatest injustice, for unalloyed pleasure is the fantasy of that man who sees himself unconditioned by any other or by his own conscience. No mere didactic lesson on restraint will temper this fantasy.

Instead, Socrates enlists his interlocutors' desire for glory as the means of directing them away from tyrannical pleasure. Very soon they come to exhibit anger when the principle of their 'city in speech' is attacked, the first signal of that force called *thumos*. The 'thumotic' expresses itself as indignation, as offence, as desire for revenge. But it is also found in passionate loyalty, in acts of self-sacrificing courage, and in honour. *Thumos* is born of the desire for recognition, but formed by the sense of justice. In forming the 'city in speech' Socrates' young associates learn the need to cultivate and nourish these passions, but also to moderate them so as to constitute useful political virtues. Without a spirited defence of the polity, and without honourable self-sacrifice, political community can only be an aggregate of biological instincts. Socrates' interlocutors are not asked to forsake the satisfaction they seek; they are shown how it is fulfilled in the political form of *thumos*. In devoting themselves to the perfectly just city, in which their thumotic passions are exhibited and sublimated, their desires are provided a deeper satisfaction, a widened amplitude of fulfilling experiences. The 'city in speech' they found acquires an impeccable structure: it displays a perfect symmetry because it builds technical craft upon technical craft, thus establishing logic and certainty in every aspect of its existence. By its completion, the 'city in speech' is a technical masterpiece. It is perfectly unified, it suffers from no contradictions. No partial perspective, no private happiness, no secret pleasure is left to disturb the proportionality of the whole. The purest political passions and the purest common good have been crafted. In this, it is the thumotic passion writ large. But by fusing individual desire and public life in this way, Socrates has risked creating a dedication to a political order which – in its excessive demand for justice (the elimination of all privacy, the exclusion of private happiness) – demands too great a sacrifice and assumes too unambiguous a character for human existence. The demand for a demonstration that justice is choiceworthy above all else and wholly for its own sake can only be met by a polity inhospitable to the complex character of human existence.

He must, then, moderate this excessive attention to *thumos*. The longing at the root of the tyrannical dream is once again brought back. The longing for wholeness continues to be a dangerous and volatile fuel. But now Socrates' young associates' souls have dispositions that are not just unformed potentiality. Because their passions have been restrained and moderated, they will experience the longing differently. The longing for wholeness is *eros*, and while they know of its first promptings as sexual desire, they are now invited to experience it through a gradual process of sublimation through which the same longing for completeness is rendered into the love of wisdom. The erotic search for wisdom continues to operate through the dialectic of speech as icons of the true and the good are brought forward to solicit and direct desire. The limitations, the rigidity, and the penurious quality of the just 'city in speech' are soon revealed by the expansive eroticism of the ascent towards wisdom. In the experience by which the transcendent order of perfection is intimated, and to whose rhythms the young souls are attuned, lies the deepest satisfaction of their longings and needs. They will possess the 'Isles of the Blessed,' albeit temporarily, in the moving image of eternity – the philosophic equivalent of the eternal happiness promised those who are favourably judged in Hades.

But the philosophizing soul must 'go down.'[7] It lives by necessity in political society and must define itself within the demands of political existence. Eros has need of friendship and its human shape is manifested in the concrete forms which friends bring to each other's attention. The particulars drawn into a horizon by *thumos* supply the images in which *eros* takes refuge. The possibility of *eros* at its highest depends definitively on the thumotic training. The moderation of *thumos* relies exclusively on the reactivation of *eros*. Eros is once again anchored in the particulars which the good illuminates. *Thumos* and *eros* modulate one another, informing each other's possibilities and limits.

The result is a soul whose reciprocating forces manifest themselves as harmony and order. Socrates' young associates are taught the art of soulcraft by seeing what experiences, what expectations, and what unities establish the soul's openness to the amplitude of reality. They have examined its lowest and highest forms, its rhythms, and the formation by which its forces are linked. They recognize what passions must be to educated to ensure a manly defence of political justice. They understand why the passions must be restrained in a regime that desires to remain free. They have seen the consequence of political fragmentation and excessive zeal. They have learned of the erotic ascent of reason towards wholeness. They have observed the proportionality with which speech is graced by reality. They know how to balance thumotic integrity with erotic openness, thumotic righteousness with erotic wonder.

Socrates did not confine himself to *explaining* this balance to his interlocutors. In the process of crafting the political forms of the 'city in speech' Socrates is, at the same time, crafting the souls of his interlocutors. He is composing the tone, sensitivity, direction, and hierarchical order of the forces of their souls to produce a character that is neither irascible nor cowardly, neither capricious nor dogged. 'Socratic wisdom' is the balance of courage and agnosticism with moderation and longing for transcendence. It is only possible if *thumos* and *eros* are artfully interwoven. But Socrates does not only tame the separate souls of his associates. He also composes the different human types he encounters into a reciprocating whole. Indeed, Plato seems to show Socrates doing precisely what the Athenians feared: engaging in the art of political rule. Arousing some and tempering others through private conversation, Socrates is at the same time performing the public activity of composing the healthy polity where different human types are harmonized to produce the self-sufficiency reflecting a comprehensive human existence. The craft by which souls are composed in this manner is explained in the image of the ruler as a weaver of the polity in the dialogue, the *Statesman*. There the political ruler is depicted as working with two distinct strands, the one soft and pliable, the other hard and inflexible. As the woof and warp of a web, they can be crafted to become a durable and supple fabric. Too much or too little of one or the other will mean that the fabric is either brittle or unyielding. Crafting two materials which have no natural affinity for one another, but which, when harmonized, actualize the highest potential of each, depends on experience with the appropriate measures. Knowing the appropriate measures is a knowledge of proportionality and symmetry. Similarly, the political ruler or educator works with two distinct strands: the restless and daring, as well as the peaceable and cautious. Unless he knows the judicious and prudent art of statesmanship, he will produce a polity given over to the extremes of intractability or total accommodation. He too must weave the strands, or the polity will vacillate between weakness and the temptation to external aggression.

There are two forms of educational influence to which Socrates exposes his charges. The first is gymnastics, the second music. The bodies of the young must be trained for strength and flexibility, while the longings of their souls must be aroused by the structured rhythms and beautiful unities of musical tone. Unless this early drawing-out of the potentialities and sensibilities of body and soul, and their integration, take place, the higher possibilities of human doing – politics and the life of reason – will be foreclosed. Gymnastics and music are propaedeutic artifices through which nature's separate purposes are crafted into unified human forms. In the process of the education, these influences which are brought to bear on the soul come to be understood as emanating from the principles of mathematics and poetry. These principles are as relevant to education as to political rule. The wholeness which *paideia* points to combines mathematics and poetry, the art that crafts proportion and symmetry with the art that expresses the human longing for the whole. Unless these are harmonized, the soul will be divided, one fragment charmed by undue confidence in its technical capacities, the other fragment enthused by any or all promises of wholeness, however baseless.

The harmonization of mathematics and poetry structuring true *paideia* is perhaps best exemplified in the dialectical art of speech. Speech is *the* form in which the distinctly human desires and longings acquire depth and coherence. In Greek, speech and reason are the same word, *logos*, holding out their mutual entanglement and edification. Speech acquires order and direction by the dividing-out and collecting-together performed by human reason; reason is illumined with human purpose by the *viva voce*. The erotic vitality of speech meets the structured ascent of reason, making possible a 'dialectic' in which the longing for wholeness is satisfied by the gradual apprehension of intelligibility in the cosmos. Dialectical speech that unifies mathematics with poetry, or reason with *eros*, is the ladder linking the human soul with the order of reality, for it reveals the consubstantiality of human longing with divine perfection.

In both the *Republic* and the *Philebus*, Socrates represents the height towards which education moves by speaking of a 'good beyond being' and of the wonder which best expresses the soul's consubstantiality with the good. The actionless and speechless intellectual intuition of goodness entails a radical transcendence of worldly form, a reverencing of mystery. But this is no starry-eyed awe, or Heideggerian 'letting be': the route is made possible through the art of the dialectic, a route which Plato describes at one point in the low but solid vernacular of 'a butcher carving at the joints.' Wonder is harmonized with craft, or *techne*; the full openness of the soul is rooted in the crafting of distinctions. The latter are not means to an end, but integral to the ballast at the core of the former.

The balance of *thumos* and *eros*, mathematics and poetry, and dialectic and wonder, prepares us for the fourth of Plato's lessons, the balance between the restraint of the passions and the life of reason. Morality has its political value for Plato but primarily it is a prolegomenon to the life of reason. Without the restraint of the passions, the soul capitulates to the immediacies of its somatic needs, 'entombed,' as Plato says in the *Gorgias*, in the 'prison-house of the body.' Without the life of reason, such restraint will lead to a harsh moral irascibility. When these 'syndromes' become chronic, participation in reality itself is at stake. Genuine participation in reality is conveyed poignantly in the image of the puppet-player in the *Laws*, which Plato uses to explain how educators and legislators must understand the principles of order by which they structure *paideia* and the laws. The Athenian Stranger suggests thinking of humans as 'puppets of the gods,' pulled by the strands of various metal cords. The measure of a man's life lies in whether the puppet-player has pulled the iron cords of the passions or the gold cord of reason. Obedience to the pull of the gold cord, as in the life of reflective thought or assent to the laws and ways of the *polis*, means a life of order. If the gold cord is to predominate, discipline must prevail before reason can operate.

In the absence of these balances, Plato knew there was bound to be political disorder and intellectual confusion. He conveyed this most vividly in his depiction of degenerate political regimes, like demagogic democracies and tyrannies. Such democracies were characterized by a condition in which all desires are allowed to grow in every direction and in which this 'many-headed beast' lacks the principles of order to be anything more than an empty vessel mirroring back the opinions and tastes of its environment. It is a condition, as Socrates depicts it, in which the extremes of frenzied energy born of a lack of direction reveal a dangerous vacuum quickly filled by demagogues, and in which political order continually dissolves into mob rule agitated by a succession of *provocateurs*. Tyrannies are characterized by utter lawlessness and licence, and a type of rule governed utterly by the dream-world of private desire. The fantasy of the tyrant's life epitomizes the final consequence of a loss of balance: loss of a sense of the order of reality. In both degenerate regimes, Plato realized, there would be the 'sham philosopher' and the sophists who will take the arts of intellectual argument and dialectic and 'misuse them as though it were play, always using them to contradict ... like puppies

enjoying pulling and tearing with argument at those who happen to be near'
(*Republic*, 539b).

Plato undertook to show that philosophy was edifying. In the *Apology of
Socrates*, ironically, the charges against Socrates are shown to be justifiable,
at least at one level. Socrates was a usurper; he was corrupting the young and
he was impious. But Plato's apology is an argument that corruption is the
prelude to human wisdom. Those whom Socrates tamed and restored to a
balanced state had unreflectively absorbed the immediacies of their environment and the unquestioned pieties of tradition. Socrates' 'politics' constitutes
a new way, a *paideia* that grasps the permanent tensions of human existence
and forms the substance and direction of the longings characterizing our
response to these tensions. It is rule by soulcraft. Plato does not allow the life
of the mind to derail into political idealism. He holds out for the perfection of
human desire through its attraction to the good. At the centre of his thought
is the self-moved psyche. Excess movement one way produces rigidity; excess
in the other direction threatens to dissolve the soul into the boundless infinite. When the two forces are in balance, the tension, and hence free self-
movement, of the psyche is preserved. Thought will display a rhythm uniting
measure and dynamism. But when one pole is abstracted and the field of
experience is no longer structured by tension, the psyche no longer moves
itself and thus loses its distinctive capacity for thought. It will incline toward
sophistry when exercising its ratiocinative power, and toward a love for tyranny when it becomes a political force.

Aristotle: Civic *Paideia* as a Window on the World

Critics of the idea of a liberal education (whether on the left or right) often
argue that it is irrelevant to our most pressing social and political problems.
In so arguing, they confuse a civic education with a politicized education. In
their view, the university is a set of intellectual and financial resources like
any other, and these resources should be deployed to implement whatever
political agenda rules the day (as long as it is their own). We agree that the
university can be tremendously helpful in contributing to economic development, and that our sense of justice as a liberal democracy is intimately connected with the accessibility of higher education to all people regardless of
origin. But we are also arguing that universities must be more than this.
They can do their share to provide economic innovation and social services.
But if their activities are made synonymous with those of economic development and social welfare agencies, universities will be bound to disappoint on

those grounds (when compared with people and institutions better equipped to undertake such activities) as well as lose their own distinctive capacity to contribute to the common good. Universities' blind pursuit of 'relevance' will not bolster their legitimacy in the eyes of the public, but rather undermine it. The core of the university's mission is civic education, and civic education is a preparation to debate knowledgeably about political choices offered in the public arena. It cannot be collapsed into partisan advocacy on behalf of any one of those alternatives.

We have considered the Platonic evocation of this search for a balance in the soul that transcends mere partisanship by equipping citizens for reasoned discourse about civic life. The idea of a liberal education that we are exploring in this study receives another of its classic expositions from Plato's student, Aristotle. It does not, in our view, differ in its essentials from Platonic *paideia*, but whereas the Platonic understanding links the harmony of the soul directly to first philosophy and an apprehension of the orderliness of the cosmos, Aristotle is more concerned with the role of civic *paideia* in everyday political life without direct recourse to the loftier controversies of metaphysics. He speaks to citizens as they understand themselves.

Aristotle gives us an enduringly clear diagnosis of why civic education cannot be seen as a mere extension of political reform or economic activity in his discussion of the sophist and urban planner Phaleas.[8] According to Phaleas, inequalities of property are the cause of all social unrest and political strife, so the solution is to give everyone an equal amount of property. But Aristotle objects that equality is relative to need. Estates can be of equal size, but so small as to lead to penury or so large as to lead to luxury. Once people's basic material needs have been seen to, only education can give them the virtues of character to make them want to avoid luxury, which would soon render the existing division of property inadequate to their expanding desires.

Phaleas provides for equal access to education, but says nothing about what the content of that education should be. He is a little like those who now proclaim that everyone has a right to an education, as if an education can be dispensed like prescription drugs or unemployment insurance. Everyone has the right to the opportunity to acquire an education, and where that right is arbitrarily restricted, our commitment to justice requires that we eradicate the restriction. But, once the opportunity is accessible to everyone, it makes as little sense to say that one has a right to the outcome as to say that everyone who has taken up painting has the right to be a Picasso.

Much like today's advocates as well, Phaleas pays no attention to the content of education, as opposed to guaranteeing equal access to it, because he assumes that the meaning of human pleasure and longing is exhausted by self-preservation. Moral and intellectual education is not a requirement of the common good, or even of political stability, if one has a materialistic conception of human behaviour – a failing common to much of the left and the right. Because Phaleas's scheme equalizes property, he assumes that this will remove anyone's motive for revolution or crime. The reasoning is very similar to that of certain Enlightenment figures like Beccaria or D'Holbach who also believe that, since the motive for crime is rooted in the frustrated desire for the basic necessities of life, if the social contract protects people's lives and leaves them free to prosper economically, crime and social unrest will fade away.[9]

But is self-preservation the only motive for violence and disorder? As Aristotle remarks, 'men do not become tyrants in order to avoid shivering in the cold.' People also commit crimes for the pleasure of dominating others, or for grand sensual passions that require violating the property and freedom of others. Phaleas's scheme assumes that politics can solve every problem, but his reforms only work for pedestrian pleasures and discontent. The need to explore the content of education arises with the understanding that a more complex account of human nature is required than political reformers can ordinarily provide, precisely if political reforms are to have any chance of succeeding. After political reform has achieved a modicum of material prosperity for everyone, Aristotle says, education is required to moderate further desires for pleasure or prestige. It does so at the highest level of principle by teaching us that the purest pleasure comes from pursuing philosophy, because the objects of philosophy's longings do not decay and do not involve us in the exploitation of other people in order to attain them. In this simple but telling way, the study of philosophy is shown to be good not only for its own sake, but for directing people away from the temptation to tyrannize over their fellow citizens. Philosophizing is the *sine qua non* of a civic education. Unequal property may not even be the main cause of social strife, according to Aristotle, let alone of extraordinary crimes or tyranny. Honour is just as important a motive. The upper classes resent the inequality of honour implied by an equal division of property (for the wealthy orders tend to confuse their superior riches with superior virtue altogether), while the lower classes – having the same natures as the oligarchs – do not simply want a single, permanent equal division of property, but long for the riches and luxuries of their oppressors. Whatever political and institutional solutions can be devised to ameliorate these tensions (the best hope being the middle-class mixed regime prescribed in Books 3 and 4 of the *Politics*), no merely political reform will succeed unless people are educated not to value wealth above everything else. If you do not employ education to moderate human passions, Aristotle says, the only alternative is fear. The desire for wealth and pleasure at the expense of others can neither be eliminated from human nature nor allowed to run riot. Neither the dictatorship of the proletariat nor the alleged generation of public virtue out of private vice can substitute for an education in the moral and intellectual virtues. Aristotle anticipates and rejects the ravages of both communism and unfettered capitalism, alike in their belief that spontaneous human behaviour can serve the common good without the crucial intermediary link of a civic *paideia*.

In Books 7 and 8 of the *Politics*, Aristotle sets forth his understanding of the best regime, the kind of politics that would best enable people to fulfil their potential for virtue. It has a host of economic and geographical requirements, but its heart and soul is a lifelong education in which the virtues are solicited and developed by successively more serious responsibilities of self-government. Here, under the best envisionable circumstances, education is not just a preparation for life, and it is not only for the young. It is life's main activity. Liberal education is not reducible to a skill such as medicine or agriculture (important as these are). It is what makes a person free. For Aristotle, freedom is not the same as an untutored whim or impulse. Instead, a liberal education develops such virtues as liberality, temperance, and moderation that free us from the passions which would otherwise drag us down to the level of beasts. It therefore enables us to exercise clear-sighted choice in deliberating about the great issues of justice and injustice, the noble and the base, and the advantageous and disadvantageous. Reasoned discourse about these matters, says Aristotle, is what it means to say that human beings are by nature political animals.[10] We fulfil our virtues at the highest level through the non-rancorous debate of principled alternative opinions about good government. If the debate is not to degenerate into shrill posturing or open conflict, a non-partisan education must provide us with the ethical and intellectual preparation for partisan argument.

Universities are the heirs to this Aristotelian educational legacy. To the extent that they provide this non-partisan haven – but only to this extent – universities are not only justified but obligated to insist on their detachment from the political agendas of the day. For, while governments represent the common good as it most directly manifests itself in the will of a current electoral majority, universities are or should be stewards for a more permanent common good passed from generation to generation – the conditions for the very possibility of informed debate among citizens.

Aristotle makes a threefold distinction between work, relaxation, and leisure. Work is serious but painful, what we have to do to make a living. Relaxation is to help us recover from work – it is pleasant but frivolous. Work and relaxation therefore both exist for the sake of what requires them and is higher than them. Aristotle terms it leisure, a word (*skole*) from which we derive our terms for school, study, and scholarship. Education is leisure par excellence. It is both engrossing and pleasant because it engages our fullest human capacities. Aristotle is not a snob, an aesthete, or an idealist. He is not blind to the need to make a living, and the harsh limitations this can place on our time and energy. Nor is he against pleasures of the body – these are harmless and even salutary when sampled in moderation. But while we use the term 'leisure time' rather flaccidly to stand for what Aristotle means by the relaxation from labour, he argues that there must be something more to a fully satisfying life than sex, sports, or entertainment.

Unlike Plato, Aristotle does not insist that education must culminate in philosophy in the sense of first philosophy and metaphysics. For Aristotle, there are different roads to the truth, just as there are different, incommensurable virtues that contribute to the composite unity of the city.[11] For the bulk of the citizenry actively engaged in the responsibilities of republican self-government, philosophical truths are more palpably connected to their lives through great poetry, art, and drama. This is the jewel of a civic education.

We must confine ourselves to a sketch. For Aristotle, art can never be a mere private avocation or personal vision, as it often is for us. Art is about the great social and civic themes of justice, *eros*, rule, tyranny, and the relationship of the family to the demands of the common good and citizenship. Poetry is closer to philosophy's search for the truth than is history, according to Aristotle, because it does not confine itself to empirical events, but draws them together into universal archetypes of the conflict between passion and justice, between power and wisdom.

In discussing the importance of art and poetry ('music') to education in the *Politics*, Aristotle cites the poet Homer.[12] Interestingly, Aristotle refers to the *Odyssey* rather than the *Iliad*, even though the latter might be more relevant to what we ordinarily think of as political issues such as war, honour, and struggles for leadership. But this is arguably why Aristotle directs our attention to the less obviously political poem. Political life even at its best, he tells us, is all too prone to reduce civic virtue to mastery in both domestic and foreign affairs.[13] Citizens do not need their passions enflamed by visions of Achillean struggle and glory. They are already too likely to harbour these ambitions. The *Odyssey* has the merit of leading us from the heat of politics and war to a more reflective stance. Its hero, Odysseus, is far more compli-

cated than Achilles, the hero of the *Iliad*. For he is more of a sagacious coun-
sellor than a soldier, and he is also a cosmopolitan wanderer and thinker.
Although he finally makes it home, he encounters and reflects on a host of
alien ways and conventions on his journey. Although in reaching Ithaca he
returns to a love of his own, it is not an unreflecting attachment or prejudice.
It has been leavened with a grasp of wider horizons, an understanding that
the good life is not necessarily synonymous with one's own land and people.
Aristotle points to the *Odyssey* as a way of liberating the thoughtful reader
from the conventional limitations of his own city without altogether destroying his attachment to the city. His loyalty to the city is secure, but he will
have a window through the poem to what is universal. Poetry is a better
medium for this educational liberation than first philosophy, because, unlike
philosophy, it does not corrode civic attachments by leaping directly toward
the Good as understood by reason alone. Because poetry evokes and appeals
to our emotions and to our flesh-and-blood attachments, it provides a more
delicate equipoise between the particular civic association and the wider
world. For Aristotle, education must be a blend of openness and civic commitment, leading us from the particular to the universal and back. It should neither undermine patriotism nor encourage a barbaric, unreasoning attachment
to one's own narrow world. Transcending one's own does not necessarily and
of itself lead to better politics or more justice. As Aristotle says, someone who
is not a member of a political community is either a god or a beast.[14] What
good we achieve, we achieve first of all as members of this political community in which we find ourselves, with its potential for good and bad. A largely
passive and attenuated 'global citizenship' conducted through media rituals
cannot substitute for this complex and nuanced engagement with a real community.

The two gods Aristotle discusses in connection with the *paideia* of the best
regime are Zeus, the god of just rule, and Athena, the goddess of reason.[15]
The lustier, more morally ambivalent deities who often enter into human
affairs in Homeric and other ancient Greek poetry are implicitly censored. At
bottom, then, Aristotle is not only recommending certain poets as models of
education. He is calling upon the poets to assume their civic responsibilities
more consciously in what they write. They should, Aristotle implies, become
allies of philosophically guided statesmanship, and let political philosophy lay
out their own tasks and parameters. Art is not for art's sake, but must serve –
while elevating – civic life.

The lesson did not go unheeded, since until this century Aristotle exercised an authority over art and poetry that can hardly be imagined today. Virgil, Dante, and Shakespeare are among his heirs, national poets who manage
both to edify and to glorify their own peoples while leaving the careful reader

to ponder the many ambiguities and doubts about the ultimate justice or virtue of their countries. The complement to Shakespeare's *Henry the Fifth*, with its heroic young king's stirring victory and charming courtship of a French princess, is the altogether darker *Henry the Fourth*, especially its second part. Here Shakespeare allows us to peek behind the blazing sun of Hal's emerging reputation to see the grim machinations and obsessions of his regicide father, and how the young man himself benefited from them (as with the dastardly ambush of Hastings and Mowbray) as well as made himself look better by the contrast between himself and earlier associates like Falstaff and Pistol, whom he ruthlessly thrusts aside. As one of our Canadian founding fathers, Thomas D'Arcy McGee, observed, there is no better education in human nature than reading Shakespeare.[16] He is an essentially Aristotelian poet, which is to say a civic poet. No one who reads him with even minimal care can argue that he is a mere propagandist for one of the exploiting races or genders.

To speak of Shakespeare in connection with Aristotle reminds us, of course, that he is not only an Aristotelian poet, but a Christian one as well, at least in the sense that his understanding of human behaviour and the complexities of civic virtue and statesmanship would be unintelligible apart from the deepening of the European soul arguably effected by Christianity. Whatever its bearing may be for today and the future, the Western conception of liberal education was profoundly altered by the exposure of classical virtue to Christian grace, and so in continuing our selective archaeology of a liberal education, we must consider the impact of that great Christian educator, Augustine.

Augustine: Will, Grace, and the Dynamics of Hope

Augustine's conversion, he tells us in his *Confessions*, was tremulous: 'I probed the hidden depths of my soul and wrung its pitiful secrets from it, and when I mustered them all before the eyes of my heart, a great storm broke within me, bringing with it a great deluge of tears.'[17] Suddenly he heard a singing child, and opening the book of Scripture read: 'Not in revelling and drunkenness, not in lust and wantonness, not in quarrels and rivalries. Rather, arm yourselves with the Lord; spend no more thought on nature and nature's appetites.'

Augustine gives voice to the deep private sorrows and anxieties which accompany the inalienable burdens of human existence. He speaks to the struggles and the sense of futility that accompany our efforts. But he also left a record of the hope that accompanied the gift of grace by which his longing for wholeness was turned around from the depravity of the flesh towards the faith of the spirit. His conversion speaks to our sustaining hope for the redemptiveness of the new beginnings ('a child is born') by which our lives are continually renewed. His theology also supplies images of salvation that shine through our inevitable human suffering. He provides in his writings the moral ballast for the mercy and forgiveness by which men endure the destructiveness of time. He makes both our sorrow and our joy the objects of education. Augustine is the other primal source of our modern being. Rome is added to Athens.

The importance of Augustine's understanding for our purposes cannot be understated. He supplies us with most of the core of our own cherished beliefs – the dignity of the person, the sacredness of life, the rich inner life of the free spirit, the uniqueness of every being, the redemptiveness of new beginnings, the nobility of the moral life, the charity with which we accept human foibles, the optimism that forgiveness will stimulate change in personality, obedience to lawful authority, and the importance of mercy – while at the same time holding out the standard by which derailments of the spirit can be gauged, such as boredom with the simple goodness of life. Like Plato he knows that the justice due to other beings emanates from the reverencing we owe to the order of existence itself. Augustine understood that the sanctity of the person was grounded in the spiritual and moral order.

What Augustine adds to our understanding is particularly palatable because his is not a philosopher's idea of education but a formation of the moral and spiritual life to which all can be called. Christian universality of the spirit transcends the contingent circumstances of our births. Overcoming the inequalities of birth is possible because Augustine believes that wisdom resides in the commonest pieties. For this reason Augustine refers to the simplicity of Scripture in opposition to the 'wisdom' of the philosophers. He appeals to the law written in man's heart. 'Truth,' Augustine writes, is 'hidden from the wise and revealed to all children.' Indeed, the life of reason can easily lead to the hubristic presumption of human power to make the world over. Thus, he warns of the dangers of 'idle curiosity.' He once quipped that those who ask the question 'What did God do before Creation?' can be furnished with the answer 'Prepared Hell for people who pry into mysteries.' The proud bearing which presumes to know the order of the whole is rebuked as nothing but lust of the eyes.

The essential tone of Augustine's writings is set by the recognition of the radical seriousness of man's fall from the plenitude of oneness with God. From this flow two important conclusions. First, since man lost the power to know God, his lot is characterized by his vulnerability – his ignorance, the hardships and sorrows of existence, his anxieties and agonies in failing to live up to what he must be. Moreover, the Fall has brought about the dispersion of humankind. Plurality reflects our ignorance. Man's weakness is, of course, also the source of what can be highest in him, for from this state can arise the virtues of humility, forbearance, charity, and patience. The recognition of our permanent imperfection is the source of moderation – neither perfect virtue nor perfect social arrangements will overcome our fallen state. The need which defines our being is, finally, the spiritual search for order in which our daily mortifications are raised up and sanctified.

Second, the Fall was due to human sin, that is, the wilful disregard of man's obligations. It is repeated in every further expression of the will to deny God – in concupiscence and in cupidity, but also in despair, boredom, and spiritual sloth. Behind each of these lies human pride, the vainglory Augustine identified as the *libido dominandi* – the will to dominate others, and ultimately the reality of God Himself. The formidable presence of sin is a reproach to the Prometheanism of classical reason; it is evidence of the lie that man is the measure of all things. The ancients overestimated the benefi-cence of *thumos*; they too readily assumed reason's capacity to convert self-love to honour. From Augustine's viewpoint, the ancients overestimated human nature because they had not adequately understood its natural weak-ness. This is not only once again a lesson in moderation (tolerance, modesty, conciliatory relations), but at the same time an explanation of man's obsti-nacy, intractability, and recalcitrance to reason. But Augustine does not mean this to be a cause for despondency. Man's power to sin is matched by his power to choose righteousness and to respond to the goodness of the created order. The capacity for disobedience may be a permanent aspect of our long-ings, but having been made in the image of God, we still share in the divine substance through our capacity to again choose God: 'For love of your love I shall retract my wicked ways.' God holds out the opportunity for redemption, thus supplying us with the ballast of hope and faith. Herein arises our spirit-ual singularity: our own private destiny, not only that of the human species as a whole, is at stake in our response to sin. Sin, but also redemption, is indi-vidual.

This double movement of fall and return, or of sin and reconciliation, forms the core of Augustine's understanding of our longing for salvation and is the pattern which defines man's moral relations with others. No similar depiction of the personal and daily tension of our spiritual existence can be found in Plato, the classical thinker with whom Augustine is most plausibly compared. Desire and joy, fear and sorrow, the considerable bitterness mixed in the cup of pleasure – these are the existential states of the heart in which the goodness of the created order is received. And thus the distinctive modalities accompanying our spiritual need – mercy and forgiveness, tolerance and compassion, hope and ecstasy – become an integral part of our search for truth. Our personal lives, those interior sentiments and the vagaries of motive and intention, are the medium for our torturous pursuit of absolute truth.

While in Plato the injunction 'Know thyself' becomes the hallmark of philosophic inquiry, Augustine's plea makes self-examination a spiritual pilgrimage: 'Have pity on me and heal me,' Augustine prays, 'for you see that I have become a problem to myself and this is the ailment from which I suffer.' Self-division and self-estrangement, tension and contradiction, are the matrix of our questioning being. Our misgivings, our anxieties and doubts, our inner torments are now proper themes of the human search for order. Nowhere is the import of Augustine's thoughts for education better revealed than in his recognition of the struggles of our will. Both error and the true vision of the soul are volitional. I see or hear because I will to do so. But the activity of the will is experienced as a tormenting struggle. 'The inner self,' he writes, 'is a house divided against itself.' The poverty of our naturally given condition compared with the sanctity demanded by God, through which we perpetually feel the struggle of our duty against our will, means that extraordinary measures must be invoked to release us from the paralyses of the will and from the will's inclination to gravitate towards domination. 'For to will is present with me,' St Paul had admitted, 'but how to perform that which is good I find not.' Augustine's theology of the will gives form to these violent contradictions which characterize our daily struggles. 'The impulses of nature and the impulses of the spirit,' as Augustine attests, 'are at war with one another.' The question is how education can respond to this war.

The answer to this comes in Augustine's writings on love. What we choose, Augustine notes, reflects what we love. We are to be understood in terms of that object whose love dominates our souls. Education is character formation and that formation must focus on the training of the will. If the will is left undirected, we will love ourselves in our pride, in our capacity to master, in our satisfaction with the immediacies of the present. Pride in any one form finally appears in every other. When we love ourselves in our pride we love the affectation of self-sufficiency and total independence (*libido*). It can manifest itself as intense self-satisfaction; alternatively, it may be a hatred of the created order and the self. As the will to dominate, it can also be directed at other men, thus violating the moral order. At its extreme, the *libido dominandi* resists reality itself and presumes that it is its author. In this, it has violated the intellectual order, for it sees itself as the source of truth. It believes in its own self-salvation. Our will, which loves overcoming and resents all limit and condition, is finally the will to power itself. It is focused exclusively on mastery and it is absorbed by the feeling of enhanced power that comes from participating in the process of change. But in loving the transient, and in forsaking the enduring, we have failed to recognize the true end of hope, which is the possession of what is good and everlasting. Derailed hope – present in the distorted longing for wholeness in all our rest-less pursuit of things of the flesh – manifests itself as spurious, unlimited desire, social fractiousness, and hatred of eternity. It is caused by the denial of permanence. The sin of Cain – wandering – is the love of fluidity and its product is but the barren waste of spiritual lassitude. As Augustine says, to love the world is to break truth with God.

We are, then, more than transient body, we are also intellect. Our needs, in other words, are not only physical but spiritual. Our wills and our loves evince a longing which the physical cannot satisfy. Our true satisfaction lies in the moral order, manifest as beatitude, and the intellectual order, under-stood as wisdom. Both are summed up in charity (*caritas*) – to love what we ought to love. That is a love which gives itself without reserve and secures the possession of the supreme good. In this it is graced by faith and hope. Augustine writes that 'truth with God' requires giving oneself away in obedi-ence. Obedience is not passive capitulation, it is the active freedom of choos-ing truth and a release from the uncertainty and paralysis of the will. Its humility assumes the abandonment of false esteem and recognition. As Augustine says, God thwarts the proud and keeps grace for the humble.

Pride and grace – each defines the other, each illuminates the other. Educa-tion and politics, while it is not given to either to undo man's imperfection, must create the conditions in which our potentiality as moral and spiritual beings, and the perfection of love called charity, can be realized. Underlying our pride is the freedom of our will to choose, a freedom that carries the mark of divine order, not in our escape from external restraints but in our power to choose rightly, to live by a higher law. But the will's addiction to endless overcoming cannot on its own bring it to that choice. Without the training of the will – the disciplining of appetite, the overcoming of the will's initial indecisiveness, the formation of the spiritual singularity of personhood – freedom becomes pride. But that training itself taps into the will's self-over coming, whose impulse it uses. The training unleashes a dynamic which, if not carefully monitored, dissolves into a slough of despair. Without the forti-tude and the constancy of beatific insight and the receptivity to moral trans-formation that comes from grace, the training of the will would cause the derailment of the will. The impulse which activates pride must be weaned from despair but held back from presumption. Such moderation can only occur with sanctifying grace. With it comes the consolation the Christian calls hope. Only in such an education is the tension between pride and grace resolved. The dynamic of hope, without which there is no solace for the burdens of our existence, depends on this resolution.

Central to Augustine's Christianity is the longing for salvation. Like Plato, Augustine holds out the prospect of the soul's liberation from the immediacies of its social existence. 'Out of the shadows and imaginings, into the truth,' Cardinal Newman wrote, paraphrasing Augustine. The longing for transcendence is satisfied through the hope of salvation. Our daily struggles are only endurable through the hope of a return to wholeness in God. 'My thoughts, the intimate life of my soul,' Augustine recognized, 'are torn this way and that in the havoc of change. And so it will be until I am purified and melted by the fire of your love and fused into one with you.' But that hope is inseparable from a recognition of the permanence of human sin. To lose hope is despair, but to assume deliverance is presumption. The balance of resignation and optimism in new beginnings goes to the heart of the Christian teaching. Patience and humility are met by beatitude and charity in the pilgrimage of our worldly lives. And this balance can be achieved only through the discipline of moral order. But the primacy of the moral life is not, for Augustine, an invitation to moralism. Augustine refers to God's law as a ten-stringed harp. Like Plato's image of the puppet-player, morality for the Christian is tied to eternal harmony. Morality does not stand apart from our intellectual and spiritual lives. Augustine holds out the prospect of a transcendence which supplies the hope we need to respond to the burdens of our existence and the puzzles of our moral relations.

The longing Augustine voices promises no immanent salvation. The revolutionary expression of millenarian hope, inspired by the Revelations of St John, that Christ would reign with his saints on earth, was rebuked by Augustine. For him there would be no divinization of society beyond the spiritual presence of Christ in his church. He repudiated the presumption implied by the millenarian position regarding knowledge of the structure of time. 'I am divided between time gone by and time to come,' Augustine commented, 'and its course is a mystery to me.' Though time itself is sanctified by the law of the created order, Augustine, like Plato, does not allow the longing for transcendence to derail him into dreams of world-transformation. Time is a mystery. In a lifelong opposition to various heresies, Augustine opposed the presumption that humans could transfigure reality. Opposing Cicero's statement that Rome is the cosmopolis, and thus the final regime of the cosmos, Augustine recalls the inevitability of human weakness and the inevitable inclination on the part of humans to worship false idols. Justice can never be fully established in any city. Justice is a transcendent standard. Acknowledging this prevents the human presumption of perfection while supplying the ballast for human charity.

Descartes and Vico: The Sundering of Mathematics and Poetry and the Transition to Modernity

The feeling that the longings for transcendence and for salvation are so futile prompts many of the moderns to find wholeness by transforming the world. Two modern thinkers, Descartes and Vico, are particularly important to our discussion because in their teachings the excesses against which Plato and Augustine warned become accepted as legitimate expressions of human longing. And where Plato and Augustine attempted to forestall these excesses by a balanced education, the modern inheritors of Descartes's and Vico's arguments find the traditional understanding too limiting. Modern activists, taking their cue from Descartes and Vico, take the disappointment with the conditions under which human life is given to us one step further, and seek deliverance from its confines and conditioning power. With Descartes and Vico, the balance evident in the perception of reality embraced in the ancient and medieval world – and comprehended under the union of mathematics and poetry – is shattered and the fragments develop on their independent paths, culminating in programs such as *The Common Curriculum*.

The first path signifying the transformation from transcendence and salvation to deliverance can be seen in the thought of Descartes and in his many followers for whom *l'esprit de géometrie* prevails over all other human longings. In his *Discourse on Method*, Descartes sets out the principles for certain knowledge modelled on mathematics as the highest form of pure reason. He makes it clear that the inconveniences of human life arise from the differences in human opinion. These differences arise not so much from the inevitable differences in perception of a complex and ambiguous reality, or from differences in human aptitude. To the contrary, reality is assumed to be simple and human talents to be equal. The problem lies with the existing intellectual traditions. Descartes's method is a solution, for it promises to be a universal method and the source of a definitive reconstruction of all human knowledge. There are two decisive steps in his method. The first is his invocation of systematic doubt: doubting the testimony of the senses and of common sense, as the bases for what is intelligible, Descartes excludes the elementary verities forming the topics of classical reason and medieval faith. Things as they are encountered in the world are now suspected of dissimulation. The soul is no longer receptive to being. It can no longer trust the appearances of the world, and it is no longer a sensorium mirroring the breadth of the created order. It is now a critical and detached instrument to be used to reconstruct the world.[18]

Under the stringent rules of the Cartesian method, the criterion of truth is restricted to what the mind itself produces. So, not only does the sheer functioning of an internal process replace the textures, densities, and shapes of worldly reality, but a single operation of logicality replaces the totality of psychic experience. Knowledge is self-validating. Mental process acting on itself replaces the common reality attested to in perception and speech. What replaces intelligibility is certainty and what replaces the textured indeterminacy of separate orders of the soul is the unity of the mind as pure reason. Clarity can only be found in the detached and isolated operations of the mind. The composite of body and soul, which in ancient and medieval experience supplied the tension and boundaries of human existence and knowledge, is superseded by an autonomous mind with no integral relation to the mechanical desires of the body. The human problems at the heart of classical *paideia* – what is the human good? what is human order? how are these reflected in crafting the political association? – at once admit of a simpler and more certain solution.

Descartes proposes a method by which complexity is first broken down into simple parts and then these parts are reassembled. This 'resolutive-compositive' process works on the assumption that complexity is inherently obscure or confused, that the observer can comprehend directly and immediately only what is clear and distinct in the simplest units, and that the whole is fully intelligible again only through the process of reassembly whereby logical order is introduced into every relation and proportion. The phenomena of the world are then no longer ambiguous or contradictory because it is we who have resolved the thing and also recomposed it, confirming the principle that we can only know what we ourselves make. Clear and distinct simplicity replaces the perception that reality is multidimensional, mysterious, and tragically dissonant. Since there can be no self-contradiction in the analytic model by which the world is comprehensively represented, there can be no self-contradiction in the world or in nature. Ambivalence, imperfection, and defect are at once overcome. (We should recall that the global environment appealed to in *The Common Curriculum* is believed by the authors of the document to display increasingly this regularity.)

The last step of Descartes's project is the assertion of the supremacy of mathematical knowledge, specifically analytical geometry, as the sole reliable model for reconstructing the world. Mathematics supplies the answer to the question 'what must reality be in order that man may be certain that he wholly knows it?' The universe is adequately grasped by mathematical 'relations and proportions,' or, in other words, by a science limited to no particular or concrete phenomena and wholly a result of forms consciousness itself produces. The world known in experience is transfigured into the world of mathematical symbols.

Accompanying this methodical reconstruction of reality is Descartes's appeal to a new moral code, reflecting a new sobriety and economy. In the *Discourse*, precipitancy and prejudgment are identified as the moral deficiencies preventing human certainty. Premature conclusions, dogmatism, and immobility in theoretical understanding are matched by wavering and inconstancy in the practice of the past. The discretionary judgment of the ancient thinkers, or the allowances for human error and frailty made by Christian forbearance, are to be replaced by the moral equivalent of Cartesian intellectual certainty. In his *Passions of the Soul*, Descartes makes it clear that the highest virtue is *générosité*, which he characterizes as 'the sensation in oneself of a firm and constant resolution ... never to fail of one's own will to undertake and execute all the things [one] judges to be the best ... which is to follow perfectly after virtue.' Resoluteness in enterprise satisfies the moral demands of collective human existence, while supplying the necessary self-regulation needed to pursue methodical inquiry.

To what end is the Cartesian method directed? In Part V of the *Discourse*, Descartes undertakes an extensive investigation of an animal heart and supplies a thermo-mechanistic physics explaining the motions and passions of living beings. In Part VI he asks how his 'general notions of physics' might promote 'the general good of mankind':

For they have satisfied me that it is possible to reach knowledge that will be of much utility in this life; and that instead of the speculative philosophy now taught in the schools we can find a practical one, by which, knowing the nature and behaviour of fire, water, air, stars, the heavens, and all the other bodies which surround us, as well as we now understand the different skills of our workers, we can employ these entities for all the purposes for which they are suited, and so make ourselves masters and possessors of nature.

The mastery of nature – human and non-human – by which the frailties and inconveniences of our state are overcome, is the certain answer to the complexities and anxieties underlying the intellectual and spiritual search of the past. For while Plato believed that human wisdom entailed the recognition that man's exodus from the cave of ignorance was fleeting and impermanent, and while the Christian realizes that his salvation rests on the understanding that it is only given to humans to 'see through a glass darkly,' Descartes saw such irresoluteness as culpable naiveté, 'similar to a blind man who wishes to fight on even terms with one who can see, and so brings him to the back of some very dark cave.' Descartes identified his own achievement as having 'opened some windows and let the light of day enter into that cave.'

When Descartes says, 'the truth of the hypotheses is proved by the actuality of the effects,' he gives licence to the systematic manipulation and mastery of the world with the intent of endowing it with logical regularity. At the centre of his political teaching is his contention that the field of medicine holds the solution to the vain strivings for individual immortality in ancient and medieval times. Descartes sees medicine as ensuring a state of health which, if not in fact enabling individual immortality, at least ensures species immortality. The 'commonhealth,' as we could name this project, is one where generations are bound together and where the individual or collective search for the meaning of the mystery of death is replaced by the enterprise of using science for man's ultimate expression of mastery – over death itself. In the mechanical Jerusalem, *eros* takes the form of a longing for deliverance, *thumos* is sublimated into resoluteness in enterprise, and the human species extends sanctifying grace to itself and acquires collective immortality.

The mathematicization of order which characterizes Descartes's teaching is rejected in Giambattista Vico's book *The Study Methods of Our Times*.[19] Vico declaims against Descartes's purely geometrical, apodeictic form of reasoning. An exposition of physics, he counters, must be eloquent, given to aesthetic charm. Metaphor, while ornamental, Vico writes, 'plays the first role in acute, figurative expression. Analogy brings matters lying far apart into a pleasing whole.' While acknowledging the contribution of the geometrical method to useful inventions, Vico finds the principles of that method to have failed to speak to the whole of man, 'as pieces of music composed in accordance with a mathematic formula give no pleasure.' A genuine representation of nature will dwell in verisimilitude, in probable approximations, and in the creative explorations of the imagination.

The centrality of 'poetry' to Vico's own preferred method of study is evident in the role he envisages for speech, namely 'eloquence.' While appealing to the ancient rhetoricians, and declaiming against the modern preoccupation with method as 'sophistry,' Vico's 'eloquence' is not one of 'great fidelity to truth and subtlety' but, as in the poetry of Tasso, is filled with 'enchantingly musical sublimity.' Vico's 'eloquence' is unlike dialectical speech, or classical rhetoric, or the consoling epistle (all of which aimed at harmonizing the individual soul with the order of existence). In their place,

Vico's 'eloquence' is a deeply sentimentalized expression of the imagination's ability to project a sense of wholeness through the sweet sentiment of existence.

This sentimentalization is equally evident in Vico's understanding of judgment. Admonishing the Cartesians for their use of 'inflexible standards of abstract right' to judge human affairs, Vico counters: 'we must rather gauge them by the pliant Lesbic rule, which does not conform bodies to itself, but adjusts itself to their contours.' Such pliant Lesbic rule, for Vico, is best exemplified in the *sensus communis*, the faculty of judgment which responds to the rhythmic changes in circumstance and which is moved by the ideals put forward by imagination. Judgment, in Vico's work, has been aestheticized into moral feeling and sentiment.

Despite this softening of Descartes's teaching, the personality which Vico wishes to cultivate by this study method is as forceful as that formed by Descartes's *esprit de géometrie*: 'the soul must be enticed by corporeal images and impelled to love; for once it loves, it is easily taught to believe; once it believes and loves, the fire of passion must be infused into it so as to break its inertia and force it to *will.*' Vico adopts the Cartesian position that the will seeks deliverance from the tensions and complexities of existence. Both thinkers picture humanity willing wholeness into a radically reconstructed social world.

The 'poeticization' of order is no negation of mathematics, but rather the perfection of its spirit. The holism to which Vico appeals, and the means by which he seeks to evoke it (charm, enchantment, sublimity), are simulacra of the past. Retrieved as simulacra of ancient and medieval forms, they are surrogates, informed by the essential Cartesian rejection of inherent purpose and unity in the whole and its accompanying balance or moderation. Over against the rigidity and inflexibility of Cartesian mathematics is set the suppleness and pliancy of poetry. Recalling our earlier discussions of Plato and Augustine, we could say that the ancient and medieval reconciliation of the body and soul through proportionality and harmony is fragmented into a dualism, each pole of which is expected to supply the wholeness of the original reconciliation. The soul is either the mind or the heart; the body is either a machine or an organic process. Each of the fragments is now susceptible to becoming the object of millenarian enthusiasm – perfect worlds held together by either mathematical precision or poetic wholeness.

The social teaching of Vico's holism appears in his prescription for an extensive preventative medicine. Criticizing the monopoly of the Cartesian *esprit de géometrie* over modern medicine, Vico proposes a far-ranging medical art which orients itself by the connection between physical and mental illness. Attending to 'intimations of future disease' revealed in the nexus of body and heart, of organic matter and imagination, the new medicine is to respond to the totality of symptoms and possible relations within which they are formed. Vico supplies the poetry missing from Cartesian mathematics. From here lies a short and direct route to the idea of a therapeutic politics linking the search for self-fulfilment and self-actualization with a comprehensive program of deliverance from the inconveniences of the human condition.

In short, Vico's release of the longing for immediacy and wholeness from structure, of imagination from speech, or of poetry from mathematics, begins the modern turn to the radical longing for the unconditioned or undetermined. This longing for deliverance in the name of the poetic voice of mankind would have a long tradition and reach its apotheosis in Rousseau's romanticism but also in the concluding years of the French Revolution, during the Jacobin Terror.

Political Modernity and the Enlightenment

With the philosophies of Descartes and Vico, we see the emergence of a characteristic modern dichotomy. It is a dichotomy between, on the one hand, the deductive universality of method and, on the other, the longing for spontaneous wholeness and release from the grid of mathematical reasoning and its methodological extension to moral and civic concerns. What classical *paideia* put together – the rigour of reason and the substantive happiness of the soul – is split asunder in this dichotomy of Cartesian formalism and Vicoan spontaneity.

The opposition between Descartes and Vico goes underground as a buried tension within modernity that re-explodes with Rousseau's romantic protest against political liberalism. The tension between Cartesian method and Vicoan beauty recrudesces as the tension between Kantian ethical formalism and Schiller's call for the aesthetic education of man. We term this great cleavage the revolution of Love and Understanding, borrowing from Hegel's diagnosis of the split, which he believed his own teleology of historical progress showed the way to healing, so that Romantic spontaneity and revolutionary longings for a millenarian flight from modernity might be tempered by a return to the substantive richness of classical *paideia* on the basis of modern freedom and subjectivity. As we shall see in chapter 5, the Rousseauan revolution and Hegel's attempt to reconcile it to the teleological unfolding of history occasion both the most dazzling hopes and the gravest dangers for the traditional enterprise of liberal education, a passage that takes us to the noblest moments of contemporary pedagogy as well as to the darkest reaches of nihilism and fragmentation. But, for now, we must regard this as a buried tension, and dwell on the considerable contribution to education of political liberalism itself. For in the encounter between Descartes and Vico, Cartesian rationalism and its extension to political life through the contractarian political philosophies of Hobbes, Locke, and Montesquieu were for a long time the clear winners.

Our interest in, and need for, liberal education arise within the specific context of liberal democracy. This context complicates the question of liberal education's content and validity for the present. For, while traditional civic *paideia* is not incompatible with liberal democracy – and indeed has been enriched by it – there is nevertheless at bottom a fundamental ambiguity about its place in a modern democratic civilization that gives priority to rights over duties. At the same time, while the connection between liberal education in the traditional sense and liberal democracy is not an easy or untroubled one, it provides much of whatever remains of the moral and intellectual integrity of democratic life in the present.

For the classical thinkers, the highest purpose of education is to enable people to approximate the eternal order of the cosmos through the moral and intellectual virtues of the soul. The consequence is a ranked hierarchy of civic responsibility and authority, famously illustrated by the tripartite class structure of Plato's *Republic*, where the wise rule over the concupiscent with the assistance of the civic-spirited. In the optimal political community, the duties of citizenship are in harmony with the most satisfying and dignified way of life for every individual. At its best, the regime does not merely protect the citizens from lawlessness or external aggression, but educates them so as to elicit each citizen's natural potential for excellence of soul.

In contrast with the classical conception of civic *paideia*, the political philosophers of the Enlightenment entertained severe doubts about this pedagogical role for government when they did not unconditionally reject it. This is especially clear when we look at the founding of the United States. The American founding was a kind of laboratory experiment for the application of liberal political theory to the real world. Because the new world was free from feudal and other pre-modern European claims to authority, the American founders state the essential doctrines of liberalism with a kind of crystalline clarity unclouded by competing or earlier concepts of legitimacy and the human good. As James Madison puts it in the tenth *Federalist*, the framers of the American constitution rejected the use of government to 'remove the causes' of faction and vice in the soul by attempting to provide a comprehensive education in citizenship.[20] In reality, Madison and the other framers claimed, these educational regimes (whether philosophic or theocratic) turned out to be despotisms imposing unbearable restrictions on the liberty of thought and action. The American framers were concerned with diluting the power of government so as to deny any person or faction the chance to tyrannize over the rest, not with expanding the authority of government so as to enable it to improve the citizens' characters. According to the tenth *Federalist*, governments should reject the traditional injunction to try to control the 'causes' of vice by educating citizens to elevate the common good over the private good. Instead, the free and open clash of selfish interests will automatically regulate the harmful 'effects' of vice as people learn from experience that their long-term self-interest is best served by refraining from violating the rights of others.

Education in the full-blown classical sense clearly has no place here. People have to be educated to elevate duty over self-interest, but no one has to be educated to seek his or her own advantage. The *Federalist* is perhaps the most anti-communitarian – and therefore, in the strict classical sense, anti-educational – treatise ever written by philosophically enlightened statesmen. In the ninth *Federalist*, Alexander Hamilton observes with relish that the ancient Greek *polis*, in contrast with the idealized version of it found in the ancient philosophers, was in reality a hotbed of tyranny and anarchy.[21] In debunking this cherished symbol of the educated and privileged classes of Europe, Hamilton is trying to win over the more toryish of his own readers who believed that the mass of Americans lacked the traditional classical education needed for republican self-government to succeed without degenerating into mobocracy. The debate in the *Federalist* over the American constitution has virtually nothing to say about the content of the new nation's education. This disregard was most strikingly confirmed by the failure of the new government to adopt Thomas Jefferson's call for a constitutionally mandated national university designed to educate the naturally most talented people from all classes of society.

Nevertheless, it would be simplistic and misleading to say that liberalism even in its pure American form had no connection at all with traditional liberal education, even if it was largely absent from the formal debate about the structure of the new constitution. The Enlightenment political philosophy from which the principles of the American founding were derived may have looked askance at the educational ideas of Plato and Aristotle with their notion of an all-encompassing pedagogical and aristocratic polity. But for all that, the Enlightenment also maintained that an education in moral character was needed if the individual liberties of the modern age were not to degenerate into licence. Adam Smith is best known for the original formulation of the 'hidden hand' argument (a variant of which is used by Madison in *Federalist* 10) to the effect that what was traditionally regarded as private vice – the pursuit of profit as the main concern in life – engenders public virtue. But Smith bases his endorsement of free-enterprise economics on the education of the 'inner man' in the intellectual and moral virtues that prevent us from being completely absorbed in making money. According to Smith, people will not treat each other decently in their commercial relations unless those commercial relations are grounded in and guided by this wider moral training based on our capacities for reason and sympathy. As its philosophical founders knew, but we all too often forget, liberalism and democracy are not simply the absence of constraint. Getting people to be productive and individualistic without being rapacious has taken centuries to achieve – a process that has involved much violence and upheaval, but also a painstaking civic and social pedagogy with conscious links to the Graeco-Roman tradition of civic humanism that transformed the human character and created a whole new civilization. In this sense, although as moderns we cannot directly imitate the educational precepts of the ancients, we can and must continue to draw on their concern with moral character to sustain our own best version of democracy.

It should be remarked in this context that the identification of liberalism with capitalism, as if the meaning of liberal democracy were exhausted by unlimited profit and productivity, is a parody of liberalism originating with its severest critics on the far left and right. Too often capitalist economics in practice have merited the criticism. But if the excesses of capitalism are to be remedied from within the moral resources of liberal democracy, then we must free our thinking about liberalism from this parody in order to encourage it to live up to its own best ideals of liberty, probity, compassion, and meritocracy. It is especially lamentable when people who call themselves 'conservatives' take the most debased account of liberalism from the far left and right as a regime concerned with nothing but profit, and openly celebrate this as if this is what it means to defend liberal democracy.

The shallowest of neo-conservatives join hands with the shallowest of leftists in believing that liberal democracy is exclusively designed to maximize the acquisition of property. But the Enlightenment thinkers such as Locke and Montesquieu from whom the American founders derived their 'new science of politics' never maintained that property rights were the basis of all other rights. The first law of nature was the right of every individual to be free from despotic and invasive treatment. The practice of this fundamental natural right entailed the right to acquire property, worship, move about, amuse oneself, and engage in political debate, so long as others' rights were not violated. Liberalism regards the right to property as one among a number of liberties that derive from, reinforce, and demonstrate our fundamental right to freedom from tyranny and oppression. Liberalism is not a product of capitalism. Liberalism permits capitalism, and justifies it only to the extent that it facilitates the liberty and dignity of every member of society.

Locke particularly favoured property rights among these various dividends of our fundamental natural liberty because of the stability he believed they engendered by transforming non-negotiable political conflicts into negotiable economic disputes. But Locke also stood for religious tolerance and more flexible approaches to education and child-rearing. He wrote:

The business of education ... is not, as I think, to make [students] perfect in any one of the sciences, but so to open and dispose their minds as may best make them capable of any, when they shall come to apply themselves to it. If men are for a long time accustomed only to one sort or method of thoughts, their minds grow stiff in it, and do not readily turn to another. It is therefore to give them this freedom, that I think they should be made to look into all sorts of knowledge, and exercise their understandings in so wide a variety and stock of knowledge.[22]

As Locke summed it up to his friend Molyneux: 'Pray let this be your chief care, to fill your son's head with clear and distinct ideas, and to teach him, on all occasions, both by practice and by rule, how to get them, and the necessity of it. This together with a mind active, set upon the attaining of reputation and truth, is the true principling of a young man.'[23]

If even Lockean liberalism is not synonymous with property rights but has a concern with moral education as well, so much more is this true of the Rousseauan strain of liberalism that enters the American founding through the views of Thomas Jefferson. Locke had maintained that people institute governments chiefly to secure 'their Lives, Liberties and Estates, which I call by the general Name, *Property*.'[24] In the Declaration of Independence, Jefferson tellingly amends Locke's concern with the protection of life, liberty, and the pursuit of property with the more expansive Rousseauan formulation, 'life, liberty, and the pursuit of *happiness*.'[25] With Rousseau, liberalism mitigates the priority of individual rights by an attempt to recapture the comprehensiveness of the classical concern with the happiness and full development of human nature within the civic association. Accordingly, for Rousseau, human liberation and moral development go well beyond what Locke envisioned. They include our freedom as citizens of a participatory republic, our autonomy in keeping with the irreducible natural dignity of every human being, and a natural sentiment of compassion towards our fellow men. These three elements work together politically and psychologically, and since they involve us in experiences of the good life that transcend spontaneous self-interest and power-seeking, they also require a more elaborate civic pedagogy. To be free, we must will the freedom of others with whom we sympathize. Although Rousseau grants that the pursuit of private property is a right, these other elements of our freedom and moral character rank high above it. We have more of a right to participate in collective self-government than we do to acquire property, and more of an obligation to be compassionate to the disadvantaged than to respect the unequal division of property.

This is a version of democratic civilization that cannot come about by allowing the clash of interests to regulate itself while instilling the bourgeois virtues in private life. Because Rousseau places much greater demands on what we are capable of as citizens of a democracy, he restores on a modern basis the classical conviction that the art of government is, above all, the art of education. In keeping with this wider vision, Jefferson called for the creation of a national university to cultivate a leadership meritocracy of the most gifted people from all classes, thoroughly educated in ancient history, the classics, mathematics, and science. This blend of modern mathematics and science with the study of ancient history and the classics to learn about the high points of moral excellence is similar to the ideals of Rousseau's own educational masterpiece, the *Emile*. Also like Rousseau, and typical of the Enlightenment as a whole, Jefferson is primarily concerned with an education in secular, as opposed to religious, morality. His appeal to the classics and to ancient history is in part an argument for excluding religious revelation:

Instead, therefore, of putting the Bible and Testament into the hands of the children at an age when their judgments are not sufficiently matured for religious inquiries, their memories may here be stored with the most useful facts from Grecian, Roman, European and American history. The first elements of morality may too be instilled into their minds; such as, when further developed as their judgments advance in strength, may teach them how to work out their own greatest happiness, by showing them that it does not depend on the condition of life in which chance has placed them, but is always the result of a good conscience, good health, occupation and freedom in all just pursuits.[26]

Here, in the *Notes on the State of Virginia*, Jefferson clearly tells us what he means by 'happiness' when he uses this word in the more widely known Declaration of Independence. Happiness is not the contentless self-expressionism of doing your own thing. The 'greatest happiness' is the freedom that a liberal education bestows to develop one's highest capacities for just pursuits, and so to rise in life according to one's natural ability, thereby escaping to the extent humanly possible the accidents of birth and fate. Jefferson's is an especially noble statement of how modern democratic meritocracy requires, and is required by, a traditional conception of liberal education. Echoing all of the most articulate defenders of liberal education stretching back through the Renaissance to Plato and Aristotle, Jefferson maintains that an educated citizenry is essential to good and accountable government: 'Every government degenerates when trusted to the rulers of the people alone. The people themselves therefore are its only safe depositories. And to render even them safe, their minds must be improved to a certain degree ... An amendment of our constitution must here come in aid of the public education. The influence over government must be shared among all the people.'[27] Unfortunately for the United States, this amendment was never added to the constitution. As we will see in chapter 6, the situation in Canada was different.

5

Liberal Education and the Fragmentation of Modernity

The Longing for Wholeness and the End of History

With Rousseau's critique of the Enlightenment, we encounter one of the watersheds of modern education and the meaning of human wholeness. The Enlightenment believed that bourgeois society allows the greatest natural fulfilment because it is the most prosperous and peaceful. Rousseau inaugurates the revolutionary notion that bourgeois society, with its routinization of competitive anxiety, keeps us further from our natural satisfaction than any other regime. After Rousseau, whenever education aims beyond the utilitarian and vocational, it is increasingly linked to a critique of 'the system' and to a promise of liberation – not merely liberation from a particular defective regime, but from all political, social, and natural hierarchies. Rousseau's is the original pedagogy of the oppressed. In our own time, when a belief in the teleological progress of history no longer seems tenable, it is Rousseau who in a way emerges in retrospect as the great divide between classical *paideia* and its questionable status today. He is the Janus who looks back behind the Enlightenment to classical antiquity and forward ahead of Schiller and von Humboldt to today's increasing politicization of learning.

Rousseau argues that the appetitive, power-seeking natural man of Hobbes and much of the Enlightenment's political and moral theory is not natural at all, but the kind of man who has already been corrupted by society and the need to compete which society imposes.[1] Man has to move into society initially out of material need. When nature is not plentiful, people must compete with or depend on the help of others. According to Rousseau, this engenders a deeper, emotional dependence on the good opinion of others. As our needs become more refined, less concerned with self-preservation, we become more concerned with prestige. We lose ourselves to others, pursuing an artificial self defined by others' acceptance of our achievements and tastes. Ambition for Rousseau is not rooted in natural man's instinctive, simple means for self-preservation, but is, as we would now say, socially constructed. Rousseau charged Hobbes, Locke, and their devotees in the French Enlightenment with helping to make society more, not less, strife-ridden. Their brand of liberalism denies us the satisfaction of genuine glory such as the ancient heroes and statesmen achieved, chaining us instead to a round of petty satisfactions. We are taught to feel anxious about surviving and prospering from day to day. The need to worry about and try to thwart the success of others makes our bourgeois competitiveness all the more pervasive for being hinged to such small, transient goals.

The difficulty which Rousseau admits with his own view of man's natural wholeness and lack of competitiveness is that society is historically too well-established for us ever to return to the state of nature. His solution is offered in the *Emile*, which can be described as the ideal education of an ordinary human being.[2] The solution is to try to preserve as much of that natural independence as possible so that man, while depending on others for those material needs which he cannot provide for himself in an already interdependent society, will not suffer from the deeper emotional dependence on conventional mores and hierarchies for his self-esteem.

Emile's needs are kept at the level of simple, natural self-preservation by keeping him in the country, preventing him from forming a dependence on the luxuries of refined society and therefore being driven to enter the competition for privileged access to them. This fails to be a sufficient safeguard, however, when Emile reaches adolescence. Sexual desire necessarily makes us dependent on other people. Since we already live in society, we cannot satisfy this urge by roaming the forest, as natural man does. We have to enter into all the alienating, conventional relationships of courtship or resort to the *demi-monde* where illicit sex is made more tantalizing by the refinement of luxury and wittiness. Once Emile follows his sexual desires, he will necessarily lose his unreflecting self-sufficiency, seeking instead to measure up to the standards set by others for his own desirability. He will become alienated from himself and will try to recover his self-esteem by competing for the vain distinctions of refined society.

Rousseau's solution to this unavoidable alienation through sexual desire is to fight it with its own weapons. He turns the artificial striving for completion beyond the self *back against* the self. He enflames Emile's adolescent imagination with the image of an ideal woman, Sophy. This woman actually exists, but Rousseau postpones Emile's contact with her until his imagination has been expanded to its limits with his ideal of her. He convinces Emile to prize in this woman the natural independence, modesty, and goodness which Rousseau has conserved in him. Rousseau persuades Emile to postpone satisfying his desire for this woman in order to make himself completely worthy of her by remaining chaste and independent, as she is. By stimulating Emile to sublimate his sexual desire into a romantic longing for spiritual union with a woman who mirrors his own best qualities, Rousseau teaches Emile to love the ideal of his own independence.

In a way, this love is totally alienating. Emile is deliberately persuaded that he will never be complete until this woman considers him worthy of her. Yet, since the ideal is such a lofty one, mirroring his own independence, Emile will pursue it in continuing oblivion to the usual attachments to society's rewards which make us the slaves of changing fashions and fickle opinions. By teaching Emile to invest all his will-power in the pursuit of his ideal of Sophy, Rousseau liberates the will only in order to head off and absorb into it those diverse forms of will-power which are ordinarily exerted in the pursuit of material comfort and social status. In this way, the will becomes the servant of, rather than a distraction from, our education in goodness and virtue.

Near the end of the *Emile*, Rousseau tells his pupil that he must learn to exercise his will against his passions simply for the sake of self-control – not just to perfect himself for Sophy. A part of moral education is to learn that, on occasion, we must perform our duty simply because it is our duty, without any hope of reward. Rousseau reveals to Emile that he will, in fact, never find in actual marriage with Sophy the sweet bliss of his imaginary longing for her. The ideal woman is actually superior to the real one. According to Rousseau, our inclinations can never achieve the satisfaction we imagine for them. Emile must learn, therefore, not to expect total bliss from the real Sophy, or from any other concrete pleasure. He must 'impose laws on the appetites of (the) heart.' He must use his will to resist dependence on the inclinations so as to avoid the bitter disappointment of learning how little they live up to the satisfactions we imagine for them.

This part of Rousseau's educational teaching deeply influenced Kant, and it obviously anticipates the categorical imperative. But it is well to remember that Rousseau's idea of education is not reducible to the universalistic and formalistic ethical maxim of Kantianism. For Rousseau, our capacity to will ourselves to rise above the inclinations must for the most part be grounded in an erotic wholeness, a harmony and equilibrium of passion and duty. In this way, Rousseau tries to restore the amplitude and comprehensive scope of classical and especially Platonic *paideia* on the basis of modern individualism and the Newtonian understanding of nature. By making Emile fall in love with an ideal woman, Rousseau not only tries to insulate Emile's natural desires from corruption by society. Rousseau transfers to Sophy as the object of Emile's dreamy romantic longing some of that sweet naturalness which otherwise could not at all survive Emile's transition from natural man to a social being. By repressing his full desire for the real Sophy in order to preserve as much of the ideal Sophy as possible, Emile achieves a beautifying aesthetic unity between the wholeness of his natural self and the object of his will. This element of Rousseau's thinking cuts him off from the pure moral assertiveness and voluntarism of Kant and links him with Schiller, who believed that in the sublime feelings aroused by art, we are able to celebrate the organic unity between the individual self and the beauty of the world into which he projects himself.

Schiller's *Letters on the Aesthetic Education of Man* is an especially important work for understanding the attempt by German thinkers in the wake of Rousseau to explore the possibility of an education in culture as a way of healing the alienation caused by modern scientific and political rationalism – an alienation not only between man and nature, but within human beings between their rational and passionate selves.[3] The very title of the work recalls the subtitle of *Emile*, 'On Education,' and thereby links it to the holistic conception of *paideia* stretching back behind the Enlightenment to the ancients. In Schiller's concern with human wholeness, echoed by Hegel's prescription for an educational 'recollection' of the classical heritage, we encounter one of the well-springs of contemporary liberal studies at their best.

Kant might be seen as a philosophical hero of modernity and of moral education. He uses the tension between reason and nature to defeat the basest consequences of Hobbesianism. If we follow the categorical imperative, we do not become sovereigns of others and masters of nature, but masters of our own natures and sovereigns of ourselves. But as Schiller and Hegel complain, Kant achieves this at the cost of a disjunction between moral reason as an anti-natural imperative and feeling which, bereft of rational form, is reduced to indiscriminate sensation. The task of modern education must be to heal this rift between arid rationality and irresponsible impulse, to find what Schiller calls a 'third condition' through education and culture.[4]

According to Schiller, whereas a life spent in fulfilling low appetites in the Hobbesian manner is 'savage,' Kantian morality creates a more complicated problem for the education of character. Having learned that reason requires us to rise above natural inclination, in the pursuit of this duty we run the risk of utterly impoverishing the world of feeling, treating its sublime and coarse expressions as equally requiring suppression by the moral will. Kantianism runs the risk of producing a prude who regards a passion for Raphael and a passion for gin as defects equally worthy of repression. Schiller therefore tries to demonstrate that there is a route to Kantian morality through an aesthetic education; that a beautiful life can entail a morally well-ordered one.

This blend of nature and morality is aesthetic culture. In attempting to beautify Kantianism, Schiller tries to restore the erotic dimension of virtue explored in Plato's *Symposium* on modern subjectivistic grounds.[5] He accepts the modern meaning of human nature as an egoistic subject. But for Schiller the pursuit of moral freedom requires not only the repression of the passions, but their sublimation and re-expression in the work of art, which reflects nature back to man as transformed, beautified, and made orderly as the home of his achieved freedom. Aesthetic culture, then, has a different ontological basis than Platonic *eros*. It is not, as in Diotima's teaching, the elicitation of erotic longing by its permanent objects in the world. Instead, aesthetic culture is man's self-conscious transformation of nature to create an organic unity between his subjective will and the sensuous embodiment of his ideal. Hence, as Schiller tells us, modern aesthetic education will have an undertone of self-doubt, moodiness, and anxiety – a quality of 'sentimentality' – that the ancients did not experience in their 'naive' conviction of an immediate openness to the permanent truth about the world. Whereas for the Platonist, the world is a rationally ordered and benevolent whole, the Romantic is prone to be tormented by the mystery of whether nature is receptive or indifferent to the beauty he both projects upon and discovers in the non-human world.

Schiller, then, tries to infuse Rousseau the solitary dreamer into Rousseau the democratic moralist taken up by Kant. According to Schiller, modernity is characterized by two powerful and contradictory forces. One is the realm of 'necessity.' As a devotee of Kant, Schiller understands the realm of nature as the realm of necessity. Its political and economic counterpart is the contractual bourgeois liberalism of Hobbes, Locke, and the Enlightenment: 'Utility is the great idol of the age, to which all other powers must do service and all talents swear allegiance.' The other great – and superior – force is the realm of freedom, which transcends the realm of natural necessity. Echoing both Kant and Rousseau, Schiller claims that our true dignity and nobility reside in our spiritual capacity to 'abandon actuality and soar with becoming boldness above necessity.' Specifically like Rousseau, he does not believe art can be a purely private concern, or a mere diversion. Its purpose is to contribute to the character and tastes appropriate to free men and women. 'Art is a daughter of Freedom, and must receive her commission from the needs of spirits, not from the exigency of matter.' Again we see how, in the wake of Rousseau, the German Idealists and Romantics try to restore the comprehensiveness of traditional civic education on the basis of modern equal rights and freedom.

For Schiller, the aesthetic is the crucial middle realm of experience between the degrading downward pull of natural necessity and the austere dictates of moral freedom. Art cannot serve the commercial interests of contractual liberalism without losing its soul. Art must contribute to mankind's progress toward the Ideal by showing that 'it is through Beauty that we arrive at Freedom.' The problem for Schiller, however, is that Understanding – the human intellect with its powers of analysis and observation – is both the ally and the enemy of culture. It is Understanding that, by discovering the categorical imperative, establishes the supremacy of freedom and human dignity over the degradation of the natural inclinations and 'the noisy mart' of liberal-contractarian politics. But Understanding also appears to destroy the aesthetic experience. Kantian morality tends to banish the aesthetic to the realm of the other inclinations, treating it as merely another selfish indulgence. Modern rationality threatens to destroy the validity of sentiment, even though the imperative to moral striving that reason demonstrates in a rigorous manner is first experienced as a sentiment in the heart of the ordinary man:

You have only to free [these sentiments] from their technical [Kantian] formulation, and they will emerge as the time-honoured utterances of common reason, and as data of that moral instinct which Nature in her wisdom appointed as Man's guardian until clear insight should bring him to maturity. But it is just this technical formulation, which reveals the truth to our understanding, that conceals it once again from our feeling; for unfortunately the Understanding must first destroy the objects of the inner sense before it can appropriate them. Like the chemist, the philosopher finds combination only through dissolution, and the work of spontaneous nature only through the torture of Art. In order to seize the fleeting appearance he must bind it in the fetters of rule, dissect its fair body into abstract notions, and preserve its living spirit in a sorry skeleton of words.

Kant, like Rousseau, believed that the basic precepts of morality comprised a 'sublime science of simple souls' likelier to be found in simple folk relatively unspoiled by civilization than in the intellectually more sophisticated.[6] Kant believed it was the duty of philosophy to use the technical capacity of rational demonstration (a part of what Schiller here terms Understanding) to raise this instinctive grasp of morality to full intellectual clarity and consciousness. Schiller, however, reminds us of the Rousseauan paradox that Kant tends to gloss over. Since reason itself – which is to say modern scientific and analyti-

cal rationality – alienates us from nature and the sentiments engendered by
the idealization and beautification of nature through art, how can reason aid
us in living closer to nature? How can reason help us achieve the 'third condition' between selfless morality and indiscriminate sensuality without
destroying it?

Hegel's answer to the question of how freedom and nature might be reconciled through educational culture is the teleological progress of history. For
we moderns, the place occupied by the soul in the classical understanding of
liberal education is somehow replaced by history. Plato had understood the
ascent up the Divided Line from sense-experience to wisdom to be a recurrent
and incompleteable journey, available at any time and place in principle. For
Hegel, the Divided Line as an eternal schema of the ascent to wisdom is
replaced by the progressive actualization of wisdom in time, accomplished by
and for the entire human species.[7] Echoing Schiller's distinction between
Understanding and Beauty, Hegel distinguished between ways of life characterized by Understanding and Love.[8] By the former, he meant the cold analytical thought premised on modern man's alienation from nature and
growing power to master it through scientific knowledge and technique.
Understanding is 'the most astonishing and greatest of all powers.'[9] In its
power to rend the world, to dissolve things and recombine them, it is the subjective engine of historical action. The political parallel of this analytical dis-
section of nature's parts came with liberalism's vision of human beings as
isolated individuals impersonally represented by the state.

Love, by contrast, boded our feeling of unity with our fellow human
beings and with nature.[10] History reconciles these two dimensions of existence. For Hegel, history is a double-sided quest for unity and fulfilment by
means of scientific and political rationality. The pursuit of Understanding
(including political rights and scientific power) itself unexpectedly brings
about the reign of Love. Mankind pursues its freedom through the conquest
of nature. But the Spirit of all history embarks on an odyssey of fulfilment
that it pursues through its locus, mankind. The result is the end of history –
the embodiment of reason and freedom in the present age.

Hegel's extraordinary contribution to modern scholarship and the modern
university curriculum must be understood in the context of this philosophical
enterprise for the reconciliation of Understanding – the whole mentality
linking political liberalism and individualism with modern scientific empiricism – with the communitarian longing for harmony with nature and with
our fellow human beings. Hegel's educational writings give perhaps the fullest and richest account of the meaning of a liberal education since Plato,
Aristotle, and Augustine. In keeping with the conditions of modern individu-

alism and freedom, however, their aim is not to cultivate the virtues of the soul so as to enable it to approximate the eternal verities. Instead, their aim is to develop our sense that we are both free individuals and members of a community, that the self-assertive, even aggressive dimension of our autonomy as individuals must be tempered by, and must compromise with, the sentiments of reconciliation and common cultural roots that link us with others.

For Hegel, the core of this educational enterprise must be a 'recollection' of the classics of Greek and Roman antiquity: 'If we make ourselves at home in such an element, all the powers of the soul are stimulated, developed and exercised; and, further, this element is a unique material through which we enrich ourselves and improve the very substance of our being.'[11] But the aim of recollecting the classical heritage is not nostalgic. There is no escape hatch from the teleological unfolding of history back into the innocent bliss of the origins. As free beings who define ourselves by our ability to assert our wills against natural, hereditary, and customary limitations, we moderns can never enjoy the unselfconscious feeling of seamless harmony with the *polis* and with nature that was given to the Greeks. For us, governments are representative; they exist to serve our interests and win our consent. We can never be unreservedly enthralled and enchanted by politics, or feel uncritically loyal to our governments, as could the ancient Greeks. But by recollecting and absorbing into our own cultural consciousness the matchless achievements of the ancient thinkers and artists in describing the complexity of human behaviour and morality, we lay claim to and appropriate that heritage to enrich our modern sense of freedom.

Moreover, precisely because our modern states are large, impersonal mechanisms for representation rather than small local communities in which we participate directly, the traditional concern of liberal education with providing a bulwark of independent-mindedness against the pressures of public opinion or tyranny takes on an even greater urgency for us than it possessed for the ancients. Modern man urgently needs an 'inner citadel' to resist the pressures of a mass society too often bent on materialism: 'Have we not seen in our own times that even states become unsteady, expose themselves to dangers and collapse, despite plenty of valuable resources, just because they had neglected and disdained to preserve such an inner citadel in the soul of their citizens, and because they were interested in profit alone and directed their citizens to treat things spiritual as mere means?'[12] Because modernity is so obsessed with the quantifiable, external relations among people as self-interested members of the social contract and as producers and consumers of commodities, liberal education is essential for giving us a depth of inner personality and conviction to fortify us against a creeping sense of our own insignificance in societies made up of millions of people largely bent on the same materialistic pursuits: '[Greek and Roman literature] alone provides the independence and firmness, the essential inwardness which is the mother of self-control and self-possession, of presence and vigilance of mind; it generates in the soul thus prepared and educated a kernel of self-dependent value, of absolute ends, which alone is the precondition of all usefulness in life and which is important to plant in all citizens of all walks of life.'

In this way, Hegel restores the direct connection between liberal education and responsible citizenship, attenuated by the contractarian political thinking of the Enlightenment. However, in contrast with the educational precepts of the classical thinkers, it is no longer a question of the place of human nature within the larger permanent natural order of the cosmos. For Hegel, the purpose of a liberal education is to help raise to consciousness our already implicit contextual relationship with the cultural heritage jointly achieved over time by mankind. However, in spite of this formal theoretical difference, the heart of education is the same for Hegel as for the classics. Education is an adventure for the soul. It should encourage the young to 'estrange' themselves from the world of the here and now in order to gain perspective on it in light of the far wider and more complicated world of historical achievement stretching back to antiquity. Just as Aristotle pointed to Homer's *Odyssey* as a way of educating people to transcend their immediate local attachments without losing all connection with them, so Hegel recommends a spiritual journey into the classics as a way of rising above our own time and place and then returning to them better equipped to take a responsible role in their affairs: 'This centrifugal force of the soul explains why the soul must always be provided with the means of estranging itself from its natural condition and essence, and why in particular the young mind must be led into a remote and foreign world. Now, the screen best suited to perform this task of estrangement for the sake of education is the world and language of the ancients.'[13]

Hegel's educational enterprise makes sense only to the extent that we are persuaded that the teleological unfolding of history is indeed gradually healing the modern dichotomy between nature and reason, or nature and freedom, making possible a return to the classical contention that education should aim at human wholeness without sacrificing modernity's gains in individual autonomy and scientific knowledge. Can we be persuaded of this historical teleology today?

When Hegel argued that history had in a sense ended by 1807, that was because he was looking back to the Terror of 1793. To him, this was the worst violence imaginable in human history, an episode so terrible it would never have to be repeated. Standing as we are on the other side of the millions of victims of totalitarianism, it is impossible for us to affirm this today. Given the horrors of the two world wars, of Auschwitz and the Gulag, is it possible to see our own world as developing toward the reconciliation of Understanding and Love? The ideological sanctions for sadism implicit in the Terror – the methodical, cold-blooded extermination of racial and class enemies – have expanded and intensified in a way that no one in Hegel's era would have imagined possible. Given that the fanatical extremisms of the Left and Right that Hegel believed would dissipate during the nineteenth century have in fact grown unimaginably worse during the twentieth, Hegel himself would probably not be a Hegelian were he alive today.[14]

Auschwitz and the Gulag make it impossible for us to return to 1807 and carry on as before. For, in order to be consistent Hegelians today, we would have to understand totalitarianism as a necessary and rational stage of human development, just as Hegel accepted the Terror of 1793 as a regrettable but unavoidable precursor for the final emergence of Spirit. For Hegel, the Jacobin Terror represented the nadir of political violence and depravity, the darkest hour before the dawn, a low point that would never have to be repeated. If even today we are troubled by the notion that the measures taken then in some way contributed to the rational evolution of modernity, who would dare to believe that the millionfold slaughters of Hitler and Stalin belong to a rational historical dialectic awaiting fruition in our own era?

The main value of returning to Hegel in our own era is not to see how we are progressing toward the end of history, but to consider how the twentieth century has shattered the synthesis that Hegel believed was imminent after the Terror of 1793 when the worst horrors were supposedly past. Looking back to the first revolution for transcending liberalism, we in the twentieth century can only see modernity as a series of sharp rifts, not as a lock-step progression of reason and freedom. All the disparate elements that Hegel thought had been at least implicitly reconciled in 1807 have blown apart in our century: religious fanaticism, nationalistic rivalries and hatreds, uncontrolled technological might, fascism of the left and right. We cannot share Hegel's conviction that the Schillerian project of reviving liberal education on modern principles is grounded in the teleological unfolding of history. Because history has not resolved the tensions between Understanding and Love, our world is more polarized than Hegel would have imagined possible between, on the one hand, the imperatives of capitalism and technology and, on the other, the atavistic and millenarian protests against these imperatives. The place of liberal education as an attempt to rise above these lethal conflicts is accordingly tenuous and fragile to a degree Hegel could not have foreseen, and the pressures to politicize education on behalf of one extreme or the other relentless. This is the ontological core of the alliance between left and right against liberal education that we considered in chapters 2 and 3. But if the great synthesis of *paideia* and modernity attempted by the German Idealists is no longer authoritative for us, the very fragmentation of our era has opened up highways to the past that in Hegel's time were thought to be no longer directly accessible. Precisely because we do not believe in progress, we can engage the classics as if they might have something directly to say to us now, free from the encrustation of intervening teleologies and adaptations. For this reason, even in the midst of this century's disasters, we in a sense live in a privileged moment – we are called upon to rethink the entire possibility of education from the classics down to the present.

For us today, the significance of Hegel's thought is not so much the synthesis culminating in the end of history as the underlying contradiction between Love and Understanding out of which this synthesis was to have emerged. Hegel argued that the inner logic of secular liberalization itself leads to terror, because of the modern state's drive to establish its sovereignty by destroying all intermediary ties of tradition (class, property, religion, regional attachment) between the general will and the abstract individual posited by liberal natural rights. The aim of the Terror was to level, by force and extermination, all distinctions of wealth and status, and all communal bonds to family, clan, region, and religion. Its goal was the reduction of man to a transparent, empty ego uprooted from every context, a being which defines itself in Kantian and Fichtean terms as the process 'I am I' – a being who is, in other words, unmediated by any inherited communal content. Such a citizen would be able to will the freedom to will, undistracted and uncorrupted by any taint of natural inclination or traditional attachment.

But Hegel also believed that the Jacobin Terror, although it took modernization to its logical extreme, would not have to be repeated because the rise of the religious spirit that had all along been unfolding in tandem with the spread of modernization would soon come to fruition, mediating the abstractness of secular liberalism with a renewed sense of historical, cultural, and social harmony. The agonizing disjunction Hegel believed his own age felt between reason and feeling – the exaggeration of reason's negative, corrosive role in the Terror – boded their imminent synthesis. In the coming synthesis, the state would be an organic mingling of political, aesthetic, religious, and cultural bonds. The state will educate and acculturate. It will restrain us only so that we can be free. It will embody our people's history and tradition so as to mediate between the abstract political relations of citizen and state formulated by Rousseau. The healing force of religion in history, reconciling the awful antagonisms between Understanding and Love, is the ultimate basis of Hegel's hopes for liberal education, which is why the *Phenomenology of Spirit* culminates in the exploration of Religious Spirit and ends with a quotation from Schiller.[15]

Hegel believed the new age was synthesizing the spheres of Love and Understanding, the spheres of community and rights. But our own experience in the late twentieth century has been of the increased polarization of secular modernization, on the one hand, and of a yearning for wholeness, on the other. In the absence of an evident middle ground or synthesis, we demand both. We want autonomy and community; individual rights and communitarian 'roots'; endlessly productive technological economies and communities attuned to 'the earth'; the freedom to define ourselves as individuals and 'the goddess.' These contradictory demands are steadily filling the vacuum left by the fragmentation of our traditional sources of *paideia*, hastening the subordination of civic education to politicized education. To the extent that liberal education has always been connected with a distinct political community, the clashing global imperatives and demands that we see ourselves primarily as parts of a global economy or of a global community-in-waiting represent the greatest challenge to its very possibility.

Today the alternatives appear to be McWorld and Jihad, as a recent essayist described it: polychrome diversity or supranational integration.[16] The nation-state as envisioned by Hegel had embodied the universality of modern constitutional liberalism in the particular context and mores of a distinct historical people. The nation-state as it evolved during the nineteenth century sought to reconcile the universal and the particular under its distinctive institutions: rule of law, sovereign constitutional authority, and electoral representation. These institutions had been elaborated by the Enlightenment's new science of politics and legitimized as a workable and just fulfilment of the human good. Today, released from the limits imposed on it by this humanist science of politics, the double process of integration and dissemination is producing a wholly novel array of identities and interdependencies quite outside the practices, institutions, and ethos of the nation-state.

Hegel believed that the near future would harmonize these kinds of contradictory yearnings for individualism and reconciliation. For us, it might well appear that their endless opposition has finally been revealed today to have all along been the very essence of modernity. We enter the darkest side of these reflections on liberal education with the question: is any form of *paideia* compatible at bottom with modernity as it appears to be revealing itself at the end of the twentieth century? Modernity is a dynamic that poses ever-new obstacles for overcoming, and whose energy and idealism feed off this sense of limitless struggle into the future. Ever since people began to describe themselves as 'moderns,' as people belonging to 'the way of today,' thus transforming a banal description of fact into a creed of the elect, modernity has issued in a series of upheavals fuelled by the conviction that if the enlightened few can make this one last Promethean effort to clear away the foolish and unjust ways of the past, all of mankind will achieve wholeness. Marxism-Leninism was one version of the modern project for the conquest of nature and corrupted human nature. Nazi Fascism was another, identifying 'the people' (as opposed to 'the party') as the vanguard of the bright new world. In Stalinism's project for re-creating human nature from above, on the one hand, and Nazism's invocation of the primordial folkish people or race to sweep away bourgeois alienation, on the other, we see the two poles of the Hegelian synthesis – Understanding and Love – fall apart into irreconcilable enemies of liberal democracy.

Those regimes are gone, but another agency of global upheaval remains – nuclear weapons. They exist with the same destructive potential as we write these lines as they did when the Soviet regime was in power. In a grotesque way, these weapons have also been a kind of Vanguard party as well as one of our major educational achievements. For they arguably represent the height of our century's capacity for scientific reasoning, and hence embody much of what remains of the Enlightenment. They are widely believed capable of creating a 'new world' by literally destroying the old one, and a 'new man' by terrorizing us out of our old aggressive traits by means of this very prospect. To C.B. Macpherson's grim but incontestable observation that nuclear weapons play a role in modern life analogous to Hobbes's Sovereign in preserving the civil peace, we can add that to some extent we seem to expect them to play the pedagogical role that the classical philosophers and their nineteenth-century German devotees believed should be fulfilled by the political community.[17] The peace movement of the eighties preserved Marxism's longing for a kind of eschatological grand reversal in which the darkest hour of danger and oppression in the present would yield a future nirvana of peace and happiness. It was an apocalyptic scenario for achieving the reign of Love that paradoxically required maximizing the threat of planetary destruction unleashed by scientific Understanding, so as to create a new personality out of thera peutic terror.

As Hegel diagnosed with still-unsurpassed brilliance, political liberalism with its emphasis on rights, self-interest, and power is rooted in a profound ontological shift in the understanding of man's place in the world. Before political liberalism emerged in its mature form in the philosophies of Locke and Montesquieu, the forces of religious Protestantism, economic individualism, and scientific methodism had already begun to rip human consciousness out of the communal contexts of the old politics, in which man saw himself as having a place within a hierarchical social and political order reflecting the eternal order of the world. Thus, by the time Locke and Montesquieu devised the kind of contractual government securing rights and encouraging commerce, the bourgeoisie-to-be was waiting for it. From the outset, the countries where liberalism took root most securely (including England, the United States, and Canada) had a head start in avoiding the traditional conflict between liberty and licence. The sober virtues and 'worldly asceticism' (as R.H. Tawney put it) of these town merchants clad in Puritan black made them well suited to exercise individual political rights, because they had already renounced most of the pleasures with which the old politics had believed people would run riot if the state gave up its traditional role as the pedagogue of civic virtue and the fashioner of souls.[18]

Nevertheless, the most amazing thing about political modernity is that the most powerful objections to it were raised as it was barely launched in Europe, and have travelled along with it ever since. Whether it be 1789, 1870, 1917, or 1932, modernizing revolutions have been intertwined with a more radical opposition, a dynamic that is pro-modern but anti-liberal. So much has the discontent over liberalism sprung up with liberalism from its very inception that we must consider this discontent to be one of modernity's built-in features, likely to accompany it wherever it goes.

If we do not believe that the present epoch embodies the perfection of reason and freedom, then we must go behind the Hegelian result to the contradiction between Love and Understanding out of which the result emerges. When you deconstruct Hegel, you find Rousseau. For it was Rousseau who first demanded of liberalism something it may well be incapable of doing, or doing fully, namely, to combine the fruits of modernization – its peace, prosperity, and individual autonomy – with a feeling of community with nature and one's fellow human beings. Rousseau was not content with the pedestrian but solid achievements of Lockean liberalism and early modern natural right. In Hegelian terms, he wanted not only Understanding but Love.

According to classical political philosophy and medieval Christianity, human beings were capable of transcending their individuality and approaching harmony with the world through knowledge and faith. This was the core of the old education. Political authorities were justified to the extent that they educated people about their duties, thus enabling them to rise toward this end. The early liberals rejected this goal as fictitious in principle and productive of despotic politics in practice. They preferred a straightforward calculation of individual interests as a low but solid motive for contractual obedience to representative authorities. Rousseau gave expression to a new synthesis – or, more precisely, to the new terms upon which the reconciliation of the individual and the community would be conceived and pursued.

The old education conceived of human wholeness as an end that resided beyond politics and society, although it could only be pursued by way of the civic virtues required by politics and society. Most people could be educated to rise at least a part of the way toward this end, and a few could approach it more closely. Rousseau transposed this transcendence from the *telos* or final end of the soul's development to the lost origins, the prehistory of politics and society. Human wholeness became nature's free gift to all, requiring no effort on our part, subsequently alienated by the distorting effects of civilization. The old education had argued that human nature was not worth much unless it was habituated to transcend its selfish base toward virtue. The early liberals argued that this selfish base should be liberated in order to energize the pursuit of liberty through peaceable commercial relations. Hence their interest in civic education, as opposed to an education in the bourgeois virtues and the social decencies, was (with some notable exceptions) limited. Rousseau rejected both. He drove a wedge between nature and virtue, insisting that virtue's austerities took us further from the lost happiness of our natural origins. But he also maintained that this austerity could, paradoxically, help level those differences of wealth and status that maximize our distance from nature's 'lovely shore, toward which one incessantly turns one's eyes and from which one regretfully feels oneself moving away.'[19]

After Rousseau's influence on 1793, modernizing revolutions would try to implement the Lockean-Montesquieuan model of limited government, rights, and economic maximization while simultaneously recanting its alienating effects. Modernity at its most revolutionary has been driven by a backward-and-forward-looking longing to shatter the constraints of the present world, a kind of atavistic futurism. This gnostic longing is what blew apart the Enlightenment as the French Revolution proceeded from its liberal to its millenarian stage. It was a longing to revoke the conditions of all established authority – not only traditional feudal authority, but the analytical understanding characteristic of political and scientific modernity – and leap back to the spontaneous bliss of the golden age.

The French Revolution was fuelled by the dynamism of the contradiction of embracing and rejecting Lockean liberalism at the same time. England's Glorious Revolution had legitimized the liberation of individual power-seeking from the remnants of the feudal world-view in order to create sensibly pragmatic, contractually limited government. By contrast, the French Revolution unleashed individual power-seeking and autonomy both to dismantle that country's deeply entrenched feudal world-view – which would have required a more violent struggle than in England in any case – and, at the same time, to wipe away the incipient liberal epoch as well. For the first time, politics was thought capable of reshaping the whole world, modern and pre-modern, in the pursuit of the lost communality of the origins. Thus, the physiocratic project of the Enlightenment to break down the feudal order so that rational commercial relations and individual liberties could flourish was harnessed to the deeper, far more radical goal of breaking down all order for-ever, of returning to 'Year One.' Because the 'past' to which one was return-ing was so distant in time, so removed from anything familiar – including the most ancient surviving traditions – getting there required the most uncom-promising futurism.

The impulse to deconstruct and reconstruct human nature from both the left and the right remains, and is at the heart of the drive to politicize education today. A new paradigm is already emerging for expressing a series of distinct but interlocking dissatisfactions with the still-dominant liberal paradigm. This new paradigm can be evoked by the current nostrum of middle-class activism, 'Think globally, act locally.' This slogan captures the dawning per-ception that, as the nation-state and its politics fade away, we experience only what is closest to us (work, family, neighbourhood, advocacy group) and what is furthest from us ('I care about this planet,' as if one could conceivably be living on some other planet). One can group under it a series of lively and spreading contemporary social movements. All of these movements, we believe, share the underlying features of deconstructed Hegelianism, the unresolved tension between Love and Understanding. Each of them begins by identifying liberal modernity as the source of its alienation and the impedi-ment to its fulfilment. Each of them posits a Rousseauan golden age of the past free of alienation and oppression. Each of them believes that one must combat the global paradigm of liberalism with its technological and capitalis-tic adjuncts in order to allow its particular local community to return to the unconditioned bliss of the origins (the realm of Rousseauan and decon-structed Hegelian Love). And yet, by returning to its own particular modality of the unconditioned, each of these movements more or less consciously believes that the shattering of the predominant liberal-democratic paradigm will allow these different local groups to inaugurate a planet-wide blossoming of greater freedom and happiness, a folkish 'millennium' (to quote a recent PBS series and coffee-table book).

Here are some examples. 1) The fascination of contemporary feminism with the age of 'the goddess,' an age of matriarchal authority supposedly preceding the rise of male-dominated Olympian Greek culture.[20] 2) The belief of 'men's rights' groups that there was also a prehistorical golden age when men were more in touch with nature and themselves, including the re-enactment of allegedly genuine tribal and shamanistic rituals. 3) The popularization of 'the age of mankind,' a prehistoric global epoch prior to the emergence of civic and commercial culture which is a historical and anthropological fact, but which also serves as a normative standard for urging people today to return to a condition of greater harmony with the earth. 4) Environmentalism itself, which often dovetails with no. 3 to suggest returning to or at least imitating the tacit wisdom of our primitive ancestors' harmony with the environment. The atavistic project to recover this harmony points the way to the complete transformation of existing modernity, so that, as US vice-president Al Gore puts it, 'saving the earth's environment' will be the 'fundamental organizing principle' of the post–Cold War era. 5) The peace movement of the eighties, according to which the entire course of Western civilization has been aimed at the pursuit of technological and nationalistic power, whose resulting nuclear terror may shock us into an advance into a peaceful future which would at the same time be a return to pre-rational tribal wholeness. 6) The 'black Athena' scholarship which locates the true origins of Western civilization with the peoples of Africa and Egypt, often with the implication that Western civilization appropriated this heritage, perverting it to serve exploitative ends.

All of these movements carry some potential for increased justice and for genuine intellectual and cultural liberation. But they also carry a potential for danger and instability that their proponents rarely acknowledge. According to their more radical advocates, the emerging new 'social movements' demonstrate that the authoritative structures of the nation-state have collapsed. What were previously 'marginals' now affect policies and behaviour in the political mainstream, demonstrating not only the value of organized mobilization but also how the traditional theoretical relation of mainstream to periphery has been confounded. For some, this is evidence of a new democratic impulse. In our view, however, this expression of optimism is ill-founded or even disingenuous. For, while they celebrate the collapse of the nation-state because it favours the emergence of new global movements, they reserve the term 'social movement' only for movements of which they approve. They conveniently forget a number of equally energetic movements emerging throughout the West which also seek release from the restraints under which the nation-state once held them: neo-Nazism, inner-city gangs, religious fanaticism, redneck vigilantism, and various neo-paganisms.

Today's progressives think that the conjunction of globalism and localism provides a synthesis of the best of the traditional era (community, meaning, and heterogeneity) with the best of the modern era (efficiency, industrial expansion, and individual freedom). For them, the dangers of globalism (homogeneity and rootlessness) and the dangers of localism (regional rivalries and hatreds) cancel one another out, though why these extremes would cancel one another out, rather than exacerbate one another, is surely open to question. Nevertheless, according to the radicals, a new era of true democracy is beginning. But we think it at least equally likely that these trends are deepening dangerous conditions that have characterized the instability of the whole twentieth century. If the nation-state is collapsing, can anyone seriously believe we will escape unscathed from such a world-historical transformation, free to retain only what we like or find edifying while keeping all the benefits and security the nation-state achieved? The collapse of the nation-state would mean nothing less than the collapse of the Enlightenment, the collapse of the West's self-understanding for three centuries. Let us not be in such a hurry to celebrate.

Despite the enormous diversity among and within the approved movements, there is a common thread. They all maintain that human life was originally not characterized by alienation and oppression. The golden age is one of harmony with the environment, peace between genders and among people, without bourgeois property relations or competition. In the most extreme formulations, Western civilization is a compendium of 'systemic' oppressions – technological, racist, sexist. Using the golden age of the unconditioned as a guide, the new global paradigm implies, we can aim for a future in which we return to the past, throwing off the shackles of the present. We need to 'reinvent politics,' 'reinvent the world.' Even though global technology is often perceived in these ideologies as the summation of Eurocentric, phallocentric, logocentric domination, these movements just as often envision using its power for their own projects of transformation. Technology may lead to disaster and oppression. But (as in Heidegger's late philosophy of *Gelassenheit*), it may also be turned against itself to release 'the earth.'[21]

This is the emerging ontological shift that underlies the debate we discussed in chapters 2 and 3 concerning the alleged Eurocentricity of the university curriculum in the humanities and social sciences. The dissolution of the Hegelian historical teleology presents both extraordinary dangers and extraordinary opportunities for the continuation and enrichment of liberal education. We have discussed the dangers at some length. If the possibility of a non-partisan education in civic virtue is tied to the possibility of the Hegelian progress of history, when that historical synthesis falls apart under the pressure of new circumstances and crises, then arguably so does the prospect of liberal education. But as we have also observed, the shattering of the Hegelian synthesis may also unexpectedly open a path directly back to the ancients themselves. To this we must now add that each of the atavistic social movements we have sketched above has the potential – to some extent already demonstrated – of enriching liberal education and expanding its canon of authoritative texts as has happened during similar periods of upheaval in the past. Every day aboriginal scholars rescue more of their spiritual and religious traditions, and those of us who are not of their community learn that those traditions rival in complexity and depth of insight what we commonly regard as the treasures of Western thought and art. Similarly, the 'Black Athena' scholarship revives a question that perplexed the ancient Greeks themselves – did the culture we in retrospect have called 'classical' originate with them, or did it build on something that originated in Egypt and Africa? But to the extent that these movements forgo the long and painstaking scholarship needed to rescue these buried insights and partly forgotten traditions, and choose instead the more immediate gratification of demanding the instant conversion and censoring of the existing university curriculum to 'represent' them as political constituencies, what remains of traditional liberal education will be threatened without the cause of non-Western scholarship being thereby advanced. Instead of working to enhance the genuine diversity of university courses, each of which tries to capture the discrete inner articulation of a different substantive tradition, we will achieve the false and empty diversity of courses that oppose the very idea of tradition in the name of a contentless self-assertion and the destructive politicization of learning. Instead of trying to dismantle the traditional approaches to liberal education, we should be developing new, non-Western approaches alongside them. For a mere fraction of what our governments spend on social services (to say nothing of their pensions and consultants' fees), and for a mere fraction of the profits our banks and corporations have made during the recession,[22] we could endow new programs and chairs in these emerging fields of study, bringing them into the heart of the university.

Ever since political philosophers began propounding the notion of a civic education devoted to the common good, we have assumed that the political community would be coextensive with a particular, autonomous nation. But the slogan 'think globally, act locally' is also evocative of a profound change in economic reality that renders the very idea of the nation-state increasingly less tenable. For today, capital is increasingly not merely multinational, but has no national basis at all. The archetypal American corporate executive of yesteryear, identifying what is good for America with what is good for his company, has been replaced by international money-markets with no executive or even physical centre. To paraphrase Foucault and Derrida, they are desubjectivized networks of (financial) power, a free play of (financial) signifiers. The millions who contribute to them through pension funds, stocks, and bonds become the joint owners of thousands of enterprises from one hour to the next as their account managers search the world for a better point spread. Thus, as economist Robert Reich puts it, the real question is not whether this global system is good for 'us' in a given country – the real question now is, 'who is us?'[23]

What all this means is that, as movements on what has traditionally been called the left gather new energy (as evidenced by environmentalism and feminism), the greatest source of stability on what has traditionally been called the right is ebbing away – a powerful sovereign nation-state that manages its own economy and social welfare. Both left and right will find this increasingly frustrating, because governments bent on global competitiveness may be unresponsive or financially hampered in advancing the social causes dear to the left, while conservatives will find these same governments unable or unwilling to bolster their own leanings toward patriotism, traditional morality, or the protection of the national economy.

Liberal education is endangered in several ways by this process of globalization. Old-fashioned accounts of the bourgeois virtues such as that of Adam Smith assumed that a talent for commerce could be placed at the service of the common good of one's country, and that the virtues of diligence, sobriety, and probity required by commerce were themselves best instilled through the character formation that comes from belonging to a distinct political association. But economic globalization appears to have snapped that perhaps always fragile link between civic character and capitalism. More crudely, the fiscal pressures placed on governments by the drive to global competitiveness, entailing the downsizing of government services and entitlements for the local citizenry, tempt governments to convert the existing resources of higher learning to those tasks. And this, in turn, further weakens the university as a haven of non-partisan reflection which might equip young citizens with a way of debating the ultimate justice and prudence for one's country of following these global imperatives uncritically.

If conservatives could ever entirely or enthusiastically identify themselves with capitalism, they manifestly cannot do so today. For capitalism is severing its link with even the rather pale and qualified Lockean and Jeffersonian appropriations of civic *paideia* to modern individualism. That 'worldly asceticism' which Tawney identified as the characterological core of bourgeois liberalism is considered to be as square and retrograde by contemporary management gurus as it was by sixties hippies. Global investment, technological R&D, and the search for low-cost labour – the whole agenda of 'competitiveness' that sums up much of what is vital in parties that call themselves conservative today – are every bit as impatient of constraints by the old structures of the nation-state, and by the old structures of linear reasoning, as are environmentalists or feminists. Capitalism is being transformed from a system of national elites of the managers of primary production into a global elite of information-processors. Class divisions within nation-states are giving way to global class divisions between information-processors, technicians, and labourers. This process unfolds in conjunction with a decentring of capital as it departs its traditional stewards in the nation-state and is dispersed into an endlessly fluid and mobile global environment. The same longing to burst the restraints of the old grammar and logic, the longing for the unconditioned, alike drives environmentalism, particle-laser weapons systems, and Disney World, where the goal is (as Umberto Eco has observed) to create a simulation of anything that has ever happened or ever could happen.[24] Laser technology, whether it serves Mickey Mouse or Star Wars, is the ultimate realization of Derridean 'différance,' a free play of signifiers in which no traditional ethical or epistemological restraint can be allowed to interfere with technology's infinite plasticity and power of creation.

We have said that the longing for the unconditioned characterizes a number of contemporary movements dissatisfied with the status quo. These movements are often also attracted to post-Hegelian (which is to say Heideggerian) ontology – the longing for non-reifying discourse, a de-subjectivized life-world, and Derridean 'différance.' This drive to go behind the copular 'is,' the constraints of linear logic and predicative reasoning, is what happens when you remove Hegelian Understanding from Love – when you attempt to liberate the longing for the unconditioned from any reliance on an analytically and politically stable conception of liberal-democratic rights and meritocracy. And yet precisely this same drive for deconstruction and intersubjectivity lies behind the most advanced processes of contemporary technology and the capitalism it serves.

In sum, the irony of the present in the West is that technological capitalism itself may be creating the de-subjectivized life-world longed for by post-Hegelian hermeneutics. The convergence between the demands of fiscal conservatism and the demands of political advocacy groups to deconstruct school and university curricula is an epiphenomenon of this disturbing new dispensation. Whether it be through post-modernist architecture, chemical-based microprocessing, or the fantasies of cyber-punk, the straight line of Newtonian physics and its political correlation in the universal rights of liberalism is everywhere giving way to the free happening of decentred Heideggerian Being. And as this global process unfolds, that great Victorian hold-over and last haven of the old education, the nation-state, appears increasingly unable to serve as a focus for retarding or limiting this process in the name of that autonomous rights-bearing human subject that was to have been the glory of the Enlightenment. This liberal subject – a blend of Puritan, Locke, and Kant with a classical education – sustained modernity for three centuries with its independent-mindedness and moral probity. But it now seems ever more peripheral to capitalism's most radical unfolding, a realm where Michel Foucault joins hands with Steven Jobs. The question we cannot today answer is whether liberal education can survive as our world dissolves into interlocking processes of money-market globalism and atavistic tribalism.

Let us be clear: we do not deny the reality of these processes. We do not deny that, like other great historical reversals and collapses, they may willy-nilly release liberating possibilities for human fulfilment. But we maintain that they are first and foremost tocsins of danger. If we passively allow them to run their course, liberal education will lose far more than it stands to gain. Whatever crudeness and harshness may lie in modern thought and practice, however much we may fail to live up to the ideals of liberal democracy, the architects of the modern age placed at the center of their concerns the humanism they found in ancient and medieval thought: for Locke as for Plato, man is the measure of all things. Reflection on the whole – nature, the universe, the world – was mediated by a conception of what was good and useful for man. We see in today's casual jettisoning of subjectivity, of authoritative distinctions, of concreteness and rootedness, and in the joyful embrace of fluidity, variability, and primordialism so evident in the call for a new 'post-humanism,' the danger of the most fundamental repudiation of personal responsibility, moral decency, and moderation. The abandonment of modernity and its ambivalent but real connection to the classical heritage is not the harbinger of a gentler, fairer humanity but points to an infinite darkness where humanity is an empty vessel.

A Nietzschean Interlude

We have now followed some of the darker paths of our reflection on the meaning and tenability of liberal education in the aftermath of the breakdown of the Hegelian synthesis of Love and Understanding. But throughout these darker considerations, we remind our readers that to confront and think through the crises of modernity should be the prelude to a clear-headed diagnosis of our current predicament rather than an invitation to passivity and despair. In leaving our consideration of Hegelianism and its fragmentation, therefore, let us try to come back into the sunlight.

The breakdown of Hegelianism may indeed mean that modern existence is and will be increasingly caught between oppressive contradictions, that there is no longer a common moral and intellectual heritage of the kind necessary to sustain the original purposes of civic *paideia*. But the fragmentation of Hegelianism, and with it the last attempt by a major European philosopher to restate the classical aims of liberal education, may also open up new possibilities. Our appreciation of the greatness of the thinkers making up the pedigree of liberal education stretching back to classical antiquity may be heightened, rather than endangered, by a fresh and reinvigorated sense of their originality and incompatibility with one another. Once the marble hall of Hegelianism has cracked or even crumbled, we may be free to re-encounter Plato or Machiavelli more directly as they understood themselves, instead of seeing them as parts of a cumulative progression toward the modern era. The fact, in other words, that these thinkers do not contribute in a lock-step fashion to the progressive unfolding of reason and freedom toward the end of history opens up their ideas to our direct study and experience. In this perspective, the shattering of the Western tradition's outward Hegelian order releases an even richer heritage of restorative possibilities for the crises and dichotomies of the present. In that spirit, then, let us look at Nietzsche's approach to educating the soul, not as if it were self-evidently outmoded by the progress of history since then, but as if it might speak directly to us and our contemporary concerns.

The hallmark of the advanced modernity in which we now live is that we have lost our conviction in the Hegelian historical teleology of the progressive actualization of freedom and reason while retaining – or seeing no exit from – our belief in the historicity of the human condition. This is Nietzsche's starting-point, and since history for us still takes the place of the soul, Nietzsche's understanding of the 'advantages and disadvantages of history for life' is first and foremost a meditation on what liberal education can and should mean in our post-Hegelian modernity.[25] In Nietzsche's treatment of the three modes of historicity and their relationship to life – the monumental, the antiquarian, and the critical – we sense an attenuated yet still real link to Plato's and Aristotle's notions of how liberal education must be a harmonizing of different states of the soul. Only now, since it is evidently not given to us to experience the soul *sub specie aeternitatis*, the great classical psychologies are replaced by a set of active stances of the self toward the world it has historically created. It is no longer a question of how best to approximate the eternal verities through our moral and intellectual virtues, but rather of how to go on being human in a world apparently devoid of permanent meaning.

Nietzsche is perhaps the greatest philosophical critic of liberal democracy and modernity. Early liberal thinkers like Locke and Montesquieu shaped the belief that liberal democracy was the only reasonable regime. According to them, since it is based on what is universal to mankind – individual autonomy and self-preservation – it allows for a truly rational politics. Under its influence, people would give up non-negotiable strife over religion, nationalism, and divine right, and in this sense act more rationally. Liberalism appeared therefore to achieve the harmony of politics and reason which for Plato remained a utopia.

The early liberal thinkers were convinced they had made a break with the past and done something entirely new. They were 'moderns' – the way of today as opposed to the Graeco-Roman and Christian traditions. So successful was the new liberal epoch that it bred the conviction that this most rational of regimes was the final outcome of all previous history, which was reinterpreted as a series of stages and half-successes leading progressively toward the present, liberal-democratic 'end of history.' Tocqueville thought that democracy was historically irreversible and the inevitable outcome of the struggle for justice throughout history.[26] Marx believed it was the inevitable outcome of man's struggle for survival and economic security, as if Hobbes's and Locke's hypotheses about the state of nature had in fact been the guiding force of history all along. Despite its imperfections, for Marx liberalism was also the harbinger of a new society which would perfect bourgeois democracy by abolishing private property while retaining its prosperity, enlightenment, and autonomy.[27]

Some, like Tocqueville, had doubts that democracy was the only good way of life, even if its victory was historically irreversible. Like Marx – although he did not share Marx's vision of the future – Tocqueville thought liberalism had robbed people of a sense of community and the security of fixed beliefs about religion. With some of the great romantic novelists like Flaubert, this disgust reaches an extreme of intensity, representative of a growing and widespread dissatisfaction with liberal modernity. *Madame Bovary* and *Sentimental Education* offer an ultimately hopeless view of modern life. Flaubert shares neither Marx's hopes for the future nor Tocqueville's belief that liberal democracy can modify its own worst tendencies in the present. For the novelist, modern individualism destroys all grand commitments by reducing man

to the 'barracks-room' of work and competition. There are no dreams or challenges. Art is vulgarized; religion is corrupt or ridiculous, as with the priest
who writes a treatise on agronomy called *Manure*. Politics is the servant of
business, whether it camouflages itself with the propaganda of the left or the
right. Flaubert thinks the socialists only want to hasten this process of degradation by destroying the remnants of personal liberty in an absolute state
that will chain everyone to their lathes (an 'American Sparta,' as it is envisioned by his revolutionary Senecal, who ends up as a police agent for the
democratic despot Napoleon III).

Nietzsche is the first philosopher to think through the principles of liberalism and its faith in history on the basis of this thoroughgoing disgust. His
writings on education are meant, in effect, to save the talented but disillu-
sioned young men and women of Flaubert's novels from their corrosive disbelief. Rousseau had already rejected modern technical rationality in favour
of 'the sublime science of simple souls.' He extolled the simplicity of the natural instincts – the individualism of natural man prior to civilization – as
against liberalism's anxiety-ridden competition for wealth and status. The
nature of the common man is, in its simple honesty, preferable to the rarest
glories of reason, which only emerge when our dependence on others – the
loss of our natural self-sufficiency – forces us to learn about them and especially how to deceive them.

Nietzsche also rejects reason, but not on the basis of some other conception of a stable human nature, as does Rousseau. Instead, he opposes reason
on behalf of 'life.' By life, Nietzsche means the passionate commitment
humans experience when they are creating something new in history.
Nietzsche is the first philosopher of commitment, a forerunner of the exis-
tentialists. He embodies a new and explosive combination. He rejects reason
and the Hegelian belief that the present age is the end result of history's progressive actualization of reason. But he does so on the basis of a more radical
historicism than that of Hegel or even Marx. Man is indeed a historical being,
a 'plastic power' rather than a fixed nature. We may sometimes envy the
beast's peace and oblivion, but in the end, Nietzsche argues, we only feel alive
when we are striving. This is why Nietzsche understood himself to be the
great enemy of Platonism. For him, Plato represents the 'super-historical'
belief that man's possibilities are naturally fixed and of eternal duration,
which is the death of striving, risk, and creativity. Hence, 'Plato is boring.'[28]

Man is historical, but the belief in the end of history prevents man from
living historically. For the belief that we are at the end of history makes us
think that nothing new can be done. It also convinces us that all past creations
– which their creators believed were absolutely true and would last forever –

were false, temporary, and of merely relative value, delusions on the way to a crowning delusion ('the end of history') that we also no longer believe in. For Nietzsche, this is all true, but it is utterly destructive of life. By exposing the relativity of values, history paralyses our belief in the possibility of absolutes, in the possibility of commitment. How, Nietzsche asks, can you worship a god which you know to be a human creation like all other gods and values? How can you give your life for your country if you know your country's cause is only relatively just, no more so than that of other countries and eras? Thus, the awful paradox: in order to make history, man must not know the truth about history. Otherwise, we give up making anything new and sink into petty materialism and laissez-aller. For Nietzsche, this is the unavowed, insidious connection between liberal democracy and the philosophy of history: historicism paralyses commitment to anything new, bold, and dangerous, and therefore bolsters bourgeois man's absorption in survival and comfort.

According to Nietzsche, the passionate commitment by which past empires, faiths, and art were created needs a narrow horizon. One must have the illusion that not everything has already been done; that not all values are relative because my value is the absolute truth. If history is to go on, first it must stop. We have to have the feeling that the past is dead and buried, that only the present counts, so we can go on from here. At the same time, we must know something about past history, because if our horizon is excessively narrow, that too can make us complacent and unimaginative, like the cow chewing its cud. The study of history shows us that, since there have been great and inspiring changes, there can be again. That is its proper relation to life.

What is there about present historical education that prevents this healthy relationship between the study of history and the pursuit of Life? According to Nietzsche, modern education is characterized by an alienating opposition between the inner and the outer.[29] A profusion of unrelated, contradictory histories makes up our external culture. Yet they do not really belong to us and we know that none of them can be lived now. We pride ourselves on catching the latest production of *La Traviata* while rejecting the heart of the opera's human relationships as sexist and patriarchal. Our eyes mist at Ingrid Bergman's agonizing choice between Humphrey Bogart and Paul Heinried in *Casablanca*, while professing to wish her character could read Marilyn French so she would not view herself as the appendage of a man. We sift through what Nietzsche calls the 'indigestible knowledge-stones' of art galleries and concerts, 'comparing their effects,' while inwardly their themes and passions have nothing to do with us. Our inner lives are confused or blank because we are cut off from any goal worth choosing in the external world.

Or, if we do resolve to choose what our world offers us, we end up gratifying our basest whims and impulses.

The divide between inner and outer finds a false resolution in the pursuit of 'objectivity.'[30] For Nietzsche, objectivity is the unwillingness to be touched deeply by anything we study. It masquerades as open-mindedness, but is really a retreat from deciding what we prefer, a disguise for indifference. Hence, in modern philosophy and classics departments, Nietzsche would observe, few can say with any great degree of conviction why they study what they do. A person studies modal logic or Attic Greek during the week and pursues a passion for sky-diving on the week-end. What is the connection? Objectivity disguises what is in truth a petty subjectivity, a desire to profess a love of great culture while fencing it off from the gratification of our whims. In looking for a way of healing the division between inner and outer produced by historicism, Nietzsche reawakens the traditional concern of liberal education with human wholeness.

Nietzsche believes we have a vague awareness that life has eluded us. He looks to the young, who have the most daring and desire for life before they are anaesthetized by education, as the hope for the future. But what should modern education and culture be replaced with? There is no clear answer here. Since man is a creator, since everything great is completely new, no clear aim can be known in advance.

More than this, the genie is out of the bottle: modern man has discovered the dread truth that values are indeed relative. He will never be able to escape this knowledge. Not only do we have to create something completely unpredictable, but we have to do so in the knowledge that it is a value, rather than an absolute truth. Since the goal cannot be predicted or justified according to the canons of eternal rationality, and since we cannot have the blissful illusion of past epochs that we are pursuing the absolute truth, the only way of being sure we are overcoming the present is through the depth, passion, and intensity of our commitment. Thus, a narrowness of horizon selectively illuminated by historical insight remains the locus of a healthy personality for Nietzsche. Knowledge of history must serve a dedication to our current life and strivings. This is why Nietzsche, far from dismissing the study of history, tries to reform it as the servant of commitment.

Let us look briefly at the three approaches to achieving the proper relationship of history to life. Monumental history consoles us in our present struggle to change and improve mankind by reminding us of past successes at doing so.[31] The enduring fame of these achievements allows us to hope that we will enjoy such fame in the future if we succeed. But every advantage of a historical education has a corresponding disadvantage. Monumental history, left to itself, isolates glorious deeds from the complex causes that made them possible for their own time and place. It can fool you into thinking that, because something great happened once, it can happen again simply through an exertion of will. In this way, monumental history does injustice to the full complexity and contingency of events. The literal-minded attempt to imitate Julius Caesar in the modern world will not produce a replica of that complex and brilliant figure, only the foolish theatricality of a Mussolini. By tempting us to rashness and fanaticism, monumental history can make us blind to the specific limitations and possibilities of the present. According to Nietzsche, we cannot copy the past. Rather, we study the complexity of past events in order to understand that current historical circumstances have a comparable complexity but a different content.

Monumental history can also lead to a hypocritical veneration of the past in order to make excuses for our failures in the present, or to suppress those who want to do great things now on the grounds that everything great has already been done. Hence, Flaubert's artist Pellerin in *Sentimental Education* venerates the old masters as a way of excusing his own failures as a painter and running down everyone else. The buccaneering businessman Jacques Arnoux justifies his coarse trafficking in art by decrying 'modern decadence.' There is nothing to be ashamed of in cheapening art or exploiting artists because all modern art is lousy.

Antiquarian history mitigates the tendency of monumental history to see the past as a marble gallery of unending glories.[32] It narrows our horizon by teaching us to venerate a specific culture of the past. The modern age does not know what to commit itself to because it knows the history of all peoples and cultures. Everything changes and passes away in a 'sea of becoming.' Antiquarian history is an antidote to this sense of dispersal. A narrow, centuries-old attachment proves that it is possible to make a single choice and stick to it. Even if we revere a tradition that is no longer viable for the present, we can look back to it from an inferior age as proof that improvement is possible in the future. Hence, the Italian Renaissance drew sustenance from Graeco-Roman antiquity in order to overcome the Middle Ages.

The problem with antiquarianism is that, if it becomes too exclusively fixed on one segment of the past, it can paralyse new creations just as surely as can too much openness to change. While confirming the possibility of a single-minded commitment, antiquarian history can become chained to this one commitment, so that man becomes once again too much like the beast grazing in the field. Reverence for the past atrophies into a kind of museum culture, cutting us off from life.

The antidote is critical history, which reveals that every epoch is only partially just, partially true to its own best vision of itself.[33] When we probe beneath the surface, we find that all societies are in some measure oppressive and all religions intolerant, and that all regimes promote one form of happiness at the expense of other plausible visions of human fulfilment. These defects always come out with time. People think of new desires or hunger for new experiences, and the old ways start to seem empty or illegitimate. When this happens, it is healthier to clear the past away than to cling desperately to the status quo, as does antiquarian history at its worst. For life reasserts itself through this destruction of the old order. It is a springboard to create something new. Nietzsche himself, for instance, abhorred the revanchist and atavistic nationalism of his era and looked ahead to a new pan-European identity.

But critical history has its disadvantages, too. Exposing the stupidity and injustice of every known era of the past can rob us of our faith in ourselves in the present, and paralyse our confidence that we can improve ourselves, since we spring from the very errors we condemn. We want to shake off the past and start over. But what if everything we are is bound up with this past, as a consistently critical historicism would have to admit? The disadvantages of critical history bear directly on our current fashionable obsession with 'demythologizing' the past. Nietzsche would agree that, in order to live up to our own best ideals, we have to shake off our smugness about what has been done up to now and realize that there was much suffering and injustice along the way. But, taken to an extreme, this process of critical deflation can lead to a revision of past history as an unremitting tale of frustrated freedom, persecution, and injustice. But if one's regime is entirely corrupt, why even hope to reform it? The current tendency to see injustice as 'systemic' is an illustration of what Nietzsche means when he argues that the healthy scepticism of critical history can be pushed to a paralysing extreme. For it implies, not merely that we have failed to live up to our ideals as a democracy (which we have, often and appallingly), but that at bottom we have no ideals at all. But if that is so, how can we appeal to them now as an adjuration to further improvement?

Nietzsche's encouragement of passionate action for its own sake is what makes his philosophy so provocative and dangerous. The Nazis invoked it as their own, staining its reputation for many years. Nietzsche would have despised the degradation and vulgarity of Nazism. But by the same token it is hard to find binding moral criteria in his philosophy that would enable one to condemn such extremism before it achieved success and showed its true character, since the rise of Nazism did involve great energy and revolutionary commitment of the kind that Nietzsche is arguably willing to see hazarded. But while we should be cautious about Nietzsche's summons to open-ended, passionate commitment, we can still benefit from studying his critique of modern historical education. We can also try to live up to his insistence that education not be an aimless rummaging through the past, but an effort to build our own characters and independent-mindedness through encountering and reflecting on the philosophy and art produced by minds incomparably superior to our own.

6

Liberal Education and the Canadian Polity

The Canadian Founding

Throughout this book, we have stressed a motif common to classical writings on liberal education and their devotees in the modern era. This is the idea that education should take students out of themselves on a journey of the soul, beyond the familiar world of our own time and place with our particular attachments as citizens, family members, and friends. Education should show us wider horizons, and enable us to entertain the limited validity of our own way of life, so that we can return to it equipped with a greater appreciation for its achievements but also with a critical standard for assessing its short-comings and making improvements where possible and prudent. Liberal education is, in short, a journey from the particular to the universal and back again. In this book, we have imitated this classical form. Beginning with the controversies over education in Canada today, we have used this concern with the common good of our own country as a window on the wider world, in the conviction that the education debate in Canada has become increasingly shallow and inward-looking. Educational experts use the latest jargon of process-learning to disguise a philistine retreat from the high universal standards of scholarship and teaching that once enabled Canadians to boast one of the finest education systems in the world.

Now in concluding these reflections, we should return from the distant shores of classical antiquity, and from the darker corridors of European nihilism, to our own Canadian shores. What we find when we look at the Canadian experience in light of the wider traditions of liberal education stretching from Plato to Nietzsche is that Canada has always been a part of those traditions. In journeying to the stars, we have been at home all along. Indeed, our country was explicitly founded in recognition of those educational traditions and their continuing worth in the modern age. By returning to our particular Canadian attachment and viewing it in a wider European and North American perspective, we find proximal sources for an understanding of liberal education in our own history and experience as a nation. Viewed in this light, indeed, the kind of Canadian nationalism prevalent during the last twenty-five years seems like a very late, and often shallow, development. Preening itself on inventing a country out of thin air, contemporary Canadian nationalism has in fact turned its back on virtually every substantive Canadian account of justice and the good life, and cut off education from a rich Canadian heritage of Hegelian and Burkean organicism – the intellectual basis for any genuine and dignified sense of how we differ from the United States. Little wonder that, as our genuine Canadian identity has been corroded, first by the continentalist liberal technocrats of the sixties and since then by the left's identification of nationalism with central planning and anti-Americanism, our state-sponsored nationalism has become ever more shrill, ever more vacuous, ever less certain in its heart of hearts that we differ from Americans at all.

Unlike the American founders, who were animated by the philosophy of the Enlightenment, the Canadian founders were moved by precedent and tradition. Canada was founded in a century, not of first principles and revolutionary optimism, but of renewed appreciation for organic ties. The eighteenth century had believed that distinctions of ethnicity and religion could and should be overcome by the universalistic principles of liberalism. But this prospect was regarded more pessimistically in the Victorian age. It ground to a halt at the borders of French Canada. Lord Durham, a classical liberal entirely at home with the ideas of James Madison, found that neither the imperial government nor the British colonials had the stomach or the conviction to implement his ill-considered and hastily conceived recommendations for the cultural assimilation of the French Canadians.[1]

In supporting the constitutional arrangement of 1867, George Etienne Cartier assured French Canada that Confederation was not a disguised plan to assimilate the French. In so doing, he summed up the moral and philosophical differences between the Victorian age and the Enlightenment: 'Nations were now formed by the agglomeration of communities having kindred interests and sympathies ... The idea of the unity of races was utopian – it was impossible. Distinctions of this kind would always exist. Dissimilarity appeared to be the order of the physical world and of the moral world, as well as of the political world.'[2]

The place of French Canada in Confederation provided from the very outset a microcosm for the new country's attempt to preserve a second way of life in North America, an alternative version of liberal democracy in the new world. For while the British colonials feared absorption into the United States, the French Canadians worried about absorption by both the United States and the British colonials. French Canadians saw in 1865, as they had seen in the days of the American Revolution, that their communal way of life was incompatible with the secularizing, homogeneous liberal republicanism of the United States. Hector Louis Langevin, in recommending Confederation to Quebec, reminded French Canadians of the fate of Louisiana under the American system: 'What has become of them? What has become of their language, their customs, their manners and their institutions? After the [civil] war, hardly a trace will remain to show that the French race has passed that way.'³

Cartier recommended Confederation to French Canada on the grounds that Canada's desire to avoid the homogeneity of American society would provide a lasting guarantee for a separate French-Canadian identity. The determination of the Anglo-Canadians to resist absorption by the Americans would justify the French Canadians' determination to resist absorption by them both, evolving a constitutional polity that preserved such communal differences rather than breaking them down as in the United States:

He viewed the diversity of races in British North America in this way: we were of different races, not for the purpose of warring against each other, but in order to compete and emulate for the general welfare ... We could not do away with the distinctions of race. We could not legislate for the disappearance of the French Canadians from American soil, but British and French Canadians alike could appreciate and understand their position relative to each other. They were placed like great families beside each other, and their contact produced a healthy spirit of emulation. It was a benefit rather than otherwise that we had a diversity of races ...⁴

Cartier did not think that such religious and cultural particularisms were incompatible with the pursuit of the general welfare and of increased prosperity, and Canadian history has largely proved him correct.

This distrust of Enlightenment universalism was not – as is sometimes implied by hostile critics of Quebec – restricted to Quebec. It was fully matched in English Canada. English-speaking conservatives like John A. Macdonald and Thomas D'Arcy McGee regarded the monarchical principle around which the new constitution would be built as a safeguard against the democratization of every aspect of life that had taken place (they believed) in the United States in the first half of the nineteenth century. Excessive democratization was connected, especially in McGee's mind, with social atomization – the erosion of all recognized standards of authority and of all social and religious distinctions. Indeed, at the time of Confederation there was a widespread and long-standing belief in British North America (going back to the Loyalists) that society in the United States was violent, lawless, and disrespectful of authority, and that American politics had a mercenary, harshly partisan character. This conviction, whether and to what degree it was accurate, served as a foil, a negative standard, for the development of a new Canadian nationality.

In one of his speeches in Canada West, Thomas D'Arcy McGee characterized the difference between British North America and the United States over the source of sovereignty as part of a more fundamental disagreement – the 'divine origin of society' versus 'the theory of its human origin, upheld by Jefferson, Paine, Rousseau and John Locke.'[5] Here in the utterance of a man who perhaps more than any other was the intellectual mentor of British Canadians of his time, we find a clear recognition of the atomistic view of society implied by American liberalism. McGee's Catholic conservatism was bolstered by the organicist philosophy of Edmund Burke. His understanding of liberal education comes directly from the classical sources we considered earlier, and his wish to make this kind of civic *paideia* a part of the new Canadian nation's character flows directly from his philosophical differences with the principles of the American founding. His articulation and defence of its value is unsurpassed by anything to be found among the American founders.

To read McGee's views on education is to be reminded of the sometimes battered but nonetheless unbroken link between the noblest versions of modern liberal democracy and the classical and Renaissance understandings of *paideia*. McGee begins by warning against looking to the United States for our literature and ideas: 'It is quite clear to me that if we are to succeed with our new dominion, it can never be by accepting a ready-made easy literature, which assumes Bostonian culture to be the worship of the future, and the American democratic system to be the manifestly destined form of government for all the civilized world, new as well as old.'[6] In this respect, and to this extent, McGee furnishes a precedent for our contemporary concern with providing for Canadian content in the electronic and print media, and in culture generally. But our nationalists of today often seem oblivious to the fact that a distinct Canadian culture must ultimately be vindicated by its intellectual and moral excellence. This excellence can only be achieved by cultivating a uniquely Canadian oasis around the great well-springs of the classical heritage, appropriating it creatively for Canadian concerns and drawing on it to on it to articulate the questions for a dialogue with the aboriginal and non-Western cultural traditions that now struggle to be heard. Canadian content must be more than a way of ensuring that Canadian business people get a share of the profits from retailing magazines, movies, and pop music. McGee's view of why Canada is different from the United States is neither self-evidently true nor wholly adequate for the present. But it is at least a starting-point for serious reflection: 'I rely on Nature and Revelation against levelling and system-mongering of the American, or any other kind. In Nature and Revelation we should lay the basis of our political, mental and moral philosophy as a people; and once so laid, those foundations will stand firmly set and rooted, as any rocks in the Huronian or Laurentian range.'[7]

Our Canadian nationalists of today are eager to protect Canada from the effects of unmitigated free trade, and rightly so. But they evince little familiarity with this intellectual heritage, except to repudiate it as Eurocentric or reactionary. And yet, while the evidence that our economic dependence on the United States has threatened our sovereignty is mixed at best, there is clear evidence that young people in Canada are increasingly devoted to American pop culture and entertainment, and have little knowledge of or interest in their own country's history or past intellectual and artistic heritage. The Americanization of youth culture cannot be unconnected with the fact that, while obsessed with economic issues like the North American Free Trade Agreement, we have largely forgotten our historical heritage and see no lessons to be drawn from it in addressing current problems. So attenuated has our connection with the past become that, while many politicians and pundits seriously argued as if a mechanism for resolving trade disputes could destroy our sovereignty, few seemed to understand that writing a new constitution was of incomparably greater significance for our prospects of surviving as an independent nation.

For McGee, education is 'an essential condition of our political independence.' Only it can provide true independence of thought and action, raising us above mere jingoistic patriotism, 'a state of public mind puffed up on small things, an exaggerated opinion of ourselves and a barbarian depreciation of foreigners.' By linking one's own people to the merits and virtues universally distributed among all peoples and individuals, liberal education, far from being Eurocentric and prejudiced, on the contrary tempers a love of one's own country with an awareness of what others have achieved. The aim of Canadian education must be:

[A] mental condition thoughtful and true; national in its preferences, but catholic in its sympathies; gravitating inward, not outward; ready to learn from every other people on one sole condition, that the lesson when learned has been worth acquiring. In short, I would desire to see ... our new national character distinguished by a manly modesty as much as by mental independence; by the conscientious exercise of the critical faculties, as well as by the zeal of the inquirer.[8]

For McGee as for Aristotle, Vergerius, and Hegel, the core of this education must be books, the kind that carry us beyond the love of our own by way of the love of our own, returning us to a patriotism that is thoughtful with respect to our country's excellences and its deficiencies in light of universal standards for the pursuit of truth and justice. Whereas for Aristotle, a poem like Homer's *Odyssey* can provide this window on the wider world, for McGee liberal education includes the Bible and Shakespeare. Reading Shakespeare is crucial to an education in citizenship, not because it teaches an uncritical love of the British tradition, but because it invites one to transcend it: 'A mind so deep and clear in itself – that easily embraces all humanity as the air does our earth – must have had profound convictions on the highest of earthly interests – the sphere and duty of government.'[9] McGee's recommendation of the Bible is interesting because, although a devout believer himself, he is careful to distinguish the educational value of the Bible from the profession of any specific religious creed. Its educational value lies in its historical, moral, and philosophical complexity, as well as its literary and rhetorical beauty.

One cannot help but compare the two founders of their respective countries most interested in the question of liberal education. Whereas Jefferson's desire for a national system of liberal education was at odds with the general view of the American framers that their constitution should be neutral toward any specific pedagogy, McGee's full-blooded defence of traditional liberal education was very much in keeping with the character of Canada as a community of communities where the rights of the individual are balanced by a substantive obligation to the whole. Canada's attempt to balance individual rights and communal duties made it easier for someone like McGee to defend the traditional concept of liberal education than it was for the American founding fathers, because Canada was founded in a different moral and intellectual climate than was the United States.

Canadian conservatism was connected to the tory democracy of Victorian British conservatism, and to this day it has an organicist character that distinguishes it from the *soi-disant* conservatism of the United States, actually the liberal 'radicalism' of pure laissez-faire and libertarianism. Canada shared in the British and European search during the nineteenth century for a way of combining liberal political rights and economic progress with a concern for social stability and heterogeneity. When McGee traced the carnage of the American Civil War to that country's unbridled egalitarianism and general lawlessness, he very likely had in mind Burke's warnings about the French Revolution as the dark side of modernity. Burke stressed the need to preserve traditional attachments to institutions, rank, and symbol, while at the same time accepting the fundamental assumptions of liberal individualism. This kind of evolutionary liberalism, developed further in the writings of Macaulay and Bagehot, was of far more importance for the Canadian founding than anything in American political thought. As we will see at the end of this chapter, it nurtured the growth of a uniquely Canadian pedagogy through the added influence of Scottish commonsense philosophy and Hegelianism on educational reformers like John Watson and George Paxton Young. The more we have forgotten the Anglo-European intellectual and ethical roots of our genuine differences from the United States, the more empty and insistent has our nationalism become, a shrill boosterism and anti-Americanism (combined with a slavish imitation of American pop culture and consumerism) with little to offer of its own.

For the Canadian founders, modern economic and democratic progress was inevitable and benevolent. But it had to be moderated by a concern for social heterogeneity and a reliance on the past as the safest guide to the future. It was in this atmosphere that the Victorian politicians of British North America consummated the project of Confederation. Even the more hard-headed of our founding fathers – the ones more interested in the economic advantages of Confederation – shared this general outlook of Burkean whiggery. The best example is George Brown, leader of the Reform party. His cause in politics was to free the expanding population of Canada West from the old system of legislative double-majority established by the Union Act of 1841 and get on with the grand enterprise of opening up the frontier to settlement and trade. Brown was as close as the Canadian founders came to a Lockean liberal and promoter of laissez-faire. For him, confederation would 'throw down the barriers of trade' and place the vast frontier at the disposal of the new nation from Lake of the Woods to British Columbia.

But even Brown was not a pure Lockean liberal in the American sense. He cherished the imperial connection as a way of pursuing the fruits of progress and liberty without committing the 'anarchistic' excesses of the republic to the south. At bottom, for Brown and his contemporaries, economic activity was not separable from their moral and emotional attachment to the British North American way of life and to a Burkean modification of Lockean liberalism in the name of pre-modern sympathies and attachments. The task of economic development was 'a great duty entrusted to their hands,' having the dignity of a civilizing enterprise that would 'maintain liberty, justice and Christianity throughout the land'[10]

As the foregoing suggests, Canada has quite unique constitutional origins, among the most interesting of any country's. The survival of Quebec in North America when the rest of French-speaking America slid into oblivion is an impressive testament to our capacity over two hundred years to combine the universality of a liberal democratic polity with the preservation of disparate and asymmetrical constitutional prerogatives meant to enhance linguistic, cultural, and religious communities. And yet, from the debate over Meech Lake and the Charlottetown Accord, one might have received the impression from our country's governing classes and news media that Canada had no historical experience to draw upon – that we were all getting together to invent a country out of nothing, guided by opinion polls and spin doctors. The Charlottetown Accord did not fail because it was not properly 'pitched' to the public, as if a constitution were something that could be sold like a sit-com pilot. The accord failed because it was an incoherent document, and its incoherence was symptomatic of the failure of liberal education in Canada. The leadership classes of Canadian society are no longer being educated to appreciate how our country's own history and constitutional experience provide us with a particular perspective, applicable to this particular polity, on the universal problems of statecraft.

Canada has never been a purely unitary state. Our provinces are sovereign in their spheres. Their authority is not merely delegated and revocable by the federal government. Although some of the Anglophone fathers of Confederation viewed it as paving the way for a unitary state, Quebec found ways of asserting its autonomy within this framework and gradually getting its special place entrenched in law, convention, and precedent. How odd it is that the loudest proponents of provincial equality and opponents of Quebec's claim to be a distinct society (such as Mr Wells and Ms Carstairs) seemed unaware of the fact that it is mainly because of Quebec's insistence on carving out its own sphere of sovereignty since 1867 that the other provinces have been able to invoke a strong claim of autonomy from the central government for themselves.

With the Constitution Act of 1982, we strangely decided to turn our backs on this rich heritage of practice and principle and begin inventing a regime out of thin air, guided by obstreperous pressure groups and exhausted mandarins haunted by a fear of bad press. The crises of Meech and Charlottetown were already implicit in the 1982 constitution, because it made the place of Quebec in Confederation untenable in a way that had never been the case before in our history. In Canada's political and constitutional evolution, sovereignty has always been a relative term. Like all the provinces, Quebec has always been sovereign, and is so now – Messieurs Parizeau and Bouchard are calling for something that already exists. It is a question of negotiating how much sovereignty the provinces have. Because the British North America Act managed to combine the basic features of a unitary state with the provisions of a compact between the two founding peoples, Quebec has always had a special status and been a distinct society. Only people like Ms Carstairs, who appeared to believe that Canada sprang into being out of nowhere under Mr Trudeau's Cartesian universalism, can regard Quebec's affirmation of these traditional realities in the context of new socio-economic circumstances as some kind of astonishing outrage and novelty. In the past, Quebec and the other provinces often wrangled with Ottawa over their respective shares of authority. But because our old constitution was more of a compact than a charter, the tensions between the unitary and provincial dimensions of sovereignty seldom called the logic of the whole Canadian polity into question as they do today. They could be dealt with through federal-provincial negotiation, legislation, or the courts' interpretation of the jurisdictional provisions of the BNA Act. But after the Charter of Rights and Freedoms, the claim of Quebec to constitute its own special arrangements for the protection of its language and heritage stood in glaring contradiction, as a matter of principle, to the universality of rights guaranteed to everyone. Whereas in the past, Quebec could assert its special status within the context of long-established precedents and conventions, in order to do so now, it may have to throw the main power switch of the 'notwithstanding' clause, jolting the rest of the country with its use of an emergency measure that the universality of the charter inevitably renders illegitimate.

We are not arguing that history and precedent can be a guide for every contemporary problem. But we do at least have to begin by consulting them. If we pay attention to the historical experience and evolution of our country's political arrangements, for instance, we will find sure evidence of our future ability to accommodate the aboriginal peoples' legitimate wish for their own share of autonomy in our past experience in accommodating the claims of Quebec. The constitution of 1982 renders this prospect more difficult because it blew apart the tacit political reasoning that had evolved throughout the history of Confederation. Canada's ability to house Quebec and allow it to preserve its way of life signified the country's deeper reservations about imitating the pure universality of American republicanism, which relentlessly converts all group-based claims into individualistic claims. We need to recover those reservations as expressed in our historical experience as a nation if we are to find ways today of accommodating the communitarian longings of disparate groups and peoples within an overarching framework of legal and civil equality. In this way, our very future as a country capable of solving its constitutional problems is linked to a restoration of liberal education as we have explored it in this book.

Canada has been a model for the attempt to evolve a nation-state in which many of the contradictory demands of human existence might be met and balanced. Its cooperative federalism was a sensible alternative to a purely unitary state. Its 'confederate' organization – what Joe Clark called the 'community of communities' – reflected a prudent assessment of the implications of either too much centralization or too much decentralization. But unless we understand why the forms of our political world are the way they are, and what principles sustain their coherence, we will doom ourselves to the same shipwreck occurring around the world as the nation-state degenerates into lethal tribalism or a reactive craving for autocracy. In a world that increasingly appears to be bound by ineluctable processes of change, where the sphere of freedom and humanity is contracted by an interlocking grid of necessary decisions, we need to remember Arendt's reminder that it always 'lies within the power of human thought and action to interrupt and arrest such processes.'[11] Thus far, we have avoided the dangerous consequences of the conjunction of globalism and localism by virtue of a strong tradition of responsible government and the rule of law, and through an education system in whose origins we can find a recognition of the centrality of virtuous character and common sense to learning. But by giving in to global pressures, are we not jettisoning the last bulwarks against the contemporary dynamic? We need to consider the Canadian polity, and its unique educational heritage, more deeply.

The Founding Educators

Like Canada's founding fathers, our first major educators identified what was of concern to them through the sensibilities of the Victorian era. For them, this sensibility required, on the one hand, the unity of the spiritual and intellectual life with moral principle and, on the other hand, the close link between education and the duties of citizenship. Their language was often the strict Presbyterian or Methodist one of 'manners and morals,' 'character formation,' and 'habit training.' While the restraint of desire was praiseworthy in itself for these educators, they were just as concerned to prepare students for their role as citizens in public life and for a life of reason. At the same time, the founding educators also recognized the importance of the sciences and of the practical arts, though these too were linked to higher purposes.

The themes which came by the end of the nineteenth century to predominate in educational debate and practice are a hybrid of many eighteenth- and nineteenth-century experiments: the Lower Canadian petit école, the Jesuit colleges, the Ecole des Arts et Métiers, the Atlantic colonies' monitorial schools (the 'Madras' schools), the Western mission schools, the Upper Canada grammar schools, and the Upper Canada common schools. The deepest roots of Canadian education extended in Lower Canada to the Ratio Studiorum of the Jesuit colleges of Europe and in Nova Scotia to England's Anglican Society for the Propagation of the Gospel. While the diversity of aims and levels of performance of these various institutions is the most conspicuous feature of their history, there were also uniting themes. Perhaps the most important of these was the need to train the human will in accordance with moral precept. But it was also maintained that morality could not be taught in the absence of religion.[12]

In Upper Canada, debate about the nature of public education intensified in response to the demands of the United Empire Loyalists. The governor, Lord Simcoe, was receptive to the educational privileges for which the Loyalists were lobbying, privileges associated with their understanding of the requirements of education drawn from their British ancestry. In this, Simcoe had strong support from the Anglican Bishop Strachan, who was to become the Family Compact's education spokesman and founder of its prestigious King's College. Simcoe, moreover, chose his advisers to the Legislative and Executive councils from a group of wealthy Loyalists, thus confining the majority of American and British immigrants to representation in the elected Assembly. In these actions were already sown the seeds of the 1837 Rebellion.

Since 1786 there had been a 'common school' system in Upper Canada, though criticism of it was extensive. The Loyalists, and especially the Family Compact, were particularly discontented with these schools. Lord Simcoe's willingness to set up 'grammar schools' for educating a potential governing class was reflected in the District Public (Grammar) School Act of 1807. The Family Compact wanted these schools to be exclusively for the wealthy; they wanted English traditions and the privileges of the aristocracy; they wanted a close connection between church and state; and the schools were, under no circumstance, to make concessions to the models current in the United States. These schools were not intended to serve the needs of the growing population of settlers. The Legislative Assembly, while cognizant of the grammar schools' inability to provide widespread public education, made no efforts to expand the mandate of the schools. The Family Compact was opposed, however, by the Reformers who wanted a reform of the common schools modelled on the schools of the United States.

J.G. Althouse reports that within ten years of the act of 1807, two hundred private schools were formed to meet the needs of the settlers. In 1816, the Legislative Council authorized state support of the 'common school' system. Boards of education were struck for each district, given local autonomy over curriculum, books, and teacher qualification. The proliferation of common schools led to the displacement of the private schools. However, there was an immediate challenge to the common schools. In 1822, Upper Canada Central School was formed, based on the experience of the Anglican British national schools. The intent of Sir Peregrine Maitland was to have low-cost national schools, under the control of the governing class, across Upper Canada. The Legislative Assembly opposed the plan, thus preserving the common schools from denominational or class control.

While the common school prevailed in Upper Canada, the idea of the privileged grammar school was also retained in a small number of exclusive schools, like Upper Canada Central School. Bishop Strachan, the most ardent defender of these exclusive schools, wanted them run by Anglican clerics and decried any concession to American schooling. 'Those sent to the United States,' he wrote, 'commonly learn little beyond anarchy in politics and infidelity in religion.'

In Lower Canada similar discontent and controversy existed. The lines were drawn between Louis Papineau's reformers and the Château Clique, and here too the issue of control over education was inextricably linked to the debate over the meaning of legitimate government. The merchants, seigneurs, and political circle constituting the Château Clique supported the *collèges classiques* formed by the British; the Patriots vehemently opposed the British model.

When the conflicts came to a head in 1837, Lord Durham was commissioned to study the causes of rebellion in Upper and Lower Canada. Out of his report came a proposal for responsible government – that the Executive Council should be appointed from members of the Assembly, that it be accountable to the Assembly, and that it retain the confidence of a working majority. In addition, Durham identified the issue of education as one of the key areas needing greater attention and, in particular, singled out the poverty of education in Lower Canada, where denominational insularity, by preventing its citizens from excelling, perpetuated their inferior status and vulnerable condition.

A number of important principles emerge from these early debates which we believe confirm the link between the traditional ideas of liberal education we have been discussing in this book and the core meaning of Canadian education. First, the success of the common schools enshrined resistance to centralized control and ensured that monopoly control over education by class or creed could be avoided. The experience of the early nineteenth century established the principle of diversity based on tolerance for religious minorities and on the education of students in their region's local history. The need to prevent sectarian control was equally evident in the rejection of the monitorial system – a system which had relied on teachers who would cater to the demands of the dominant class or sect – in favour of teacher independence.[13] Moreover, the argument for a plurality of avenues to education acquired greater legitimacy at the Quebec Conference in 1866 with the support of Thomas D'Arcy McGee. The Dominion Act of 1867 finally established formal recognition of religious tolerance and local autonomy in education.

Secondly, an interesting case was made, as a part of the argument on behalf of plurality, for schools catering to the most intellectually advantaged. The argument for exclusive schools was not intended to defend the privileges of the few, but instead to channel their ambitions into a constructive public life. Strachan's impassioned defence of Upper Canada College recognized the importance of educating the ambitious passions. This argument would also appear in the provisions in Lord Durham's report for changes to the form of government, for he too recognized that,

as long as personal ambition is inherent in human nature, and as long as the morality of every free and civilized community encourages its aspirations, it is one great business of a wise Government to provide for its legitimate development. If, as it is commonly asserted, the disorders of these Colonies have, in great measure, been fomented by the influence of designing and ambitious individuals, this evil will best be remedied by allowing such a scope for the desires of such men as shall direct their ambition into the legitimate chance of furthering, and not of thwarting, their Government.[14]

As late as the end of the nineteenth century, defenders of Upper Canada College would still argue that the point of these schools was to channel the potent passions of the ambitious so that they did not produce social disorder. George Parkin Grant would argue that the advantage of Upper Canada College was that it resisted 'the mental and moral suffocation from which it is well-nigh impossible to guard boys in rich and luxurious homes.'[15]

The third and fourth principles emerging from the early educational debates stressed unity rather than diversity. The schools had to sustain the free and accountable politics that had been achieved with the institution of responsible government. As Thomas d'Arcy McGee had argued, government cannot work without a virtuous citizenry, for in its absence there could not be the attentiveness to reasoned political debate upon which legitimate authority rests. Education had to form civic-mindedness and the virtues requisite to political participation.

Finally, the early educators, notwithstanding their dispute over whether the Presbyterian, Methodist, or Anglican strand should take precedence, agreed that the moral and spiritual dimensions of education could not be treated separately from the life of the intellect. Reverence for the supreme being was the guarantee of moral virtue and sound science. One influential educator after another insisted on the relation between religion and intellectual achievement. Thus concluded John Dawson in an 1863 university lecture: 'But lastly I would direct your attention to the duties of the educated man in his relation to his God, and to the example that he sets before his fellow-man. The religious life of a people is its only true life. If this is wanting, or if it is vitiated by infidelity, by superstition, or by any of the idolatries which are set up between man and his Maker, nothing will avail to give prosperity and happiness?'[16]

Likewise, the principal of Bishop's College in 1857, in a public lecture, asked: 'Where else will you find the man you require, but among those whose powers of mind have been carefully nurtured under a system which took pains with the formation of character, which stamped that character with a firm and lasting outline, by giving to it an abiding sense of the fear of God and desire of His favour?'[17]

For these educators, religion was not construed as mere conformity and obedience to dogma. They did not see religion as inimical to the meaning of liberal education. The spiritual longings to which religion gave voice were understood as stimulating and broadening the meaning of intellectual achievement. Moreover, liberal education was seen as safeguarding equality and political order by instilling respect for others and modest expectations. A committee of the Upper Canadian Assembly determined that liberal education 'should be the source of intellectual and moral light and animation, from which the glorious irradiations of literature and science may descend upon all with equal lustre and power.'[18] Thomas McCulloch (1776–1843), president of Dalhousie University and later principal of Victoria College, and the propounder of a liberal education curriculum based on Christian intellectual tradition, insisted that although liberal education temporarily removed the mind from the immediacies of daily existence, it returned the individual with an invigorated commitment to the good of the whole community. 'Its primary object,' he wrote, 'is knowledge which could not be easily acquired in any other way: its ends, the improvement of man in intelligence and moral principle, as the basis of his subsequent duty and happiness.' Liberal education, he argued, formed 'barriers against barbarism.' Such barriers could only be formed if individuals acknowledged that they were not the creators of their own existence or of social and political order. Rising above doctrinal partisanship, and acknowledging divine perfection as well as the importance of spiritual longing, were paramount in liberal education.

This connection between education, religion, and politics was in no way restricted to Upper Canada and Nova Scotia. Prompted by Lord Durham's report, the voices of two major Lower Canadian writers on education were soon heard: Dr Jean-Baptiste Meilleur and Judge Charles E. Mondelet. Mondelet was the more vocal of the two. One of his major themes is the important link between education and political order:

Common or primary schools are one of the most interesting institutions in any well organized society ... No community is safe without them; no government is secure if it neglects or proscribes them. An enlightened people will, in most cases, guard against the corrupting influence of bad rulers. It will be equally free from the snares of ignorant, or of intriguing and unprincipled demagogues. In either case, the governed will escape the tyranny of the one, that of the few, or the tyranny of the many. The cause of education is, therefore, the cause of liberty.[19]

An education producing this kind of independence of character would, Mondelet insisted, have to be free from control by political rulers, by mass opinion, and by religious sectarians. Educators, he wrote, must be 'uninfluenced either by the frowns of the government, or the clamour of the people; they will acknowledge no authority but that of the law and their conscience.' For Mondelet, the guarantee of such independence was the moral foundation supplied by the Bible. But while 'there must be a religious foundation or basis ... in the classroom,' Mondelet wrote, 'it should be such as to secure the assent of all, and affect the good of all classes and all religious denominations.' Hence, one of Mondelet's proposals was that representatives of all religious denominations in Lower Canada would meet and select biblical passages to be collected into books used in the schools. Mondelet saw the major principle of his writings as non-partisanship:

National, religious, sectarian and other absurd and injurious distinctions have been denounced, and I have, I hope, suggested means of soothing down prejudice, restoring confidence, diffusing elementary and practical knowledge, and securing to all classes, whatever may be their origin, their religious creed, or their politics, a full and complete guarantee, for their rights and privileges. Knowledge being the universal right, the universal duty, and the universal interest of man and government, what other but a system of education calculated to maintain inviolate that right, ensure the discharge of that duty, and work in the interest of man and government, can be attempted with any chance of success, to be set in operation, on this side of the Atlantic?[20]

In this, Mondelet was setting the tone for nineteenth-century French-Canadian nationalism, marked, as many historians have pointed out, by a resistance to the abstract principles of the French Revolution and to English commercialism. Much of his thinking would deeply influence the Thomism of Louis-Adolphe Paquet and Louis Lachance, the major architects of French-Canadian nationalism in the twentieth century.

From this general perspective, we wish now to focus on three particular forces in Canada's history of education: the Scottish commonsense educators, Egerton Ryerson, and the Hegelian Rational Idealist educators. It is in the creative tension and cross-fertilization of these forces that the distinctive identity of Canadian education was formed. Although these educators represented distinct philosophical alternatives, they joined in defining themselves against scientism, utilitarianism, empiricism, and pragmatism. Moreover, they were at one in stipulating that moral principle and public duty took precedence over individual rights and autonomy. Thus, we argue, at the core of Canadian education lie the main ideas of liberal education we have been discussing throughout this book.

The first significant influence on Canadian education was the Scottish Presbyterian commonsense school, whose main thinkers were Thomas Reid, Francis Hutcheson, and Sir William Hamilton. As W.J. Rattray chronicles in *The Scot in British North America (1804–1894)*, the contribution of the Scottish to nineteenth-century Canadian life was 'immense.'[21] Leading Canadian educators – John Strachan, Thomas McCulloch, Thomas Liddell – were touched by the commonsense school's account of human understanding and its moral philosophy.

The two general features of commonsense philosophy were the defence of 'the ordinary convictions of mankind' and the rejection of the early liberal notion that individuals were isolated atoms and inherently apolitical. The arguments of Reid, Hutcheson, and Hamilton were an effort to resist both dogmatism and scepticism at the intellectual level and hedonism and contractualism at the level of politics and society. Commonsense, as they understood it, supplied both those truths necessary to endow practical life with reason and those intimations of moral right and wrong that were the bond of civic life. In these arguments, the commonsense thinkers believed they had found the way to defend social and religious custom against the corrosive materialism of Darwinian evolutionary theory.

Disavowing the speculativeness of metaphysics, and thus restating their

Presbyterian acknowledgment of the irreversibility of the Fall and of human sin, the commonsense thinkers held that even in the absence of the mind's capacity to know the essence of things, it was sufficiently given in human experience and sense to understand how personal and political existence is mediated by reason. This appeal to 'common understanding' was an inherently democratic notion – common experience supplied a sufficient fund out of which human understanding could be formed. The natural limits to human knowledge affirmed the essential plurality of human understanding. Its further social implication was that education ought not to be reserved for a privileged few, but should be for all.

This same caution was evident in the resistance to abstract principles of political right. Rejecting the revolutionary implications of social contract theories of the state, commonsense thinkers were inclined to see in the gradual patterns of custom, sensibility, and judgment the forms of practical reason and sound understanding.[22] Identifying the role of reason in this way accorded well with the Augustinian understanding of the natural condition of human dispersal and ignorance after the Fall, as well as with the natural theology that found intimations of God's design in the rhythms of everyday life. To assume self-evident truths was a reflection of an excessive desire for unity and certainty. What was given to human beings were the promptings of reason based on probability and plausibility rather than self-evident compelling truths.

Interestingly, the same principle of limited reason underlies the argument that there is a substantive public purpose for government beyond protecting the equal rights of individuals. Recognizing the inevitable recurrence of sin as the obstacle to spontaneous human cooperation meant that education had to work at overcoming human unsociability by actively fashioning people's social nature. The commonsense thinkers were in overall accord when they identified the primary purpose of politics and education as sustaining civic virtue.[23]

We can see this focus on civic virtue in two ways. Writers on the Scottish commonsense school have been inclined to dwell primarily on one of these, namely Reid's and Hutcheson's postulate of man's inherent moral sense. Enfolded within commonsense, for them, lies a natural benevolence towards others, from which, even in the absence of a rational apprehension of the good, moral principle is intuited. Thus Hutcheson posits our natural sense of moral approval, a disinterested passion that recognizes the beauty of benevolence. Human beings, he writes, have 'a moral faculty which points out the rights and obligations of this state, and shows how far any appetite or passion can be indulged consistently with the inward approbation of our souls.'[24] This is commonsense philosophy's answer to the materialism and pragmatism of social-contract theorists, whose postulate of man's natural shrewdness is rejected as providing only a conditional sense of obligation. While humans have 'moral sense,' however, it is not spontaneous. The task of liberal education, then, is the cultivation of this natural benevolence, either as moral sense through an apprehension of the beauty of benevolence, or as conscience informed by our obligations to God's law and divine will.

There was, however, another aspect to civic virtue as the commonsense thinkers understood it. Commonsense was not merely the application of universal rules to particular circumstances, but rather a sense of historical appropriateness, cultural sensibility, and the discretion and tact accompanying prudence, akin to what Aristotle called *phronesis*. It was an inherently civic or political faculty, in that it provided the basis for thoughtful and virtuous citizenship. The commonsense philosophers denied the radically speculative capacity of reason, recognizing the limits inherent in our embodied and historical existence. Commonsense was situational, taking its bearings from within a reality characterized by contingency and ambivalence, by error and relativity. But one must not see in this emphasis on the situational a prescription for simple conformism to the social world. Just as 'moral sense' was not merely a mirror of social taste, 'commonsense' was neither mere whimsy nor an aggregate of shrewd guesses and hunches. Central to commonsense philosophy was the role of judgment. As the commonsense thinkers understood it, judgment was consistent with the rational requirements of clarity and order, for while it did not have the critical detachment of speculative reason, it was still discriminating and coherent in its responsiveness to wider political and historical meanings.

Thus educators were mandated to form the capacities for judgment appropriate to participation in the civil association, where politics was seen as the art of the possible, rather than of the necessary. To form such capacities for judgment entailed exercises whereby prudence and rhetorical persuasiveness were given substance by the appreciation of historical fact and cultural meaning. And while there were orderly measures governing judgment, these were not products of the Cartesian self-certainty of the speculative reasoner, but a worldly interaction with others through discerning that common reality arising when a variety of human perspectives on what is useful and good are measured against one another.

The tenets of commonsense philosophy vindicated ordinary men and women, whose talents were not superlative, who were not flighty and unstable, but were of 'the middle degrees of capacity.' For them especially, as participants in a free society, there was a special need for judgment and moral sensibility. Liberal education at once gave them the confidence that their everyday experiences in the world were intelligible and the capacity to judge those experiences. Education formed in them an active concern for public life and even the potential for public leadership.

The second major influence on Canadian public education was Egerton Ryerson. His father was a United Empire Loyalist, but one who had little sympathy for either the Family Compact or the Reformers. In 1827, Ryerson converted to Methodism and spent a year spreading the word of Methodism. He was himself educated in the milieu of the Scottish commonsense school.

Three elements loom large in Ryerson's educational writings. First, he understood the task of education to be the formation of moral beings capable of participation in universal civilization. But, just as importantly, he focused on the shaping of citizens who would play a role in their country's affairs and contribute to the common good. Second, neither morality nor politics could be based solely on the observable facts of social life. The Scriptures contained the foundation of political rights and civil liberties. Moreover, Ryerson took seriously the Christian teaching of the Fall and thus saw the task of education as raising individuals above their fallen condition, guiding them in the direction of their original pre-fallen state. As a Methodist, he shared John Wesley's disavowal of dogma and his distaste for sectarianism. And like Wesley, he believed that the truths of Scripture were experienced through the faith of the heart and spirit; that reason was the vehicle of God's revelation; and that man's lot was not predestined, but rather the perfectibility of man made the grace of God available to all. Third, Ryerson saw the need for a liberal education responding to the student's physical, mental, and moral faculties. The immediate aim of his educational proposals was to alleviate the plight of the Irish famine immigrants. He hoped to bring education within their means, thus ensuring their sound moral conduct. These educational 'facilities' would combine liberal, classical, and practical education to form 'good men and useful members of civil society.' As he would frequently repeat, the integration of spiritual, moral, and vocational components in schooling aimed at ensuring that 'those principles and precepts of morality will be carefully inculcated and enforced which will guard the pupil from the contagion of vicious practice and example and will lead him to the love and practice of virtue.'[25]

'By Education,' Ryerson states, 'I mean not the mere acquisition of certain arts or of certain branches of knowledge, but that instruction and discipline which qualify and dispose the subjects of it for their appropriate duties and employments of life, as Christians, as persons of business, and also as members of the civil community in which they live.'[26] The liberal curriculum he proposed to meet these aims included English language and literature, ancient languages, mathematics and the physical sciences, moral science, rhetoric and belles-lettres, and theology.

There are three further features of Ryerson's thought which reveal how deep was his understanding of this comprehensive liberal education. First, education should be practical. In his *Report on a System of Public Elementary Instruction*, he argued that education had to address those aptitudes which students would need in their vocations and enterprises, and to this end they would need to be exposed to the modern sciences – to 'an extensive knowledge and observation of facts' – and to the 'every-day duties and the business of life.' But what he meant by 'practical' extended beyond technical skill, for to be educated was to have the 'requisite qualities to apply that knowledge in the best manner,' which Ryerson explained as entailing the correlation of our 'moral, intellectual, and physical culture' so that it 'should harmonize with the design of our existence.' So while for Ryerson the 'practical' entails, to a considerable extent, the skills needed in the 'business of life,' and thus involves 'the development to a certain extent of all our faculties', and 'an acquaintance with several branches of elementary knowledge,' and while there is no question but that Ryerson was particularly fearful of 'asymmetry' in character if this need for vocational preparedness was not met, the 'practical' also 'includes religion and morality.' Vocational training has to be linked with a sense of obligation and a pious disposition.[27]

Indeed, Ryerson warns of the consequences of failing to put moral science and theology at the core of the practical. He approvingly quotes Samuel Young's condemnation of the pragmatism reigning in New York's school system: 'The exaltation of talent, as it is called, above virtue and religion, is the curse of this age. Education is now chiefly a stimulus to learning, and thus men acquire power without the principles which alone make it a good. Talent is worshipped; but, if divorced from rectitude, it will prove more of a demon than a god.'[28] Schooling might make a child grow up 'shrewd, intelligent, and influential,' 'but yet a slave to his lower propensities.' Technical competence alone, Ryerson argues, in the absence of moral order and a 'pious disposition' leads to a dangerous magnification of irascible desires and a dangerous 'vainglorious' presumption of human perfection.

Second, Ryerson stipulates that education must include religious instruction, though he is insistent that such instruction must avoid all sectarianism, thus preventing the 'army of pugilists and persecutors' whose dogmatism defeats not only social order but the spiritual life itself. Ryerson's argument for religious instruction again refers to the testimony of Samuel Young. America, Young admits, is a society for whom the *vox populi est vox Dei*, and the consequence is that it is shaken by disagreement and collision at every juncture, by sectarian partiality, by the perpetual vanity of individuals who 'perceive not a single cloud in [their] mental horizon,' by a dictatorial and despotic public opinion, and by knowledge, 'severed from its relations to duty.' Religious instruction, Young and Ryerson agreed, answered to all these sources of personal and political disorder. But Ryerson also makes it clear, in the appendix to his *Special Report of 1847*, that by religious instruction he does not mean dogma and doctrine. There is 'a wide common ground of principles and morals, held equally sacred, and equally taught to all, and [this is] the spirit which ought to pervade the whole system of Public Instruction, and which comprehends the essential requisites of social happiness and good citizenship.'[29] By religious instruction, Ryerson intends primarily the formation of a sense of moral duty and of the piety which comes from attentiveness to divine perfection.

Finally, Ryerson stipulates that liberal education should be universal and meritocratic, as much for those intending to go on to a religious ministry as for those who will be lawyers, doctors, and merchants. He asks why the farmer should be 'destitute of the nobility of knowledge,' and why the mechanic should be 'a mere operative at his bench,' when 'by the higher powers of a cultivated mind, he might equally contribute to his country's intellectual wealth and civic advancement.'[30] Ryerson's concern here is two-fold. First, as we have already noted, is his worry about a technical 'talent' which has not been linked to 'a sense of obligation' and a 'pious disposition.' The farmer and the mechanic must be saved from presumption. But, just as important, for Ryerson, liberal education is the great equalizer. The principles upon which it is based are all 'within the grasp of ordinary minds.' Indeed, this is why rhetoric, the art of speaking well, continues to be so important for Ryerson:

Speech is the great instrument of intercourse between man and man; and he who can speak well, both in public and in private, on all subjects in which he may be concerned, possesses a power more enviable and formidable than that of the sword; he possesses an empire over mind, the more admirable as it is entirely voluntary – the more elevated as it is the force of reason in man's immortal nature – the more formidable as it controls the very springs of human action. Knowledge itself cannot properly be said to be power, without the appropriate power to communicate it.[31]

'Knowledge even with poverty,' Ryerson notes, 'is preferable to riches with ignorance.' We might find ourselves mere 'hewers of wood and drawers of water,' but 'a pauper in intellect ranks the lowest of the order of paupers.'

Central to Ryerson's idea of a liberal education is that symmetry and balance of character we examined in our consideration of *paideia* in chapter 4. Failure to evoke the ancients in 'matters of taste' is like 'a blind man's denying the beautiful and variegated splendours of the rainbow,' a denial that 'would prove nothing but his own ignorance and presumption.' But an appeal to the ancients was not antiquarianism. It was intended to add breadth and stimulus to 'the business of life.' Liberal education for Ryerson unites ancient 'illustrious' example with modern enterprise 'to impress both the mind and the heart of the pupil with the conviction of the dignity and duty of uniting personal industry and enterprise with genius and learning in all the private and public relations of life.'[32] It aims at the highest so as to enhance all dimensions of human existence. While he saw the need for fitting knowledge to the 'active duties of life' he stipulated that such a linkage must be one in which 'the mental symmetry is preserved and developed; and the whole intellectual man grows up into masculine maturity and vigour.'[33] The 'apprenticeship of the mind' in liberal education, Ryerson comments, 'develops and harmoniously matures its latent faculties, and directs their skilful application to the varied and noblest objects of human pursuit.'[34]

The third major force in Canadian public education arose in reaction to the commonsense school. It denied that moral sense was susceptible of rational defence and concluded that despite that school's opposition to utilitarianism and pragmatism, its 'commonsense' was in fact little more than a combination of shrewdness and naiveté, incompatible with comprehensive ideas of personal responsibility and moral initiative. Those resisting commonsense philosophy found a more satisfactory account of education and morality in German Idealism and particularly in the thought of G.W.F. Hegel. Hegelianism had no extensive effect in the English-speaking world until J.H. Stirling's publication in 1865 of *The Secret of Hegel*. It would have a major impact on a generation of scholars – including T.H. Green, Lewis Nettleship, F.H. Bradley, Josiah Royce, Bernard Bosanquet. The two most influential of these, however, were John and Edward Caird, who introduced Hegel's thought into Scottish intellectual life. For them, commonsense was the 'mere opinion of ordinary intelligence.' Hegel's thought, moreover, held out the the prospect of a reconciliation between philosophy and science (especially important in the wake of Darwin's evolutionary theory) which commonsense philosophy could not.

Hegel's thought had prominent adherents in North America, especially in the St Louis School where William Harris and William Brokmeyer made Hegel's thought accessible to American intellectuals. The Hegelian influence was, however, even more strongly felt in Canada. Two Canadians, James Cappon and John Watson, studied under Edward Caird at Glasgow University.

When they returned to Canada, the predominance of commonsense philosophy was already weakening. In the intellectual milieu fostered by George Paxton Young and John Clark Murray, professors of ethics and metaphysics at University College and McGill University respectively, there was already discontent with the reigning orthodoxy. The leading commonsense philosopher, Sir William Hamilton, was roundly criticized by them. John Watson's return to the chair of philosophy at Queen's University heralded the beginning of a philosophical alternative, and with Young and Murray, Hegel's Idealism and his understanding of liberal education were absorbed by the general Canadian intellectual climate.

Watson shared with Caird a discontent with tradition for its own sake. The commonsense school, in Watson's words, allowed men simply to 'jog along contentedly, with no very strong faith and no very disquieting disbelief.' From Caird, Watson learned to conjoin Socrates with Christianity, to find 'the kinship of Greek Philosophy and the Christian Religion.'

At the centre of the Canadians' attraction to Hegel was his argument for the essential unity and interconnectedness of all things: philosophy and science, thought and nature, reason and experience. These diverse phenomena and forms of knowledge were in truth one. In this, the appeal of Hegelianism was prepared for by the general nineteenth-century attraction to natural theology, whose tenets were called upon to justify on religious grounds the prominence of the sciences at many Canadian universities. Hegelianism revealed that there was design and purpose in the universe, and thus was compatible with the findings of evolutionary science. It also coincided with the active presence of movements dedicated to fostering a Christian social conscience in Canada. Hegelianism offered a reconciliation between the demands of religion and those of science, between the demands of reason and those of sentiment, or between man as a natural and man as a spiritual being.

This reconciliation had important ramifications for the study of politics and morals. Not surprisingly, Canadian Hegelians attacked the atomism of liberalism, finding in Hegel's writings a means of discussing human interrelatedness. They disavowed the dualisms of spirit and matter, mind and body, religion and philosophy, that had played so prominent a part in modern empiricism, and even in Kant's moral philosophy. Hegel's thought supplied an organic view of reality, identifying unity both in life and in its development. The idea of such an organic political community based on the moral precepts of rational Christianity led John Watson to write: 'It is still true that only in identifying himself with a social good can the individual realize himself. And the reason is that in the community the idea of humanity as an organic unity is in the process of realization ... Hence the individual man can find himself, can become moral, only by contributing his share to its realization.'[35]

Watson attacked Thomas Hobbes's highly atomized individualism: 'We can no more speak of what man would be apart from society,' he wrote, 'than we can speak of an organ as independent of the whole body. In the one case as in the other, the nature of the parts is determined by the nature of the whole, as the nature of the whole is determined by the nature of its parts.' But he also opposed Herbert Spencer's Darwinian understanding of social evolution, for it conceived of development in wholly mechanical terms, reducing the higher to an epiphenomenon of the lower. Spencer's social Darwinism was predicated on the selfish motives of individuals. Watson retorted: 'only by the sacrifice of all petty vanity and other baser forms of egotism – can a nation be truly great.' Spencer had also advocated the centrality of science as the preparation for 'complete living' in an industrial age. History, Spencer had noted, is the progressive adjustment of human character to the circumstances of living and thus education had to entail industrial and vocational skills. But for Watson, as for Hegel, human historical development was a spiritual odyssey. The present times had brought about the possibility of a freedom and a social good transcending narrow self-interest and pragmatic calculation. Preventing the disintegration of this achievement was the task of liberal education in the modern age.

For Watson liberal education entailed defending the requirements of 'civilized community' against the pressure for an education dedicated to preparing students for the workplace, a defence which manifestly needs to be recalled in today's debates. 'Is it possible, then,' he asked, 'for men living under the complex civilization of modern times to limit themselves entirely to their practical avocation in life?'[36] Abdicating the need to inculcate social and political duties, Watson held, would 'lead to a despotic form of government or to the direst anarchy and confusion.' Especially in a representative government there was a need for the cultivation of 'a high intelligence by the people.' An uneducated citizenry will allow the nation to 'sink into a contemptible obscurity.' A training merely for technical life, Watson writes, tends 'to superinduce a host of personal or class prejudices.' And unless the mind is 'trained in the proper direction, it inevitably seeks a downward path for itself. If it is not filled with great and ennobling thoughts, it will seek to find satisfaction in what is mean, and petty and evanescent.' Moreover, to have a society based purely on technical knowledge would require 'an entire revolution of the present order of society.' Only liberal education could counterbalance this presumption that a society could be formed in which judgment, the deliberative faculty Aristotle referred to as *phronesis*, was unnecessary. Watson's evocation of liberal education at the dawn of our century reaches back through Hegel to all the major themes of *paideia* that we examined in chapter 4, beginning with Plato, suitably modified for the conditions of modernity.

Watson saw the purpose of ethics as reconciling freedom and necessity. Rejecting the empiricist and narrow liberal view that freedom was 'the exemption from all external influences and restraints,' Watson saw it instead as conduct 'regulated by the highest laws of our nature.' 'He ... who regulates all his actions by eternal principles of duty, may seem to be bound by the chains of necessity, but he really enjoys the highest liberty. For he is not subject to any external necessity, but only to the inner necessity of his own nature, in obeying which he purifies and strengthens his will and becomes a master where others are slaves.'[37] Appealing to Kant, Watson argues that morality is acting 'as if we belonged to a "kingdom of ends"; in other words, each individual must conceive of himself as a member of a social organism.'[38] Like Hegel, as we saw in chapter 5, Watson made no romantic appeal back to tribal times: 'The industrial life of modern times, with all its imperfections, is more fitted to nourish and develop the intellectual and spiritual life of the individual, and to foster a high tone of public morality, than any other; and in this alone lies its right to exist.'[39] Just as for Kant, for Watson this higher public morality would demand the simultaneous education of the intellect and training of the will.

Watson's influence was significant in academic circles. But he would also have an indirect impact on the public life of Canada. For example, Adam Shortt was a student of his in the 1880s at Queen's University. In 1908 Shortt was hired by Mackenzie King as civil service commissioner, and his mandate was to rid the civil service of patronage. He pursued this aim by introducing civil service examinations. The philosophy component of the exams was marked by Watson. In addition, both Shortt's and O.D. Skelton's receptivity (through Watson) to T.H. Green, Bernard Bosanquet, L.T. Hobhouse, and Graham Wallis set a distinct tone of civic humanism especially at the University of Toronto and at Queen's University, an outlook which would make important inroads among the Pearson Liberals.[40] There was, moreover, a general legacy of Hegelianism, traceable to Watson, evident in the works of Charles Cochrane, George Sydney Brett, and the early works of George Grant.

The field of education also absorbed Hegelianism through an interest in Friedrich Froebel. It is here that a healthy and vital progressive movement in Canadian education was formed, which could hold up a truly holistic understanding of human longing against dogmatic teaching methods and doctrines. The enduring theme of Froebel's work was the organic order of the universe within which humans exist. Family and society were integrated into a whole which displayed progressively higher levels of complexity. The task of educators was to form a self-consciousness which would see the connection between a person's particular place and the encompassing organic unity: 'Education consists in leading man, as a thinking, intelligent being, growing into self-consciousness, to a pure, unsullied, conscious and free representation of the inner law of divine unity, and in teaching him means thereto.'[41] The task of education was to help the fullness of human possibility flourish in each person: spiritual longing to guide the emotions, the study of nature to create an awareness of reason in the whole, and mathematics to clarify human experience with images of universal order. How remarkably closely this idea of liberal education follows the prescriptions of Plato and Augustine, while being given a modern form through German Idealism!

This idea of liberal education was embraced by James Hughes, Froebel's major Canadian disciple and author of *Froebel's Educational Law for All Teachers*.[42] In this book, he discusses the child's growth through stages, tracing the modalities of harmonious development and elaborating on how the child's appreciation of the unity of things determines the child's harmonious relationship with reality. Central to Froebel's teaching methods, Hughes explains, was 'self-activity,' but Hughes distinguishes this from an absence of restraint. Self-activity is so structured that the curiosity activated by education is only for the correct objects. Childhood spontaneity is thus channelled into acceptable social and moral behaviour. While 'child-centred,' Froebel's idea of education is one in which, as Hughes wrote, 'the whole intellectual and spiritual being is invigorated, and through which the stable forms of reality are progressively revealed.' Human development can occur only if an individual's spiritual faculties moderate the desires of the body. Central to education was the training of the will, a training that resulted in a freedom which neither cancelled itself in conforming to authority nor overextended itself in seeing itself as the source of its own value and truth. Canadian Froebelians like Hughes were significantly influenced by John Watson's Hegelian conception of an organic community. Thus, while their idea of education was 'child-centred,' in contrast to the meaning that term has taken on today, it entailed the subordination of the individual to the community and insisted on the centrality of intellectual and spiritual longings. Here we see a distinguished example of the genuine holism and recognition of diversity which we identified in chapter 3 as central to liberal education.

The unfortunate turn in Canadian education occurred when the progressivism stemming from Watson was corroded by breakaway fragments which became autonomous movements pushing for radical reform in education. It is here that the right- and left-wing camps began to undermine the real meaning of liberal education as we have discussed it in this book, either by opting for dogmatic doctrinairism or by burdening education with the extravagant task of perfecting all individual and social life. In either case the erosion of a true liberal education dedicated to forming mature citizens and guiding intellectual and spiritual longing was inevitable. What we find particularly objectionable is how some of the most powerfully negative movements of recent European thought (stemming from Foucault and Derrida) have been allowed to undermine the richness and soundness of true Canadian progressivism. This corrosive post-Hegelianism, especially as it is encountered in the practice of deconstructing the forms of what we know to be civilized education, is what drives so much of today's radical educational reform.[43]

In his book *The Idea of Canada*,[44] Leslie Armour makes an important observation. Examining the differences between the French-Canadian Thomist Louis Lachance and the English-Canadian Anglican Hegelian John Watson, two thinkers who so significantly influenced Canadian political culture, he finds that, despite surface disagreements, their works share a common understanding of how to overcome the dualisms of the modern age – freedom and community, reason and sentiment. Lachance begins with a recognition of the intractable imperfection of human wisdom, reflected both in the insuperable diversity of human beings around the world and in the insurmountable divisions within the individual soul. Yet he also knows that humankind as a whole responds to some pull towards the centre. For him, that centre was revealed in the Incarnation, a particular moment in history in which the potential for human salvation is disclosed but not fulfilled. However humans respond to their spiritual longings for divine perfection, Lachance realizes that perfection will not become an immanent reality. The human world will remain a plural world, though there is a meaning to the whole in which all humans can participate and thus endow their own communities with order. And in working towards actualizing this order, individuals actualize their freedom as 'responsibility.' Watson's Hegelian position also seeks to reconcile diversity with the unfolding of the Absolute. While the process of history is a progressive reconciliation of reason and nature, Watson resists both the assumption that such an unfolding implies homogeneity, especially through the suppression of national independence and individuality, and the assumption that the Absolute completes itself within the phenomenal world.

Both Lachance and Watson reject the subjectivism of isolated, selfish individuals and narrow, insulated nationalism, but both also reject global homogeneity. Both appeal to the idea of a nationalism mediated by reason.

Lachance's and Watson's nationalism was rooted in the idea of a concrete political community, based on the modern achievements of constitutionalism and self-government, which held together the individual and the community, the particular and the universal, in mutual interdependence. The concrete community is a rational and coherent whole, while at the same time it affords the recognition of both individuality and plurality. Finally, their thought shares the assumption of an uneasy harmony between immanence and transcendence. This means that the thought of neither issued in a messianic call for epochal world transformation. Neither Lachance nor Watson believed social engineering could fulfil and exhaust the longing for transcendence.

We see the emphasis on harmony common to the thought of Lachance and Watson as a continuation of the balance we analysed in chapter 4 – the Augustinian dynamic of will and grace, the Platonic crafting of *thumos* and *eros*. It is a harmony which can hold together traditionalism and progressivism, order and transcendence, allowing each to act on the other and thus moderate one other. It is a reciprocity that permits the longing for perfection without extravagant projects for world transformation. There is a synthesis of plurality with unity, particularity with universality, and order with process, but without the millenarian dream of a perfected state. By contrast, today's radicalism, as we saw in chapters 2 and 3 of this study, reveals a dangerous fragmentation of that synthesis, taking indeterminacy and perpetual fluidity to be freedom and taking its own messianism to be the final creed of the elect. Whereas Lachance and Watson realize that individual and social imperfection will never be overcome and thus see the need for a liberal education which moderates and sublimates human longings into noble virtues, the radicalism which we discussed in chapter 3 has rejected all the stable and permanent forms of civilized life and education. Contemporary radicalism assumes that all social ills will be overcome and the human desire for wholeness will be fulfilled when we all participate in the *frisson* of permanent revolution. Such a project, we think, threatens to extinguish the cautious and commonsensical exercise of judgment and makes the prospect of extensive human indecency a real danger.

Radicalism now dominates modern educational practice. But today's radicalism, with all its shortcomings, has a distant antecedent in that wiser and richer progressivism which is rooted in Hegelian Idealism. The link is a fragile one, but still, we believe, recoverable. We have emphasized the idea of reciprocity in Hegel's Idealism, by which we mean the reciprocal interaction of process and order, of Love and Understanding. It is only recently that progressivism has degenerated into the fragment we have called radicalism. We believe it is time to restore the balance, by retrieving the noblest possibilities that lie within the Hegelian legacy. That legacy has deep roots in the tradition of Western humanism stretching back to Plato and Augustine. It is epitomized in the life of Thomas d'Arcy McGee, who, as an eloquent admirer put it,

strove with all the power of genius to convert the stagnant pool of politics into a stream of living water; who dared to be national in the face of living selfishness and impartially liberal in the face of sectarian strife; [and] who ... sowed broadcast the seeds of a higher national life, and with persuasive eloquence drew us closer together as a people, pointing out to each what was good in the other ... [and] one who breathed into our new Dominion the spirit of a proud self-reliance, and first taught Canadians to respect themselves.[45]

7

Conclusion

Our pride as Canadians has a defensible core. Our heritage is filled with political achievements which make this country, despite its imperfections, a model of free government and of justice. A detached analysis of our origins, and of the debates which justified the institutions of responsible government we put in place, reveals how judicious, prudent, and far-seeing our founders were. The same qualities informed the establishment of public education in Canada. Educators like McCulloch, Ryerson, and Young designed curricula and teaching practices which balanced individual needs with social responsibility, common sense with moral principle, and freedom with culture.

We have allowed this legacy, both at the level of politics and in the schools, to fossilize into dogma. If the founding experiences by which this country was formed are to remain vital, they must be renewed and shown to illuminate our present circumstances. We have not done so. Instead, we have permitted a sterile set of binaries to control our public debate: individualism versus communitarianism, traditionalism versus progressivism, the status quo versus global forces. These paralysing oppositions have created a vacuum where responsible civic discourse is silenced. Rushing in to fill it, innumerable advocates, lobbyists, and special-issue sectarians have expressed their private grievances and offended feelings, and have been allowed to dominate the debate with their narrow agendas. In shying away from substantive debate, we have left our public discussions barren. Our debate is degenerating into a form of defeatism and cynicism which ends by merely flattering the loudest voices and which refuses to face up to the complex tasks of statesmanship.

If we are to restore a sense of balance to education, it will not do to dwell only on the contributions being made to Canada through gender, race, and ethnic identities. We must also emphasize the opportunities present within the Canadian polity for all Canadians. We should not dwell exclusively on the connection each of us has to our culturally different origins, but also on the connections we can forge together.

Moreover, it will not do to gape uncritically at other school systems like Japan's, admiring its high performance rate in scholastic exams and low drop-out rate, while ignoring its poor record of promoting a sense of freedom and participation. The founders of Canada and of Canadian education made certain choices. We have argued that these were sensible choices and ones that can still offer guidance.

A loss of balance is evident when educators take the primary task of schools to be that of supplying efficient units prepared to assimilate themselves to the demands of the socio-economic environment. Despite its pretensions of hard-headedness and relevance, in our estimation, this outlook constitutes a refusal to take full responsibility for education. Liberal education supplies a vision; it civilizes by taking us beyond our immediate circumstances. We must allow for what J.A. Corry has called the periodic withdrawal from the 'clamour of the immediate.'[1] Matthew Arnold expressed the meaning that lies at the heart of liberal education: 'Culture [is] a pursuit of our total perfection by means of getting to know, on all the matters which most concern us, the best which has been thought and said in the world.' The abdication of responsibility for teaching these foundations, once understood as necessary for an independent mind and a judicious political life, has led to bankrupt education.

Today's progressive reformers have identified our current malaise as stemming from racism, violence towards women, lack of relevant skills, insufficient attention to global competitiveness, lack of adaptability, and too much hierarchy and authoritarianism. Significant as these issues are, we would point to other syndromes of spiritual illness that are at least as prominent in contemporary life. We see boredom with the simple goodness of life, cynicism, unfulfilled longings for transcendence, unchannelled political passions, untamed erotic desire, unguided anxiety regarding death, feelings of impotence, despair over the inner divisions of the self, an unanswered need for respect. Students are not satisfied and they carry the lie of contemporary educational reform in their souls.

We have argued that the source of our misguided reforms is millenarian enthusiasm. We regard this enthusiasm as the syndrome of an intellectual and spiritual illness in which a fantasy version of perfection and wholeness is allowed to obscure those real conditions of existence, those burdens and responsibilities of life, to which human beings must critically and decently respond. Millenarian enthusiasm takes the form of a wilful eclipse of those cardinal elements of reality we sought to elaborate for our readers when we discussed the importance of such thinkers as Plato, Aristotle, and Augustine, as well as their modern counterparts. To recall the terms of that discussion, today's reforms vacillate between the Cartesian *esprit de géometrie* and what Vico terms a 'pliant Lesbic rule.' They vacillate, in other words, between an excessive hope that technical competence will solve all our problems and an equally excessive appeal to a poetic but structureless wholeness which dreams that nothing need limit us. In either case, what has been lost is balanced judgment concerning the aims and scope of education. We see no promise in today's calls for endless 'restructuring' that a way will be found to stem these excesses.

In our view, there will be no cessation of the ills we have diagnosed without the antidote of liberal education. Such an education balances creativity with tradition, usefulness with transcendence, the longing for wholeness with the requirements of human order; or, to use the terms of an earlier chapter, *thumos* with *eros*, will with grace, and love with understanding. We cannot abandon the judicious balance at the heart of liberal education without inviting peril to our democratic heritage.

Notes

CHAPTER 1 INTRODUCTION

1 As quoted in Andrew Nikiforuk, 'Fifth Column: Education,' *Globe and Mail*, 30 October 1992, p. A26.
2 Rose-Marie Batley, 'System's Broke so Let's Get on with Fixing It,' *Ottawa Citizen*, 15 March 1993, p. A9.
3 As reported by Michael Valpy, 'The Three Rs versus Citizenship,' *Globe and Mail*, 12 October 1993.

CHAPTER 2 THE CRISIS IN CANADIAN EDUCATION

1 See Robert M. Stamp, *The Schools of Ontario 1876–1976* (Toronto: University of Toronto Press 1982), and Donald M. Cameron, *Schools for Ontario* (Toronto: University of Toronto Press 1982), chap. 10. In 1960, the federal government passed the Technical and Vocational Training Assistance Act.
2 Between 1955 and 1975, the Canadian gross national product increased by a factor of 2.5, while personal per capita income doubled in real terms. See Walter C. Gordon, *What's Happening to Canada* (Toronto: McClelland and Stewart 1978), pp. 9–10.
3 In part, it would seem, because they would like the school system to pay for training that they are unwilling to pay for themselves. Canada reportedly ranks nineteenth among twenty-two countries surveyed for support for on-the-job training of workers in the industrial sector. Michael Valpy, 'Just What Are Schools Preparing Students For?' *Globe and Mail*, 14 October 1993.
4 See James Shields, Jr, ed., *Japanese Schooling* (University Park: Pennsylvania State University Press 1989), and Sterling Sishman and Lothar Martin, *Estranged*

Twins: Education and Society in the Two Germanies (New York: Praeger Press 1987). In recent years, private schools like the Waldorf-Schulen have emerged in Germany that focus on child-centred learning.

5 Dennis Raphael, 'From Bad to Worse: Student Achievement in Ontario,' *Globe and Mail*, 27 April 1993.

6 As reported by Andrew Duffy, 'Do Gifted Students Need a Special High School?' *Toronto Star*, 7 July 1993. Mr Cooke announced in April 1993 that UTS's government grant will be terminated in 1994.

7 According to a recent survey of Canadian private schools, UTS has the highest admissions standards, admitting only 9 per cent of applicants in Grade 7. As reported by Scott Feschuk, 'Guide to Private Schools an Open Book,' *Globe and Mail*, 5 August 1993.

8 Even within the NDP, these policies are provoking a bitter controversy. For a detailed critique of the Rae government's agenda, see 'Robert K. Rae, QC, Should Resign,' *Ottawa Citizen*, 7 April 1993. The writer, Rob Martin, is a law professor at the University of Western Ontario and was a candidate for the federal NDP in 1989 and 1980. The Rae government, he argues, has 'abandoned all pretence of acting on behalf of ordinary men and women ... Rae lavishes money on a horde of officially certified 'victims,' counsellors, facilitators and the like. What distinguishes these beneficiaries is sneering contempt for the working people of Ontario ... The Rae government has been tireless in promoting racial consciousness and racist ideology ... It also favors "educational equity"; this means racial quotas in schools and universities ... The Rae government is determined to make skin color the central focus of each person's existence. It wants to create our very own system of apartheid.'

9 Not surprisingly, more and more parents are sending their children to private schools as the public system declines. Private school enrolment has doubled in the past twenty years, even though the cost per year per student can run as high as $20,000. As reported by Jennifer Lewington, 'Private Schools Increasingly Seen as Real Alternative,' *Globe and Mail*, 5 August 1993.

10 See the informative account of how destreaming is proceeding so far by Pat Bell, 'Combined Grade 9 Gets Good Marks,' *Ottawa Citizen*, 16 October 1993. Oddly, the reporter's observations at Osgoode Township High School in Metcalfe, Ontario do not seem to justify the article's upbeat title and generally enthusiastic tone. In one Grade 9 math class, learning abilities range from the Grade 10 to the Grade 4 level. The brightest students will be given 'interesting tasks' to *prevent* them from 'hurrying on to Grade 10 material.' They will also be conscripted to help out the less-gifted students. Their teacher reports: 'At times the students will work in groups and each group will have at least one student who knows the material and they'll help each other.' But how can the less-gifted students learn more

from a student their own age in occasional groups than they would from a teacher who could devote an entire class to teaching them at their own pace, as would be the case with streaming? However, the point is as much ideological as pedagogical: 'The reality in life is that nobody works alone,' the teacher asserts. 'You don't have to be best friends. You just have to work productively together.' But don't we all have to 'work alone' sometimes? And don't the greatest achievements in economic innovation, the sciences, and the humanities come at least as much from solitary inspiration and diligence as from teamwork? Why should the schools give special status to the concept of working in groups as opposed to cultivating one's individual excellence as well as cooperating with others?

11 The best recent figures available are from 1991, when, according to the statistics branch of the Ontario Ministry of Education, there were 15,571 gifted students out of a total of 680,563.

12 'Introduction,' *The Common Curriculum: Grades 1–9*, February 1993, p. 3, distributed by the Ontario Ministry of Education, under the name of David Cooke and Charles Pascal.

13 'Memorandum,' Carleton Board of Education Corporate Services, 24 November 1992.

14 As reported in *Ottawa Citizen*, 12 December 1992, p. B3.

15 *Ottawa Citizen*, 29 November 1992, p. A11.

16 'Mind over Matter: Fortis Boss Sees Need for Less Facts, More Wisdom,' as reported in *Evening Telegram*, St John's, Newfoundland, 9 July 1993, p. 14.

17 'Educational Aims Outdated, Charges Economic Council,' as reported in *Evening Telegram*, St John's, Newfoundland, 6 July 1993.

18 'Corporate-Style Schools May Kick-start Education,' *Province*, Vancouver, 22 July 1993, p. A38.

19 One example is a July 1993 report by the New Brunswick Coalition for Human Rights Reform, which calls on the education system to stop distinguishing hetero- from homosexual relations. The education system should further the understanding and acceptance of a diversity of sexual orientations, the report reads, as part of junior and senior high school curricula.

20 Ron Brandt, 'On Outcome-Based Education: A Conversation with Bill Spady,' circulated by the Ontario Secondary School Teachers Federation, 1993.

21 Ibid.

22 William Daggett, *Preparing Students for the 1990's and Beyond* (Schenectady, NY: International Center for Leadership in Education 1992), p. 25.

23 Ibid.

24 Ibid.

25 George Grant, 'Thinking about Technology,' *Technology and Justice* (Toronto: Anansi 1986), p. 15.

CHAPTER 3   THE ASSAULT ON EDUCATION

1 'Memorandum,' Ottawa Board of Education, 26 January 1993.

2 As reported in *Ottawa Citizen*, 1 November 1992, p. A1.

3 Statistics Canada reports show that in 1991–2 private-school enrolment was double that of twenty years ago. The biggest increases were in Christian fundamentalist private schools. Cf. 'Private Schools Increasingly Seen as Real Alternative,' *Globe and Mail*, 5 August 1993, p. C1.

4 Teachers have expressed considerable opposition to the parents' demands. They claim that province-wide testing is little more than a form of teacher evaluation. It seems to us, though, that such evaluation is preferable to the much more extensive and vague accountability that arises from teachers' bearing responsibility for 'behaviours and attitudes' related to 'learning outcomes'. Nevertheless, the Ontario Ministry of Education is opposed to it as well: 'The problem with standardized testing is they [*sic*] don't work,' stated Tony Silipo. 'The big drawback of standardized tests is all they tell you is how a student does on a particular test. Those tests don't actively reflect all that a student has learned, nor can they ever really.' (As reported in *Ottawa Citizen*, 6 February 1993, p. B2.) On 4 April 1993 the Ontario Ministry of Education, responding to parents' discontent, announced an 'interim-measure' province-wide series of tests of reading and writing ability based on a two-week food and nutrition course.

5 As noted in the Queen's University Forum on Education, broadcast on CBC Newsworld.

6 'Foisting Racism Woes on Schools Irks Group,' *Windsor Star*, 16 July 1993, p. B8.

7 As reported in *Ottawa Citizen*, 29 November 1992, p. A11.

8 'Parents to Get Say in Reform of Schools,' *Toronto Star*, 18 June 1993, p. A11. Concern regarding the diminishing of power among incumbent players was immediately heard. The Ontario Public School Boards' Association indicated disapproval, claiming the council would only duplicate local school boards. The Metropolitan Toronto Public School Board stated that it saw no sense in the council: 'the variation of what parents expect from the school system differs so much across the province,' retorted its chairperson Ann Vanstone. Barb Smith, president of Quality Education Network, was, however, content. Parents have no special interests to protect, she said, and 'we have no other agenda except seeing a good education provided our children.'

9 As reported in *Ottawa Citizen*, 28 November 1993, p. F4.

10 As reported in 'Letter of the Day,' *Ottawa Citizen*, 18 November 1992, p. A10.

11 As reported in *Ottawa Citizen*, 1 November 1992, p. A1.

12 'Overview of Research on Pilot Projects – (Unedited),' released by Sue Borowski, Director, Educational Services, Ontario Institute for Studies in Education, 11

March 1993, a summary of a study done under Andy Hargreaves and Kenneth Leithwood for the Ministry of Education.

13 Ibid.

14 'Teacher In-Service Program Criteria: Grades 7, 8, and 9 (Transition Years),' Memorandum to All Secondary Principals, the Carleton Board of Education, Instructional Support Department, 11 September 1992.

15 Some of the more suggestive titles are *Minority Education, From Shame to Struggle, Decoding Discrimination: A Student-Based Approach to Anti-racist Education using Film, Empowering Minority Students, Global Teacher, Global Learner,* 'Transition Years: Preliminary List of Resources,' Ministry of Education, 1992.

16 As reported in *Ottawa Citizen*, 10 November 1992, p. E2.

17 In passing it should be noted that Oakes also identifies 'truancy' as a problem; in Ontario, questions of discipline appear not to be discussed.

18 In her study *Improving Inner-City Schools: Current Directions in Urban District Reform*, advocating child-centred, 'effective' schooling, Jeannie Oakes candidly concludes: 'Very little is actually known about the effects of these reforms' (Madison: Center for Policy Research in Education, Rand Corporation 1987), p. 58. See also Andrew Nikiforuk, 'Fifth Column: Education,' *Globe and Mail*, 4 December 1992, on the US government's ten-year study Project Follow-Through which demonstrated that 'progressive' educational techniques tended to penalize economically disadvantaged and multicultural students, while the highly structured 'direct instruction' and performance-based approach produced higher gains in skills, as well as self-esteem.

19 On the one hand, we have gone from the Hall-Dennis principle of learning experiences in line with student's own perception of needs to learning outcomes demanded by the workplace consonant with the student's sense of self-esteem. But, in another way, *The Common Curriculum* simply completes and perfects the spirit of the Hall-Dennis Report. The school for Hall-Dennis is to have an atmosphere that is 'positive and encouraging ... The punitive approach must give way to a more relaxed teacher-pupil relationship ... Going to school will be a pleasant growing experience ... As he [the student] enters and passes through adolescence he will do so without any sudden or traumatic change and without a sense of alienation from society.'

20 'The Transition Years: A Report for Schools in the Carleton Board of Education,' Carleton Board of Education, 1 December 1992.

21 Memorandum to School Principals: School Achievement Indicators Program, Ministry of Education, 25 September 1992.

22 'The Transition Years: A Report for Schools in the Carleton Board of Education,' Carleton Board of Education, December 1992.

23 From one of the recommended source materials distributed by the Ottawa Board

of Education: Willard Daggett, *Preparing Students for the 1990's and Beyond* (Schenectady, NY: International Center for Leadership in Education 1992).

24 Ironically, the assumption that future trends can be forecast, and the 'learning out-comes' approach built on that assumption, are based on the work of Jeannie Oakes, who concludes her study *Educational Indicators: A Guide for Policymakers* as fol-lows: 'Much of this confidence, and our hopes for indicators, may be exaggerated. Educational organizations may be far more complex, dynamic, and interacting than data about discrete, or even mechanically-linked parts can convey. We may have a great deal of trouble capturing and measuring their most important fea-tures. "Successes" detected by indicators may be so short-lived that, by the time they are reported, they no longer exist. Educational planning based on indicator data may fail to bring about intended results and have contrary, unintended, and unpredictable consequences. Moreover, it is hard to imagine that collecting, reporting, and interpreting indicator data will be free of political influence.' (Mad-ison: Center for Policy Research in Education, University of Wisconsin 1986)

25 Benjamin Bloom, *Taxonomy of Educational Objectives* (New York: McKay 1969).

26 Daggett, p. 23.

27 While *The Common Curriculum* allows for optional, or discretionary, learning outcomes, the directive, at the same time, is that 'all aspects of school environ-ment, operations, and program must contribute to the common curriculum.'

28 George Grant, *Time as History* (Toronto: Canadian Broadcasting Corporation 1969), p. 41.

29 The political significance of millenarian movements is discussed in Eric Voegelin, *The New Science of Politics* (Chicago: University of Chicago Press 1987); Norman Cohn, *The Pursuit of the Millennium* (Oxford: Oxford University Press 1961); Theodor Olson, *Millenialism, Utopianism, and Progress* (Toronto: University of Toronto Press 1982); and Bernard Yack, *The Longing for Total Revolution: Philosophic Sources of Social Discontent from Rousseau to Marx and Nietzsche* (Princeton: Princeton University Press 1986).

30 *Cf.* Eric Voegelin, 'Wisdom and the Magic of the Extreme: A Meditation,' *Col-lected Works of Eric Voegelin*, vol. 12, *Published Essays, 1966–1985* (Baton Rouge: Louisiana State University Press 1990), pp. 317–75; and also Norman Cohn, *The Pursuit of the Millennium.*

31 *Cf.* Mircea Eliade, *The Forge and the Crucible: the Origins and Structures of Alchemy* (Chicago: University of Chicago Press 1956), and *Rites and Symbols of Initiation*, trans. by Willard R. Trask (New York: Harper Torchbooks 1958). For a discussion of 'liminal' states, see Victor Turner, *The Forest of Symbols: Aspects of Ndembu Ritual* (Ithaca: Cornell University Press 1970), especially chap. 4, 'Be-twixt and Between: The Liminal Period in *Rites de Passage*'; and Mary Douglas, *Purity and Danger* (Harmondsworth: Penguin 1966).

32 For a discussion of how values education is contributing to this process of homogenization, see Peter Emberley, *Values Education and Technology: The Politics of Dispossession* (Toronto: University of Toronto Press, in press).

33 David Warrick, 'Nurturing Illiteracy,' *Ottawa Citizen*, 18 April 1993.

34 Robert Davidson and Luc Rainville, 'Higher Education under the Microscope,' *University Affairs*, May 1993.

35 Christine Tausig Ford, 'A Solid Showing,' *University Affairs*, April 1993.

36 Stuart Smith, *Report of the Commission of Inquiry on Canadian University Education* (Ottawa: AUCC 1991).

37 In making this suggestion, we emphatically do not wish to see an end to our noble Canadian experiment of conjoining high university academic standards with public funding. But we do believe that universities need both the freedom and the responsibility to open themselves up to the wider world, both to reinvigorate themselves and to regain some degree of financial independence from the government of the day, and from the pressures the government is under from both the left and the right to use the university to achieve their agendas. Privatization could be both a voluntary and a limited option. Some universities might boldly try to go all or most of the way toward self-financing. Others might do so selectively while remaining mainly dependent on public funding. Equality of access and opportunity for students could be maintained through scholarships and student loans. Indeed, to the extent that universities become self-financing, more public funds could be freed up for these purposes. We have nothing to lose and everything to gain by encouraging this kind of diversity to flower, so as to release the university from an increasingly monolithic, intrusive government-dominated 'system.'

38 Enrolments increased by 34 per cent during the 1980s, as funding declined in real terms. Remarkably, enrolments increased during the 1980s at an annual rate of 3 per cent even though, during this same decade, the number of eighteen- to twenty-four year-olds shrank by 13 per cent. See *Trends: The Canadian University in Profile 1991* (Ottawa: AUCC 1991).

39 Paul Davenport, president of the University of Alberta, has recently proposed deregulating tuition fees to solve the university's increasingly severe financial problems. The danger to accessibility posed by uncapped fees, he argues, could be offset by government loans based on student need. The alternative to deregulation, he goes on, will be to save money by turning away students through the establishment of 'rigid quotas.' Such measures 'will limit accessibility to a university education much more than higher fees.' But, according to a government spokesperson, the government of Alberta 'has no plans to deregulate university tuition fees.' As reported by Farhan Memon, 'University Report Proposes Deregulating Tuition Fees,' *Edmonton Journal*, 24 June 1993.

40 This issue was still unfolding as *Bankrupt Education* was being completed in early

October 1993. On 7 October Ontario Education Minister David Cooke announced guidelines that would require all university governing bodies to be made up of external representatives of visible minorities – women, the disabled, francophones, and native people – and internal representatives of faculty, students, and campus staff (at least two members from each of the three groups). Since October 1992, when earlier draft guidelines were first issued that appeared to be aimed at legislation, Ontario's universities had been lobbying to persuade the government not to legislate the guidelines but to make compliance with them by the universities voluntary. In apparent acquiescence to that lobbying effort, Mr Cooke has given the universities until 31 March 1994 to comply with the final version of the guidelines he announced on 7 October 1993. The ministry must approve each individual university's plan for making its governing body conform to the guidelines. Presumably, if some or all of the universities fail to comply in the ministry's judgment, it could still legislate the guidelines. The Council of Ontario Universities appeared to believe that, by making this arrangement for voluntary compliance, it fended off an assertion by the government of direct control over the universities such as the ministry exercises over Ontario's community colleges. However, as far as we can judge, whether the guidelines are complied with voluntarily or given the force of law through legislation, the result will be the same: university governing bodies will now be the administrative creatures of Queen's Park, and universities will therefore effectively be directly controlled by the government as are the community colleges. (As reported in 'Ontario Colleges Told to Diversify,' *Globe and Mail*, 8 October 1993.)

41 Alexis de Tocqueville, *Democracy in America*, trans. by George Lawrence (Garden City, NY: Anchor Books 1969), pp. 668–70.

42 In considering the role of the university, we recommend to our readers the essay by J.M. Cameron, *On the Idea of a University* (Toronto: University of Toronto Press 1978).

43 Cameron is eloquent on the character of the teacher-student relationship: 'Teaching and learning constitute a natural relation, one that is needed for survival – much that is in the other animals instinctive (such as swimming) is with us learned behaviour – and, once survival is safeguarded, for satisfying the needs of civilization ... One understands why among the Greeks the relation is portrayed through the image of an erotic relationship and is also thought, by a metaphor, to be a kind of midwifery.' Cameron, *On the Idea of a University*, pp. 68–9.

44 Leah Bradshaw, 'Universities: Looking For What's Best,' *Globe and Mail*, 3 June 1993.

45 As Andrew Nikiforuk reports, even environmentalist activists are taking a hard look at the way environmental issues are being taught in our schools. He cites the observations of Patricia Poore, editor of an environmentalist journal who surveyed

hundreds of classroom materials on this subject: 'Patricia Poore was dumbfounded by "the repetitive topics, the emphasis on social problems rather than science background and the call to activism ..." Ms Poore was also shocked by the apocalyptic nature of this curriculum. If acid rain doesn't do in the human race, then overpopulation, nuclear waste or holes in the ozone will ... [M]uch so-called "eco-education" has had a difficult time separating cant from fact, thought from action and science from awareness ... In this regard, so-called environmental education merely reflects what is wrong with most social curriculums in the schools. Whether dealing with racism, AIDS, the ozone layer or homosexuality, issues generally get reduced (or politicized) to well-intentioned topics devoid of context, history and argument. [As Ms. Poore observes:] "Activists simply don't make good educators, no matter what the cause, for the agenda of an activist is to promulgate propaganda."' Andrew Nikiforuk, 'Environmental Education Could Clean Up Its Own Act,' *Globe and Mail*, 16 July 1993. For a discussion of related issues, see Mr Nikiforuk's book, *School's Out: The Catastrophe of Public Education and What We Can Do About It* (Toronto: McFarland, Walter and Ross 1993).

46 Robert B. Reich, *The Work of Nations* (New York: Vintage Books 1992), pp. 174–6.

CHAPTER 4   LIBERAL EDUCATION AND THE MODERN WORLD

1 Pier Paolo Vergerio, 'Concerning Liberal Studies,' in *Vittorino da Feltre and Other Humanist Educators*, ed. by W.H. Woodward (Cambridge: Cambridge University Press 1897), p. 102. For further discussion, see Waller R. Newell, 'How Original Is Machiavelli? A Consideration of Skinner's Interpretation of Virtue and Fortune,' *Political Theory*, November 1987.

2 Ibid., p. 110.

3 Ibid., p. 105.

4 Ibid.

5 See the discussion of Nietzsche below, in the second section of chapter 5, 'A Nietzschean Interlude.'

6 Plato, *Gorgias*, trans. by W.C. Helmbold (Indianapolis: Bobbs-Merrill Educational Publishing 1952), 508a.

7 Plato, *The Republic*, trans. by Allan Bloom (New York: Basic Books 1968), 519d.

8 Aristotle, *Politics*, 1286a–1287b.

9 See, for example, Paul Heinlich D'Holbach, 'The Priestly Religion,' pp. 60–3, and Cesare Bonesana, Marchese di Beccaria, 'Of the Proportion between Crimes and Punishments,' pp. 141–2, in *The Enlightenment*, ed. by Frank E. Manuel (Englewood Cliffs, NJ: Prentice-Hall 1965).

10 Aristotle, *Politics*, 1253a.

11 For further discussion, see Waller R. Newell, 'Superlative Virtue and the Problem of Monarchy in Aristotle's *Politics*,' in *Essays on the Foundations of Aristotelian Political Science*, ed. by Carnes Lord (Berkeley: University of California Press 1991), and 'Machiavelli and Xenophon on Princely Rule: A Double-Edged Encounter,' *Journal of Politics*, November 1983.

12 Aristotle, *Politics*, 1338a24–27.

13 Consider Aristotle, ibid., 1324b24–41 and 1334a11–40.

14 Ibid., 1253a.

15 Ibid., 1339b5–10, 1341b1–10.

16 McGee's contribution to Canadian education is discussed in chapter 6 below.

17 All quotations are from Saint Augustine, *Confessions*, trans. by R.S. Pine-Coffin (Harmondsworth: Penguin Books 1961). See also Michael Ignatieff, *The Needs of Strangers* (Harmondsworth: Penguin Books 1984), for a thoughtful account of Augustine and our spiritual needs.

18 A most thoughtful assessment of Descartes's thought is offered in Hannah Arendt's *The Human Condition* (Chicago: University of Chicago Press 1959), chap. 5, from which the following account in considerable part derives. All quotes of Descartes are from René Descartes, *The Philosophical Works of Descartes*, trans. by Elizabeth S. Haldane and G.T.T. Ross (London: Cambridge University Press 1973 rep.)

19 All quotations are from Giambattista Vico, *On the Study Methods of Our Time*, trans. by Elio Gianturco (New York: Bobbs-Merrill 1965).

20 James Madison, No. 10, *The Federalist Papers*, ed. by Clinton Rossiter (New York: New American Library 1961), pp. 78–84.

20 Alexander Hamilton, No. 9, *The Federalist Papers*, pp. 71–6.

22 Quoted in *The Educational Writings of John Locke*, ed. by James L. Axtell with introduction and notes (Cambridge: Cambridge University Press 1968), p. 58.

23 Ibid., p. 59.

24 John Locke, *Two Treatises of Government*, ed. by Peter Laslett (New York: New American Library 1965), p. 395.

25 Our emphasis.

26 Thomas Jefferson, *Notes on the State of Virginia*, intro. by Thomas Perkins Abernathy (New York: Harper and Row 1964), p. 141.

27 Ibid., pp. 142–3.

CHAPTER 5   LIBERAL EDUCATION AND THE FRAGMENTATION OF MODERNITY

1 Rousseau sets forth this argument in his discourses on the harmful effect of the revival of the arts and sciences on morality and on the origin of human inequality.

Jean-Jacques Rousseau, *The First and Second Discourses*, ed. by Roger D. Masters (New York: St. Martin's Press 1964).

2 Jean-Jacques Rousseau, *Emile, or on Education*, trans. and ed. by Allan Bloom (New York: Basic Books 1979). For further discussion, see Bloom's introduction to his translation of the *Emile* and his discussion of Rousseau in *Love and Friendship* (New York: Simon and Schuster 1993).

3 Friedrich Schiller, *On the Aesthetic Education of Man*, trans. by Reginald Snell (New York: Frederick Ungar 1974), pp. 23–8.

4 Hegel pays generous tribute to Schiller: 'It is Schiller to whom we must give credit for the greatest service of having broken through the Kantian subjectivity and abstractness of thought, daring to transcend them by intellectually apprehending the principles of unity and reconciliation as the truth, and realizing them in art.' Quoted in Schiller, ibid., pp. 11–12.

5 The reader should bear in mind that we are discussing Schiller's characterization of a certain aspect of Kantianism, which is not necessarily the same thing as the full meaning of Kant's philosophy. A full consideration of Kant's philosophy would have to include his own aesthetic theories in *The Critique of Judgment* and *Observations on the Feeling of the Beautiful and Sublime*. Schiller is well aware of this: the dichotomy between Understanding and sentiment, he observes, 'is by no means in the *spirit* of the Kantian system, but it may very well be found in the *letter* of it' (Schiller, ibid., p. 68, n. 1).

6 Rousseau, *First and Second Discourses*, p. 64.

7 G.W.F. Hegel, *The Phenomenology of Mind*, trans. by J.B. Baillie (New York: Harper and Row 1967), pp. 71, 227.

8 The following discussion is drawn in the main from Hegel, *Phenomenology of Mind*, pp. 71–94, and *Early Theological Writings*, trans. by T.M. Knox and Richard Kroner (Chicago: University of Chicago Press 1948), pp. 304–13.

9 Hegel, *Phenomenology*, p. 93.

10 Ibid., pp. 81, 93; *Early Theological Writings*, pp. 312–13.

11 *Early Theological Writings*, p. 325.

12 Ibid., p. 326.

13 Ibid., p. 328.

14 There is an exceptionally rich and thought-provoking scholarly literature on Hegel, and some of the best of it is by Canadians. It is too large to survey here, but we suggest the following as a core list: Emil L. Fackenheim, *The Religious Dimension in Hegel's Thought* (Boston: Beacon Press 1970); Alexandre Kojève, *Introduction to the Reading of Hegel*, trans. by James H. Nicholls (New York: Basic Books 1969); Hans-Georg Gadamer, *Hegel's Dialectic: Five Hermeneutical Studies*, trans. by P. Christopher Smith (New Haven: Yale University Press 1976); Charles Taylor, *Hegel* (Cambridge: Cambridge University Press 1975); Tom Darby, *The Feast:*

Meditations on Politics and Time (Toronto: University of Toronto Press 1990); Barry Cooper, *The End of History* (Toronto: University of Toronto Press 1986).

15 Hegel, *Phenomenology of Mind*, p. 808. Although we refer to the best-known English translation of Hegel's book, 'spirit' is, strictly speaking, a better translation of the German word *Geist* in Hegel's title than is Baillie's translation 'mind.' 'Spirit' suggests a moving and multifaceted process – as well as evoking the Holy Spirit of Christianity – and is therefore true to the meaning of Hegel's thought. 'Mind,' by contrast, sounds too static and formalistic in the manner of Newtonian or Cartesian rationality, whose validity would, for Hegel, be limited to the 'Understanding' side of the dialectic.

16 Benjamin R. Barber, 'Jihad vs. McWorld: How the Planet Is Both Falling Apart and Coming Together and What This Means for Democracy,' *Atlantic*, vol. 269, no. 3, March 1992, pp. 53–63.

17 C.B. Macpherson, *The Political Theory of Possessive Individualism* (London: Oxford University Press 1970), pp. 276–7.

18 Consider R.H. Tawney, *Religion and the Rise of Capitalism* (New York: New American Library 1954).

19 Rousseau, *First and Second Discourses*, p. 54.

20 For a judiciously sceptical view, see Mary Lefkowitz, 'The Twilight of the Goddess,' *New Republic*, 3 August 1992.

21 On Heidegger and the breakdown of Hegelianism, see Waller R. Newell, 'Heidegger on Freedom and Community: Some Political Implications of His Early Thought,' *American Political Science Review*, September 1984; 'Philosophy and the Perils of Commitment: A Comparison of Lukacs and Heidegger,' *History of Political Ideas*, vol. 9, no. 3, 1988; 'Politics and Progress in Heidegger's Philosophy of History,' in *Democratic Theory and Technological Society*, ed. by Richard Day, Ronald Beiner, and Joseph Masciulli (New York: M.E. Sharpe 1988).

22 Gail Lem, 'Second-Quarter Profits Leap 60%,' *Globe and Mail Report on Business*, 9 August 1993.

23 Robert B. Reich, *The Work of Nations* (New York: Vintage Books 1992), p. 301.

24 Umberto Eco, *Travels in Hyper-reality* (New York: Continuum 1986).

25 Friedrich Nietzsche, *The Use and Abuse of History*, trans. by Adrian Collins (Indianapolis: Bobbs-Merrill 1957). See also Waller R. Newell, 'Zarathustra's Dancing Dialectic,' *Interpretation*, Spring 1990.

26 Alexis de Tocqueville, *Democracy in America*, trans. by George Lawrence (Garden City, NY: Anchor Books 1969), pp. 9–20.

27 See Waller R. Newell, 'Reflections on Marxism and America,' in *Confronting the Constitution*, ed. by Allan Bloom (Washington, DC: AEI Press 1990).

28 Friedrich Nietzsche, *The Twilight of the Idols*, in *The Portable Nietzsche*, trans. by Walter Kaufman (New York: Penguin Books 1976), p. 557.

29 Nietzsche, *The Use and Abuse of History*, p. 23.
30 Ibid., p. 39.
31 Nietzsche, *The Use and Abuse of History*, pp. 13–16.
32 Ibid., pp. 18–20.
33 Ibid., pp. 20–21.

CHAPTER 6 LIBERAL EDUCATION AND THE CANADIAN POLITY

1 Consider Chester New, *Lord Durham's Mission to Canada*, ed. by H.W. McCready, Carleton Library No. 8 (Toronto: McClelland and Stewart 1963), pp. 167–215, and Janet Ajzenstat, *The Political Thought of Lord Durham* (Montreal: McGill-Queen's University Press 1988).
2 *The Confederation Debates in the Province of Canada 1865*, ed. by P.B. Waite, Carleton Library No. 2 (Toronto: McClelland and Stewart 1967), p. 50.
3 Province of Canada, Legislature, *Parliamentary Debates on the Subject of the Confederation of the British North American Provinces* (Quebec 1865), p. 361.
4 *Confederation Debates*, p. 51.
5 Speech delivered at Cookshire, 22 December, p. 8; Public Archives of Canada.
6 *1825 – D'Arcy McGee – 1925: A Collection of Speeches and Addresses*, ed. by the Honourable Charles Murphy, KC, LLD (Toronto: Macmillan Company of Canada 1937), p. 18.
7 Ibid.
8 Ibid., p. 2.
9 Ibid., p. 43.
10 *Confederation Debates*, p. 60.
11 Hannah Arendt, 'The Crisis in Education,' *Between Past and Future* (Harmondsworth: Penguin Books 1977), p. 195.
12 The most comprehensive guide to the history of Canadian curriculum theory is George S. Tomkins, *A Common Countenance: Stability and Change in the Canadian Curriculum* (Scarborough, Ont.: Prentice-Hall 1986). See also A.B. McKillop, *A Disciplined Intelligence: Critical Inquiry and Canadian Thought in the Victorian Era* (Montreal: McGill-Queen's University Press 1979), and Leslie Armour and Elizabeth Trott, *The Faces of Reason: An Essay on Philosophy and Culture in English Canada 1850–1950* (Waterloo: Wilfrid Laurier University Press 1981).
13 Cf. J.G. Althouse, *The Ontario Teacher 1800–1910* (Toronto: W.J. Gage 1967).
14 The Earl of Durham, *Report on the Affairs of British North America*, printed by the House of Commons, 11 February 1839, p. 112.
15 Terry Cook, 'George R. Parkin and the Concept of Britannic Idealism,' *Journal of Canadian Studies*, vol. 10, August 1975, pp. 15–31.
16 Ibid., p. 15.

17 Ibid.
18 As quoted in McKillop, *A Disciplined Intelligence*, p. 13.
19 Charles Mondelet, *Letters on Elementary and Practical Education* (Montreal: John James Williams 1841), p. 6.
20 Ibid., p. 55.
21 W.J. Rattray, *The Scot in British North America (1804–1894)*, 4 vols. (Toronto: Maclear and Company 1880), vol. 1, p. 6.
22 There was considerable interest in post-revolutionary France in Scottish common-sense philosophy as an antidote of moderation to the extreme ideological fervour in educational innovation during the revolution. Walter Bagehot, too, was much impressed with its cautious generalizations, whose tone he attempted to convey in his work on constitutionalism.
23 Cf. Douglas Sloan, *The Scottish Enlightenment and the American College Ideal* (New York: Teachers College Press 1971); George Elder Davie, *The Democratic Intellect: Scotland and Her Universities in the Nineteenth Century* (Edinburgh: Edinburgh University Press 1961).
24 Francis Hutcheson, *A System of Moral Philosophy*, in *Collected Works*, vol. 1, prepared by Bernhard Fabian (Hadesheim: Georg Olms Verlagsbuchhandlung 1969), p. 283.
25 Egerton Ryerson, *Inaugural Address on the Nature and Advantages of an English and Liberal Education* (Toronto 1842), p. 13.
26 Ibid., p. 9.
27 Egerton Ryerson, *Report on a System of Public Elementary Instruction* (Cobourg 1846), p. 22.
28 Ibid., p. 31.
29 Cited in J. George Hodgins, *Documentary, History of Education in Upper Canada*, vol. 6 (Toronto: Warwick Bro's and Rutter 1899), p. 261.
30 *Inaugural Address*, p. 25.
31 Ibid., p. 23.
32 Ibid., p. 15.
33 *Report on a System*, p. 56.
34 It must be added that Ryerson was attracted to the work of Johann Pestalozzi, to whom some contemporary educators trace the origins of child-centred and social-reform-minded education. While Ryerson was responsive to Pestalozzi's teaching methods and his views concerning the aims of education, he did not overlook, as do today's radicals, Pestalozzi's pessimistic view of the inevitability of human sin and his unequivocal rejection of the idea that reform could eradicate human imperfection. Accepting the fact of human weakness, Ryerson saw the evident educational ramifications. Ryerson had learned about Pestalozzi through Horace Mann and through the ideas of Johan Herbart, a widely admired educational

thinker whose ideas had been adopted in many of Canada's normal schools. Herbart was particularly attentive to the sinful tendencies of the human will. While education was to respond to the particular needs of the child, the authority of the teacher was paramount, particularly in constraining and disciplining the will. Because the Hebartians took human weakness seriously, refusing to believe that self-control arose spontaneously, they recognized the importance of habit and character-formation. The lesson was not lost on Ryerson, so evident in the moderate progressivism of his Canadian National Series of Readers, the 'Ryerson Readers.' We wish that *The Common Curriculum* exhibited a similar sense of balance in its attraction for child-centred education.

35 John Watson, *An Outline of Philosophy* (New York: Macmillan 1901), p. 88.
36 John Watson, *Education and Life*, An Address Delivered at the Opening of the Thirty-Second Session of Queen's University, Published by the Alma Mater Society of Queen's University, 1872, p. 5.
37 McKillop, *A Disciplined Intelligence*, p. 196.
38 Ibid., p. 198.
39 *Education and Life*, p. 11.
40 We are indebted to Professor A.B. McKillop, Department of History, Carleton University, who in conversation pointed these influences out to us.
41 Friedrich Froebels, *The Education of Man*, trans. by W.N. Hailmann (New York: D. Appleton and Company 1899), p. 2.
42 James Laughlin Hughes, *Froebel's Educational Law for All Teachers* (New York: D. Appleton and Company 1903).
43 B. Anne Wood, *Idealism Transformed: The Making of a Progressive Educator* (Kingston: McGill-Queen's University Press 1985). Wood chronicles how the Watson-inspired idealism of the New Education was betrayed by the progressive education system. See also Robert Hughes, *The Culture of Complaint: The Fraying of America* (New York: Oxford University Press 1993).
44 Leslie Armour, *The Idea of Canada and the Crisis of Community* (Ottawa: Steel Rail Publishing 1981).
45 As quoted in A.G. Bailey, *Culture and Nationality* (Toronto: McClelland and Stewart 1972), pp. 147–8.

CHAPTER 7 CONCLUSION

1 J.A. Corry, 'The University and the Canadian Community,' in *Farewell the Ivory Tower* (Montreal: McGill-Queen's University Press 1970), p. 33.

Index

Vico, Giambattista, 95, 98–100, 101, 168
Virgil, 88
virtue, 3, 37, 38, 47, 72, 74, 86, 92, 97,
   103, 120, 121, 130, 150, 153, 154
Voegelin, Eric, 48
von Humboldt, Alexander, 107
voucher system, 54, 68

Warrick, David, 51–2, 67
Watson, John, 143, 158, 159–61, 162,
   163–4

Weber, Max, 46–7
Wells, Clyde, 69, 144
will, 92–4, 99, 109, 117, 134, 161, 162,
   164, 168
wonder, 52, 82

Young, George Paxton, 143, 159, 166

Zeus, 88